STANFORD'S

River Thames

STANFORD'S

River Thames

A Companion and Boating Guide

GRAHAM HAYWARD

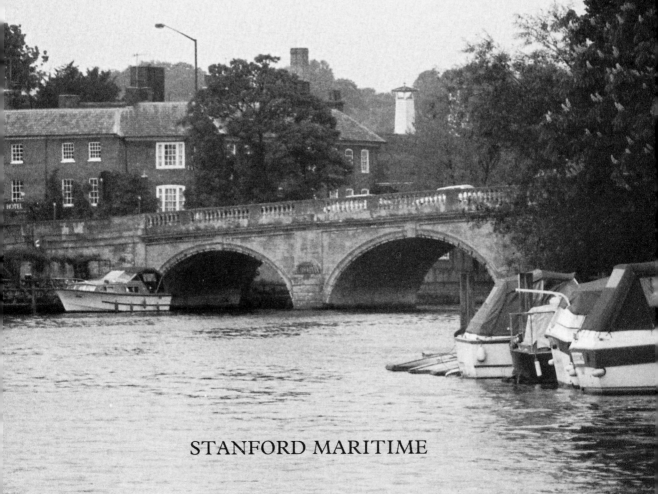

STANFORD MARITIME

Stanford Maritime Limited
Member Company of the George Philip Group
27a Floral Street London WC2 E9DP

© Graham Hayward 1988
Photographs © Graham Hayward and Adrian Morgan
unless credited

British Library Cataloguing in Publication Data
Hayward, Graham
    Stanford's River Thames: a companion
    and boating guide.
    1. Thames, River (England)—Handbooks,
    manuals, etc.
    I. Title
    914.22′04858   DA670.T2
    ISBN 0-540-07428-4

Typeset and Printed in Great Britain by
Butler & Tanner Ltd, Frome and London

for
STANTON GEORGE HAYWARD
1900–1971
this small memorial

ACKNOWLEDGEMENTS

IT WOULD NOT have been possible to write this book without the co-operation of Thames Water. I am most grateful to the staff at all levels of that organisation for their ready help and kindly understanding. The Chief Navigation Inspector, his District Inspectors and all the lock keepers and their assistants, from St John's to Teddington, were unfailingly patient and courteous, and several made helpful contributions to what appears within these pages. In particular, I am indebted to John Redmond, Deputy Chief Navigation Inspector, and Mike Hall, archaeologist, for their assistance and advice; to Ian Burgoyne for much fascinating information on the upper river; and to Brian and Mary Rogers for talking a great deal of sense and for casting boaters' eyes over the descriptions of the locks.

Thanks are due to Oxfordshire County Library in Oxford, for permission to reproduce photographs from the Taunt Collection, and to the staff at the library for their helpful understanding, and to the Bodleian Library for the photograph of Medley Weir from the Minn Collection, and to Thames Water for the photograph from their 1927 Collection reproduced on page 11, and for the Buoy diagram on page 143.

I am grateful to Commander K Cooke, Steward of Christ Church, for information about that college, and to Mr John Eyston for details of Mapledurham. Dr David Bird of the Surrey Archaeological Unit was most helpful in sifting the possible from the highly improbable in connection with the Abbey River, Coway Stakes and Saxon Kingston, and Mr Paul Larkin of Chertsey Museum did the same apropos Chertsey Monastery and other aspects of the Abbey River. Background to iron-age Sinodun and Dorchester was provided by Mr Arthur MacGregor of the Ashmolean Museum.

Others there were who helped with fact or advice who, for professional or personal reasons wish to remain anonymous.

My son Andrew, and especially the twins, Kate and Annabel, have been my frequent companions during the gestation and birth of this book, which they have also read, corrected and criticised with great enthusiasm.

Adrian Morgan, my editor, also voyaged with me, the more thoroughly to check my observations! I am indebted to him for many of the photographs and for his enthusiasm and forbearance.

Finally, Maureen Ergeneli, who interpreted my sometimes damp and blotchy and always wildly implausible sketches of the locks, and drew them into coherence, has also been a constant source of support and encouragement. No hour has been so dark, no concept so awkward in its refusal to flow comprehensively, that she has been unable to coax and enthuse into light and simplicity.

CONTENTS

LIST OF MAPS AND LOCKS

INTRODUCTION

THE RIVER THAMES runs, literally and psychologically, to the heart of the English nation. Through the centuries it has served as frontier, defensive line, attack route, communications link, trading highway, water supply, food source, sewer and, for the last hundred years, adventure playground.

In world terms, the Thames is a remarkably insignificant river. It is navigable for a mere 200 miles or so, at most. But then, these are remarkably insignificant islands, geographically. The importance of the river lies in the consciousness of the island race. So much so that if an Englishman speaks of the River, he means the Thames, a cause of some confusion to foreigners.

This book deals with the Thames as a river for cruising upon; the non-tidal, locked river, originally tamed and developed for the convenience and expedition of trading barges. These have now been replaced by road and rail, leaving a smooth running system for the joy of the thousands who own a boat or hire one, and who set out each year to unwind the tensions of modern life upon its waters.

The River has been intimately connected with the development of Britain, certainly since the beginning of written history, probably much earlier. The Romans recognised the importance of London, are thought to have bridged the river at Staines (which they called Pontes), and built a camp and town alongside the iron-age fortifications at Dorchester (Dorcicon).

These same fortifications are overlooked by the massive early iron-age works by the Wittenham Clumps, Sinodun. The pre-historic Ridgeway Path, as important to Britain before the Romans as the M4 motorway is to us today, crosses the Thames at Goring. Who held the ford at Goring could exert great influence on trade over a wide area of surrounding country.

The Romans and the British were displaced by the ferocious but surprisingly cultured and domesticated Saxons, during the fifth and sixth centuries. Despite the later ravages of Dane and Norman, it is still largely a Saxon river, a circumstance chiefly attributable to the energy and example of one man, Alfred the Great. He formed a defensive line along the river and, from that base, fought the Danes to a standstill. The legacy of Saxon influence that has come down to us lies in a string of places named after them and their leaders: Sonning, Reading, Goring: and words like weir and eyot.

The Normans brought further developments, notably the establishment of castles like those near the Saxon villages of Windsor and Wallingford, and at the youthful but promising place of learning that had begun to develop at Oxford.

With the Normans came also the great increase in the influence of the monasteries. There grew major monasteries at Oxford, Abingdon, Reading and Chertsey, not to mention St John's at Lechlade. For five hundred years, almost all the serious investment, planning and initiative towards the organisation of the Thames as a trading route came from the Church.

About two hundred and fifty years ago, the management of the river, which had previously been undertaken haphazardly, began to devolve upon a central Authority, which in 1770 became known as the Thames Commissioners. This was a large, unwieldy organisation, which tried to balance all the conflicting interests involved in the river and its environs. In the circumstances, they did remarkably well, until the Industrial Revolution brought the Railways, which took the trade from the barges. Faced with bankruptcy, the Commissioners were disbanded and replaced, in 1857, by the Thames Conservancy. This body was placed on a firm financial footing by the government, given control of the stream from Teddington to the source, and the necessary powers to exercise such control.

It was the Conservancy that developed the Thames to its present state of excellence. Professional lock-keepers; smartly painted locks, gates and fences; the river patrols; these are the outward and visible marks of the Conservancy. Behind them lies systematic dredging, bank stabilisation and organised flow control over the whole of the locked river. In 1974, management of all the water services in the Thames Valley passed to the Thames Water Authority, and the role of the Conservancy was taken over by a Division of this authority, where it now resides.

People have no doubt always boated on the

The lock-keeper Mr J Dunston at Bell Weir, 1926. Thames Water.

river for pleasure. It was not until the middle of the nineteenth century that this activity began to take any particular form. It was the railways, by a strange irony, that brought about a revolution in boating for pleasure. Suddenly, large numbers of people could journey cheaply to the country from London, and back in a day. They came in droves, especially to Maidenhead. Sculling and punting soon became arts perfected by the most unlikely people.

At the same time, people started to camp out. They equipped their boats with canvas covers against the elements, took a bedroll and certain basic foodstuffs, and sculled away for weeks at a time. To a cruiser captain, it seems a primitive and uncomfortable way to spend a holiday. It is actually great fun, and it is a delight to witness a revival of this type of river cruise in the last few years.

Among the early adventurers were Mr and Mrs Hall, in 1859, who wrote a book about it; Henry Taunt, who was regularly a camper for the next forty years and took hundreds of photographs, which now provide us with a priceless record of his river; and Jerome K Jerome, whose immortal *Three Men in a Boat* is as fresh and as apt now as it was a century ago.

In the nineties, steam launches began to be a regular feature, as well as the large passenger steamers, such as those run by Salter of Oxford. By the 1920s, motor-cruisers provided a more comfortable way of camping out. Nowadays, the best equipped of these are so comfortable that camping out is no longer the right description. They are true all weather boats.

Weather is the one unchanging feature of the Thames. Anyone who takes a holiday in England must expect the weather to be unreliable. When it is not, one may be agreeably surprised. The advantage of any water holiday is that rain and river are the same element. Providing that one dresses appropriately, weather need not be a major factor affecting enjoyment. It is rare indeed for a whole day to be unrelievedly wet. Even the dreadful summer of 1985 had more dry periods, and even sunshine, than rain. I spent most of it standing in the open on the poop of my narrow-boat. It was distressing to come across a number of

Summer Eights at Oxford on one of the few glorious days in 1987.

crews that were depressed by the rain to the extent that they had almost come to a stop, while they waited for the holiday to end. Yet, in oilskins and boots, I never got wet and by starting early and sometimes stopping early, I kept to a steady schedule and had a great deal of fun. As with so many things in life, it is largely a matter of attitude. It is also a good idea to plan a voyage so that there is never any need to press on in the teeth of bad weather, simply because you have run out of time.

The literature about the Thames is naturally extensive. A bibliography of some of the more interesting and reliable of the books currently available will be found on page 186. This book is unique in that it addresses itself exclusively to the needs of the boater. It was the lack of such a book, to meet my own realised needs, that decided me to write it.

The book is designed to be referred to while actually cruising. The description of the river is based on Stanford's River Thames map,

Salter's launch Wargrave, *a coal-fired steamer now converted to diesel.*

which is reproduced. This description keeps close to the river itself, to those features the boater can see or passes over. It is not my experience that one strays very far from one's boat, in practice, so details of nearby towns or historical features, while interesting, are not strictly relevant.

Whilst a good deal of the information is meant to be of use for all boaters, regardless of experience, I am keenly aware of the lack of available information for the beginner. The basic arts and terms are therefore included, for the benefit of those for whom they may be of use.

The two greatest books written about the Thames in modern times are undoubtedly Henry Taunt's *Illustrated Map of the Thames*, of which I have the 1897 edition, containing much material from as early as 1869; and secondly, Fred S. Thacker's *The Thames Highway*, published in 1919. Both these gentlemen, Rivermen to their fingertips, are reliable authorities. They are not always right. Who is? They do have the priceless gift for a later researcher, of being honest. Thacker,

*A pill-box reinforces the pre-Roman
earthworks at Dorcicon, by Day's Lock and
provides shelter.*

particularly, carried out the most exhaustive and detailed investigation, and set out his reasoning into the bargain.

I have drawn greatly on these two for historical detail of the river bed itself. As will be seen, there is a remarkable amount of river history still discernible to the informed searcher. I am sure there is a great deal more to be found (and perhaps to be published in later editions!).

While dealing with history, it seemed right to include details of the line of forts, 'pill-boxes', built along the upper river in 1940, to act, it was hoped, as a stiffening of a possible defensive line against the invading Hun. This latest use of the Thames for war would have exactly mirrored the Saxon line of Alfred, being on the north bank, instead of the south. Further, it included the earthworks at Dorchester. So, we might have seen the defensive ditches of the ancient Britons being used nineteen centuries or so later to repel another invader. Fortunately, the Germans did not come, for I do not think the line would have held for very long, and some fine old bridges would have been destroyed as well.

When I have been unable to write what I believe to be fact, I have tried to make an informed guess, which may well stimulate others. In the latter case, I have declared that I am guessing. If that is not particularly scientific, it is at least done in an effort to be positive. As is probably inevitable in a river that passes through Oxford, there has been a good deal of negative guesswork about the River. One idea is that it does not rise where everyone expects it to, at Thameshead, but rather at Seven Springs, which everybody has always thought to be the source of the Churn. This argument is reinforced by the continuing reduction in the amount of water at Thameshead, which is nowadays an exceedingly feeble place to start a river, being about as dry as anywhere in England. Nevertheless, there used to be a good spring at Thameshead, a hundred years and more ago, and the Thames/Churn confluence still finds the stripling Thames the senior partner.

A more serious and more insidious argument concerns the very name of the river. According to this hypothesis, it is not the Thames, it is the Isis. If this is too much for the public to swallow, it is the Isis when it flows through Oxford; or, it is the Isis until it joins the Thame

Isis (with light fitting) and Father Thames look up and down from Henley Bridge.
Right: *Swans feeding.* Jon Eastland.

at Dorchester: Thames/Isis = Tamesis; or, it is the Isis as far as Henley Bridge.

All this is based on the testimony of one Leland, who is an early, interesting but frequently unreliable chronicler of the Thames. He lived in the sixteenth century. He wrote that the Thames was known as Isis, 'beyond the memory of man', which was a medieval way of avoiding the need for fundamental research.

The problem is that the word Thames or Thame or Teme is a British word, meaning 'river'. So, the fact that the Romans called it Tamesis, 1500 years before Leland, is not as conclusive as it might seem. All it proves is that, when the Romans asked the local Britons what it was called, they replied: 'the River'. The Saxons were given the same message. Isis has never been accepted, or even seriously suggested, for the lower river. It appears only to have had local provenance, mainly around Oxford. In that case it should fail, on the grounds that it is a confusion, a barrier to simple understanding. It is interesting that the Englishman's insistence on calling the Thames the River, already discussed, is not merely another example of exasperating idiosyncracy. Rather, it has a tradition going back at least 2000 years. We have always called it the River!

THE THAMES MILE-BY-MILE

Well rowed! Well rowed!

PREAMBLE

THE THAMES as a cruising river stretches from Inglesham Bridge, about one mile above Lechlade in Gloucestershire, to Teddington Lock, between Richmond and Kingston, in what is now called Greater London. This is a distance of 125 miles. That is to say, it takes the Thames 125 miles to cover the 63 miles between these places.

From the edge of the Cotswolds to the edge of London, the stream explores a rich and varied segment of English countryside. The journey divides rather well into four parts, each markedly different. The lowest 16 miles lie in London's commuter belt. Here the close proximity of large numbers of people is clearly evident, although, as will be seen, this section still has a great deal to recommend it. From Bell Weir, near Egham, to Reading, is about 40 miles. It is the sophisticated river, with all the best known centres; Windsor, Maidenhead, Cookham, Marlow, and Henley. The third section, from

Tea by the River at Henley.

Reading to Oxford, also 40 miles, is much less crowded in mid-summer, passing through Pangbourne, Goring, Wallingford and Abingdon. Lastly lie the 30 miles from Oxford to Lechlade, mostly open countryside and so wild and empty of people that the river touches just two villages, Kelmscott and Buscot, and otherwise only seven pubs, eleven locks and one boatyard.

The chief difficulties with any guide to the river are that the ideal of starting at the beginning and travelling steadily to the end is most unlikely to occur in practice; and that it is awkward to follow a narrative that is running one way if one is travelling in the opposite direction. I have tried to reduce these difficulties in several ways. I have written the guide the wrong way up, from the lowest point of the river upwards. This is simply because most of the boats on the river are kept at the London end. Secondly, the description of the passing scene is indexed mile by mile to Stanford's River Thames map. Thirdly, dividing the chapter into four sections is intended to help the reader quickly to find the right place.

Although it is sensible to describe the River from the bottom to the top, since most people and their boats are in the lower reaches, there is no denying that any river is best appreciated as an element if studied from source to sea. If you cruise up the Thames, you will move from vista to vista as the countryside unfolds before you. If you cruise down river you can determine much more readily *why* it unwinds the way it does. In short, you become almost a part of the stream, involved in its life-force. It is a different experience altogether. For this reason cruising up and down a section is far more a continuing experience than a repeat of the same experience.

It appears that the Thames used to flow north-east, linking perhaps with the Great Ouse, and becoming a tributary of the Rhine somewhere off the coast of Holland. The impact of the American continental plate and the action of the last ice-age seem to have been two factors which caused this flow first to form a lake in the centre of Middle England, and then to break out across the barrier of the Chiltern Hills to take up its present course.

Where the breakthrough was made became a gorge, which allowed the lake to drain, and is now a valley, steep in places but usually relatively gentle. The breakthrough is called the

The Goring Gap with Goring Lock and Streatley Woods.

Goring Gap, because it starts quite clearly at Goring. The river above this point runs through a flat plain. There are low hills from time to time but there is never any major clash of interests, as it were. The river goes on its way, particularly above Oxford, without any obvious rhyme or reason. It is a skittish river, apparently exploring the countryside out of curiosity rather than as a result of any grand design. When hills appear, as at Nuneham Courteney or Wittenham, they do not seem to dictate the course so much as to run alongside it.

At Goring, all this changes quite dramatically. Time and again, as you run down with it, you see clearly how the way forward is barred by one great hill after another, and the river is forced to change its course accordingly. The final flourish of the Goring Gap is at Cliveden. It is also the most spectacular, for here is a true cliff, with which the river has obviously fought savagely for supremacy over the eons of prehistory, finishing with the natural compromise that give us so much pleasure today.

Below Maidenhead, the country is flat again and the Thames makes its way with measured majesty and occasional wild frolic to the sea.

A good deal of the information in this chapter has accrued over the last forty years or so, but details of moorings, locks and pubs were the subject of two surveys carried out specially, to make them as accurate as possible. The first of these surveys was done during five weeks in July/August 1985, and covered the river from Bell Weir to Lechlade. I used my own boat, which is 40 feet long and draws 1 ft 9 in. The second took place in October 1986, for which I hired a boat of 31 ft, drawing 2 ft 3 in, and covered the section from Bell Weir to Teddington. On both trips the river was full but not high, the current was never fast and the weirs which control the flow were never more than half open. Information about locks was finally checked, by advice and observation, in 1987.

If I say there is a mooring, it means that I went alongside. Where I could not come alongside because someone else was there, I have indicated this. Where I could not come alongside but I think a boat drawing rather less would do so, I have indicated this by calling it a shallow mooring. I have only included those places where it is difficult but highly desirable to land, such as Wallingford for example.

From all this it should follow that, if your boat does not exceed either dimension of mine but is less in one of them, you will no doubt find other moorings. Equally, if your boat exceeds either of my dimensions you will not be able to use all the moorings I have indicated. You should not assume however that there *will* be other moorings if your boat draws less than mine. This is particularly important where I have said there are no moorings between two locks or features. It is also the case that you will be less likely to find additional moorings the higher up river you go.

I found it was usually true that moorings came in groups; only a few are isolated. You will find they tend to be on the outside of bends and upstream of them. Broad, straight stretches are often frustratingly bad for mooring, all up the Remenham (left) bank at Henley for instance. The exceptions are generally where the river has been dredged specifically so that you can moor, at some public mooring places.

Please note particularly that I have referred to the right and left banks as they are when heading upstream. In this I have broken the convention that left and right should be taken in a downstream direction. I have done this to avoid chaos! The only exception to this rule is, when writing of bridge arches, the suggested arch takes into account your direction of travel. The advice: 'Use the right-hand arch going up and coming down', for instance, does not mean: 'Use the same arch both ways', rather: 'Use the arch on your right whichever way you are going.' Since this is the only exception, I hope it follows that the observation: 'the channel is on the right, going up' clearly indicates that it is on the left coming down.

NOTES ABOUT THE LOCKS

Information about each lock is given, as far as possible, adjacent to the reference in the Travelogue. The following explanatory note will serve as a guide to this information.

The diagrams accompanying the descriptions of the locks are not drawn to scale. This is because the measurements of the locks plus their tying up facilities do not fit a manageable space unless the lock is drawn too small.

The direction of the steps is shown, as discussed on page 150.

Wooden pilings and walings are shown with the correct number of uprights. Uprights are roughly 25 ft (7 m) apart.

Where the tie-up is to a hard-stand, the bollards vary in incidence, but 8 ft (2.5 m) is an average. The total number is shown, to allow an estimate of the length of the lay-by.

I have only shown stream direction arrows where they are likely to be a factor in the successful navigation of a particular lock. In many cases I have experienced these effects. In others, they are indicated as a result of discussion with the lock-keeper.

Wind is frequently a major problem, mostly above a lock: i.e. when heading downstream. For this reason, the north bearing is shown for each lock. The prevailing wind over the Thames is south westerly.

The dates shown are those for the first pound lock on the site. They are taken from *The Thames Highway*, vol. 11, except for King's and Eynsham.

The terms DEEP and SHALLOW are meant to indicate whether one can reasonably expect to step or scramble lightly ashore in an empty lock, or to experience difficulty in so doing. I have taken 4 ft as the cut-off point between these two, and have included the words in the descriptions so that the boat skipper can inform himself at a glance.

Where I have said that a particular weir is not a problem, this should be taken to refer to normal conditions. In severe stream conditions, particularly when the red boards are up at locks, *all* weirs have to be treated with great respect.

Overnight mooring is sometimes available at locks, and I have indicated these. There may be others at which the lock-keeper will allow it. In all cases there is a fee payable.

I have occasionally been asked if one should tip lock-keepers. The answer is no. Interestingly, there is a long and proud tradition, going back certainly to the days of the Thames Commissioners, that Thames lock-keepers never have accepted tips.

Part One

TEDDINGTON
TO
STAINES

TWO hundred and fifty yards below Teddington Lock, hidden discreetly away in a glade beside the tow-path, stands a monument known as the Boundary Stone. It was erected in 1909 to mark the landward limit of the Port of London Authority and the lower limit of the Thames Conservancy. It is typical of the serious yet relaxed attitude of Authority to the Thames River that the stone is quite grand for a marker, nicely worked and arresting to the eye, and yet is so placed that you certainly would never see it unless you were looking for it carefully.

The Boundary Stone.

The same applies to the London Stone at Staines, as we shall see. The first section of the journey to Lechlade is almost a tale of two stones, for the London Stone represents the limit of the jurisdiction of the City of London over this length of river from its settled beginning, in 1285, to its end in 1857. This jurisdiction, and control, firmly but usually lightly exercised over the centuries, mainly for the greater benefit of the City itself but surprisingly often in a spirit of altruism which stands to its great credit, has left an indelible mark upon the river. To a Middle Thames man, like myself, the stretch from Teddington to Staines might as well be a different river to that which follows, so strange does it look and feel.

In 1197, King Richard I, finding himself short of money, applied to the Corporation of the City of London to provide it. They did, and asked for the Thames in exchange. With his usual lack of thought for the future, the King granted their wish by means of a document marvellously vague and all enveloping, with which the City proceeded to crush at law any challenger, including several monarchs, for the next seven centuries. Fortunately, the City was normally on the side of the angels, 'though Richard had no way of knowing that.

Although Richard's Charter appears to refer to the whole river, and although the City occasionally expressed its wishes and complaints concerning the middle and upper river, for practical purposes their jurisdiction never extended beyond Staines after 1285. There was no new charter or royal amendment, no obvious reason in fact why this happened. My own view is that, in the end, the City settled for that which it could control. Staines became the upper limit because it was a day's ride from London, or a day's row by barge, if you started early and finished late.

We tend to forget, in these days of strong central government, backed by local police forces and, in need, the army, that things were very different in the Middle Ages. Then, the King could enact laws, impose penalties, require action, but he could not ensure obedience unless he appeared in person, heavily backed by force. Since kings were almost always fighting the Welsh, Scots, French, Saracens or each other, they had little time for enforcing domestic laws. On the other hand, the monasteries and local landlords were not to be trifled with. Private armies were the rule. Local people were either owned by their lord, or knew better than to upset him.

In these circumstances, I cannot see how the City of London could have expected to control the River in the face of certain opposition from the riparian owners out of their immediate, physical reach. Royal officials sent to enforce the law were normally either bought, advised to keep riding west, or met with unfortunate, terminal accidents. City messengers had even less hope of being obeyed. I think the City fathers made a pragmatic decision to manage only that part of the river they could readily patrol. To celebrate their decision and to give notice of their determination to protect their rights, they raised the stone at Staines in 1285.

One of the enduring policies of the City over the centuries was to set its face against locks in the lower river. They believed it was better to have a free flow than to allow weirs of any kind to be erected. They were helped in this by the flatness of the countryside, which meant there were few rapids to contend with, and also by the action of the tides, which flowed some way above Teddington, and slowed the flow of the river above their highest point, causing it to back up significantly with each high tide.

This policy became finally untenable during the second half of the eighteenth century, when a number of shallows began to cause increasing difficulties to the barge-owners, who compared the City's river unfavourably with the Commissioners' stream and its locks. Early in the nineteenth century therefore, it was decided to build six locks. Acting with their usual energy and despatch, they completed the first at Teddington in 1811, and the last, at Molesey, in 1815. All six lock sites are still in use and suffice to this day.

MILE
0

Teddington is the lowest true lock on the Thames, since the lock at Richmond only operates when the tide barrier is in use. There are in fact three locks here; the barge lock, which can be divided into two enormous halves, each of which dwarfs the 'large' launch lock alongside it; and finally the skiff lock, unique on the river, which is only wide enough for a skiff, and long enough for two of them.

Teddington is so named because it was the farm (tun) of Tuda, who was the first of many

TEDDINGTON 1811

Fall 8' 10": 2.68 m | Deep

Upstream The lock is on the left, almost opposite Tough Bros yard, which you will see first. The launch lock is up to the right of the barge lock. The tie-up is to a high level gantry on the left.

Downstream The lock is on the right. There is no lay-by, only a number of pilings against the bank, about 40 ft apart. You do the best you can with those. The weir is not a problem, although it does run down the cut for some way, provided that you use the width of the cut to keep away.

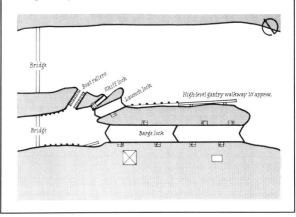

Saxons we shall meet on our journey. He may have been a local chief, if the 'ing' is a Saxon suffix, in which case it was 'the farm of the people of Tuda'. There is considerable doubt, in this case though, so it is safer to discount the possibility.

Teddington Weir is the most impressive on the river. The main section has a massive concrete gantry over it, on which are mounted the electric motors which control the sluices. The lock cut is fortunately the widest on the river, so one can keep a respectable distance from the weir when leaving the lock. There is a boom between you and it for greater reassurance.

There is a mooring on the left, opposite the top of the weir, pleasantly situated against a green bank, and overlooking the Lensbury Country Club opposite. This is a good place from which to examine the Boundary Stone, or indeed Teddington itself, since there is a footbridge (or more accurately two, in line) half way down the cut. There are two pubs at the end of these, The Anglers and The Tide End Cottage. Curiously for a journey across England from east to west, but typically, as we shall soon see, we have started in a south-easterly direction! However, we now turn south for the next $2\frac{1}{2}$ miles, and come at once to a major feature of this section of the Thames. Trowlock Island, on the right, is covered in chalet bungalows, which do nothing for the view. They, and similar ticky-tacky, will be a regular blot on the landscape all the way to Staines, so it is as well to mention about them.

For the romantic soul, the ideal of boating on the Thames is mile on mile of wood and meadow, past the occasional great house, with another boat to meet and greet every hour or so, as one slips peacefully along. Actually, one can do that at certain times of the year and on most of the river. On the other hand, if few people used the river, Thames Water would soon find it impossible to justify the cost of maintaining the Navigation. Looked at another way therefore, a certain amount has to be tolerated. Here are hundreds of people who so love the river that they have gone to great lengths to have a bit of bank to live on, or at least to use at weekends. Almost all of them have a boat moored alongside. I estimate that perhaps three-fifths of all the boats on the locked river are kept between Teddington and Staines. Furthermore, such is the River and the traditions that govern it, there are plenty of visually pleasant, quiet moorings to be had, like the one we have just left, and there is always a feeling of freedom, of distance from the crowd, in the busiest, most built-up places. For an outsider though, I would advise cruising this area from Monday to Thursday, for it must be prodigiously busy on a summer weekend. That is without taking into account all the organised activity.

At the head of Trowlock Island are three boat or yacht clubs, including Tamesis, with Kingston Rowing Club almost opposite. There is another, The Small Boat Club, at the tail of Steven's Eyot. You can pass both sides of this island, and moor at the head of it. Opposite, on the left is the Boater's Inn, which is hardly that, more a restaurant. It has a landing-stage.

The black topped chimneys of Kingston power-station are now plainly visible ahead.

Canbury Gardens are on the left. Mooring is not practicable. The bank is poor and covered in concrete, making it impossible to drive spikes anyway. The Teddington shore is rather smart, with a number of attractive houses on it.

Kingston Railway Bridge has three arches, only the centre and left hand ones being available. The right hand arch can be full of moored boats, as can the right hand bank and a good width of the river as well. Between this bridge and Kingston Bridge, on the left, is the boatyard of R J Turk & Sons, which is the lowest yard from which you can hire a cruiser. They also offer all main services to passing craft.

Once through Kingston Bridge, which is a handsome, soft stone colour, built in 1828, and where you can use any of the three centre arches there are a number of moorings giving access to shops or pubs or both. On the right, the pleasantest of the lot, is a Thames Water mooring at the start of Hampton Court Park which is but a step from the White Hart at Hampton Wick. On the left is a mooring adjoining the Ram. Kingston market is just round the corner from here. The Gazebo pub has a mooring, as does the Kingston Mill. There is another mooring, to a quay, with shops behind, and the main Kingston Town moorings, to a series of jetties. Here is a Notice: 'Public Moorings. Welcome to Kingston-upon-Thames. Short term moorings available, subject to bye-laws.' These include a maximum stay of 24 hours, and a table of charges.

Kingston-upon-Thames is named from the Saxon 'Cyninges tun', 'farm of the kings'. Here, it is claimed by some authorities, were crowned a number of Saxon kings: Athelstan, 924; Edmund, 940; Edred, 946; Edwy, 955; Edgar, 959; Edward the Martyr, 975; Ethelred II, 978 (the unready, or uncounselled); and Edmund II, 1016, to name but a few. It may be true. There is no evidence that they were not, and it seems probable that, it being a royal estate, some kings would have lived here. There is no reason to suppose that the Kings' Stone, carefully preserved as a Coronation Stone, was in fact any such thing. It seems more likely that those authorities who wrongly translated Kingston as Kings' stone then looked round for a likely stone to fill the role.

On leaving the Kingston moorings, there are no more on the right until opposite Ravens

Eyot, where there is a good one. On the left there are a series of steps leading up from the bank, with two rings at each set. There is no question of mooring anywhere else because of the impossibility of driving stakes through the concrete, but if these places are available there seems no reason not to use them. They are some way from the shops however.

Take note of two ferries in this reach, at mile $2\frac{1}{2}$ and at the head of Ravens Eyot.

3 The route has now swung south-west, although it will be another half mile before we reach the same longitude as we started from. The right hand bank is parkland, the same park in which 'the little gentleman in the velvet coat' dug out his heap of earth, causing King William III's horse to stumble and throw that unfortunate and unpopular monarch to his death. For us it is a great, green lung. The left bank has a high wall along it and signs of industry beyond.

Thames Marina offer most facilities including mooring, as do Maidboats. Mid-week you may be able to moor at the latter yard and walk into Thames Ditton, which is a pretty little village, deuced hard to get at. Maidboats have a notice proclaiming that they are: 'THE Hireboat people'! There's confidence for you.

There is a remarkable bungalow just here, beautifully built under a fully tiled roof—floating on a pontoon. It takes the term house-boat to its logical conclusion.

Opposite Maidboats there are now a series of moorings to Hampton Court Park. They stretch right round the sharp bend that swings us north-west, up to the tail of Thames Ditton Island. There is another, on the same bank, half way up Thames Ditton Island itself. Those sections of the bank where mooring is possible appear to be the lengths capped with wood, as opposed to concrete or grass.

It is possible to circumnavigate Thames Ditton Island, which is actually two islands, although the channel is to the right of it (going up). Do not try to pass between the two islands. You can moor at the Swan, which is as close as you can come to the village. The fine Georgian house to the left is now called 'Home of Compassion', and is run by nuns. Basic shopping can be done in the village, which has a dear old church. Thames Ditton is called Ditton to denote 'farm by the ditch or dyke', and Thames

to differentiate between this place and Long Ditton, a mile or so to the south.

The island has a bridge for the use of residents, who have so covered it in houses and it is so narrow anyway, that some of the houses seem to be perched precariously on the edge. The houses are noticeably smart, as are some of the attendant boats.

Above the island, on the left, the Albany 4 Hotel is well worth a visit, although mooring to the travesty of a jetty is a great test of rivermanship. The landlord tells me he has it in mind to sort this out, which would make his pub even more popular.

There is now open space on both sides but no mooring until just before the confluence of the Mole, on the left, where the piling is noticeably higher than the stone wall. Here is a pleasant grassy bank. Opposite is 200 yards of short stay mooring, for visitors to Hampton Court Palace.

The Palace at Hampton Court was built by Cardinal Wolsey, and represented the summit and consummation of his success. So much so that it signalled the start of his downfall, for it began to be said that he lived greater than the King, and Henry was not one to put up with that. Hampton Court is perhaps the saddest great house in England.

With the disgrace of its builder, Henry VIII moved in himself, in 1529. Here Anne Boleyn was courted, married and doomed. Here Jane Seymour gave Henry a sickly son, and died doing so. Here Catherine Howard betrayed her king and husband, and died for it. Perhaps Wolsey cursed the man who made and destroyed him. If so, his curse was spectacularly successful.

For two hundred years the Kings and Queens of England lived here, some more than others. It was the home of Mary, whose hated memory lies deep in the English subconscious, expressing itself in deep suspicion of the Church of Rome, and still remembered nursery rhyme. Charles I lived here, and was later imprisoned here. Charles II held Court here. William III caused Wren to make major alterations to the house, and the two greatest gardeners of the day, London and Wise, to lay out the formal gardens after the manner of the French.

After William's fall over the mole-hill, Anne lived here, and finally George II, chiefly famous, as I remember, for being the last English king to lead his army into battle. With his death, in 1760, the house ceased to be a royal home. For two hundred years it has stood, full of grandeur and precious things, but empty of the bustle and throb of the life it was designed for. Only 'grace and favour' apartments are now occupied. What sort of life is that for the palace of the great and proud Cardinal?

Three things can give us solace for Hampton's fate. The great mansion is still Tudor, with Stuart and William and Mary additions. Nobody since has cared enough to ruin it with further improvements. The public rooms and courts and gardens are full of loveliness, and open for us all to see. Lastly, there is of course the maze. Here the immortal Harris, according to Jerome K Jerome, offered to act as guide to a relative, and ended up leading about twenty people and a keeper absolutely nowhere and nearly getting himself lynched by the mob! I was last there in 1948, and remember it as one of the great disappointments of my life, it being exceedingly moth-eaten and impossible to get lost in for a second. However, the twins were there recently, and report that it was 'quite good'. So is Hampton Court itself, and well worth a visit.

Above the Palace stands Hampton Court Bridge, which is about as fine as any other on the Thames. It is relatively new, being built by Edwin Lutyens and opened by Edward, Prince of Wales, in July, 1933. Use any of its three arches. There is a mooring on the left, immediately above the bridge, from which to reach the local shops, which are a short distance down the middle street. There is a grocer, greengrocer and butcher.

Molesey Lock is 150 yards above the bridge. There is a lovely view of Hampton Court Palace from the lock, with the bridge complementing the mellow brick of the old house.

Molesey Weir is one of the more awe-inspiring on the river. It comes down almost to the lock. At the head of the weir, on an island, are T W Allen & Son, who offer most services and hire cruisers. They are unique in that their yard can only be approached by water.

5   Molesey Boat Club is on the left, and you can pass either side of Tagg's Island, which is lined with house-boats of all shapes and sizes, some quite grand. None so grand as the vision that is

MOLESEY 1815

Fall 6' 1" : 1.85m | Deep | Sanitary station & Pump-out

Upstream The lock is on the left. Prepare as you pass Hampton Court Bridge. The lay-by is on the left, and is short. If the lay-by is full however there is plenty of room to manoeuvre above the bridge. The lock is wider than the gates, which are offset, so if going in on the left, allow for this. I found no effect from the weir below the lock.

Downstream The weir runs down the left of the cut for 50 yards or so. The easier tie-up is to a concrete lay-by on the left. The problem with this is that the weir runs right up to it, so you have to keep off this and then turn in sharply once you are past, tricky in a strong stream. The right bank has a number of pilings with chains slung between them. Alternate piles are higher than the bank, the others are cut off level with the top. The pump-out is at the lock end of this right hand tie-up.

Do not move into the lock cut unless there is room to tie up.

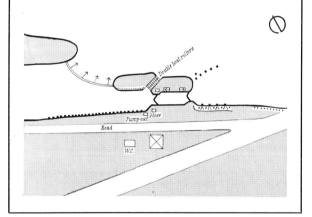

moored on the right bank, beyond the island, which raises house-boat design to an art form.

Garrick's Temple now lies on the right, built by him to house a statue of Shakespeare by Roubiliac, which is now in the British Museum. David Garrick lived in a villa beyond the road, which he loved and on which, and the gardens attached to it, he lavished great attention. The island above is called Garrick's Eyot while Hampton Church, nestling in its village on the

House-boat above Tagg's Island.

right, makes a welcoming sight. There is a public mooring, 24 hour, allowing access to the Bell Inn and the shops, reached by means of Station Road and about five minutes' walk away. Hampton is 'farm in the great bend in the river'.

Here is Constable's yard, where Mark Edwards makes skiffs and punts in the traditional way. He seemed very busy, I am pleased to say. You can hire such boats by day or for camping from the yard.

Back on the river, Hampton Sailing Club is in the middle, opposite the church. There was a cormorant on the point of Garrick's Eyot as I came down. He was still there next day, looking black and sinister in the evening light. He had been joined by 12 Canada geese.

There is occasionally a ferry from Hampton Wharf to West Molesey.

6   There is a mooring on the left, opposite Hampton church, to a grassy bank: not bad. The course now swings south-west by west and

Platts Eyot is ahead. It is possible to pass both sides with equal ease. Ambrose Marine who hire cruisers and offer pump-out and other services to casual visitors, are on the island, which is connected by an iron suspension bridge to the Hampton bank.

There is a mooring on the left bank, opposite Platts Eyot, above Ambrose's yard. The wall becomes distinctly higher. It is a place called West Molesey Wharf, and is not the best mooring on the Thames. This area, Molesey Hurst, has had a chequered history in the last two hundred years. The books at the turn of the century always regret the close presence of Hurst Park Racecourse and its large grandstand. I managed to lose money here once, on a horse belonging to the Queen Mother in fact, but I forget its name. Now the racecourse has gone, its place taken by one of the earlier, and I am afraid rather ghastly ticky-tacky estates. This at least has the decency to stand back some way from the river, but the land between has a forlorn air, as though it has no role to play.

Racing has taken place here for longer than

A glimpse of Hampton from Molesey Hurst.

you might think. Fred Thacker reports that the first lock-keeper at Molesey, one John Nash, was 'killed by a racehorse on Moulsey Hurst', in 1820. Before racing was held here there were prize fights and, even earlier, it was a favourite spot for duelling. Presumably with both these activities, the approach of the enforcement officers of the Surrey Magistracy would lead to escape to Hampton by river!

Molesey was 'Mul's Island'. Presumably the River Mole was also named after him.

7   Above Platts Eyot there are reservoirs on both banks, particularly to the left. Aquarius Sailing Club is on the right, shortly before mile 7. Some particularly pleasing houses stand on the right before Purvis Eyot, but the standard is not maintained for long. Sunbury Court Island is built upon, and the channel to the right is lined with boats, some of which are quite large. Nevertheless, I came to a sticky end near the top, and had to back out, with massive loss of dignity! The left bank has plenty of tree cover, so that the reach is quite pleasant to pass along. I was accompanied down it by a fleet of

'best boats' from Molesey Boat Club. It was one of those occasions when you do not know whether to press on or wait, and always end up making the wrong decision. There must have been a dozen of them, each stopping from time to time to discuss technique with someone on shore, or simply to rest. Every time I decided to overtake a boat it instantly started again, and a potential collision had to be avoided. It all makes for interest.

The reach ends with Phoenix Island, which is open space with a swimming pool in the middle of it, and no mooring. Whether Phoenix Island was named after the Phoenix public house or vice versa, and why, I do not know. Thacker calls it Collingridge or Swan's Nest Ait, so its present name is a recent adoption.

Turks of Sunbury lie at the tail of the weir-stream, one of three branches of the same family running separate boatyards. They hire cruisers and offer services to passers-by.

The Sunbury Mooring is up the weir-stream,   **8**

and is a good one, to a sloping bank, planted with trees. The village is perhaps five minutes' walk, (to the right and first left) and has two butchers, a grocer, greengrocer, baker (milk), two newsagents, a hardware store, a laundrette, and Barclays Bank, but no great character. Its name means 'Sunna's stronghold', which starts an interesting train of thought. Was this the Sunna whose 'people' settled at Sonning? If so, did he establish himself at Sunbury and then send home for the women and children before moving on? Or was it a descendent of his who left the family settlement at Sunbury to explore further inland, with his tribe? Or was it simply a common name and no connection existed between the two?

Both the pubs in the weir-stream, the Phoenix and the Magpie have moorings for clients, but the official mooring is so close that it matters little if these are full. A plaque at the Magpie commemorates the first meeting of the Grand Order of Water Rats, in 1889.

Sunbury Lock is unique in that it is actually two locks alongside each other. The one on the right still has the 'old fashioned' ship's wheel type of sluice gear, which we shall not see again until King's, 90 miles away. It was built in 1856, to replace the 1812 lock, which stood half way up the cut, above the present lock, opposite the fine lockhouse. The City celebrated with a plaque: 'Sunbury Lock re-built 1856', which is on the ground beside it. The City always had more style than the Thames Commissioners, but then they always had more money too. The old lock now acts as a relief for the new, which was opened on July 6, 1927.

The weir continues the disconcerting habit, to the Middle Thames man, of accompanying you half way down the cut on the way down, and forcing adoption of a prudent course in mid cut on the way up. This is a feature of all the locks until Romney.

The Weir Hotel at the top of the cut has a mooring for clients. A little above, Thames Water Navigation Headquarters is on the island to the right. There is a weir between this island and the one above it, and another at the top of that island. The inference is that the channel behind the islands was originally man-made, probably to serve a mill erected at the higher end. Thacker places Barringer's Weir at this point, a structure first mentioned in 1776

SUNBURY 1812

Fall 6' 2" : 1.87m | Deep

Upstream There does not appear to be any weir effect. The concrete lay-by is on the left. The left hand lock is the one normally used. If the other one is to be used, this will be obvious.

Downstream The weir leads you into the cut, and continues down it for 50 yards. The piling is on the right, and turns to the right at the approach to the lock. So make sure your approach is firm and decisive. The right hand lock is the one normally in use.

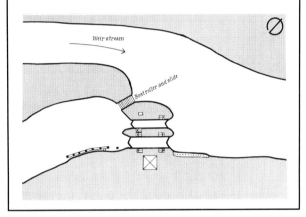

---

although, again by inference, probably in position since 1623. In his day, there was only one island here, the middle weir seems to be a recent development.

The Walton Town Wharf is in front of the Angler's Inn, and can be moored against. It has two mooring rings, about 50 feet apart, which are a little awe-inspiring, but closer inspection reveals an anchored chain about six feet back from the edge, to which a boat can be tied.

Shepperton Marina, on the right, have cruisers for hire, but do not offer services for casual callers. Walton Marine do, on the left, just before the bridge.

Walton Bridge is easily the ugliest on the whole river up from Teddington, and I do not exclude all the unattractive railway bridges. Its only relieving feature is that it presents no difficulty to the navigator. It was not always so, although Taunt refers to 'an iron girder structure', which is the best way to describe the present edifice. A print of 1794 shows an

Walton. Could this be the ugliest bridge on the Thames?

extraordinary latticed affair, rising to a marked point in the centre, rather after the design on a willow-pattern plate. It appears to have stood for over half a century, as did its successor, a fine structure of four arches which attracted the attention of J M W Turner RA. This fell down in 1859 and was replaced in 1863 with the one to which Taunt refers. It was quite elegant, iron or not, and appears to have used the same footings as its predecessor.

Walton means 'farm of the serfs', by which the Saxons who named it may well have meant the Britons, whom they invariably regarded in that light. There is a public mooring on the

left above the bridge. The position is pleasant enough, although a bit close to the bridge and road.

A quarter of a mile above Walton Bridge we come to the start of the most recent man-made channel on the Thames, the Desborough Cut. Named after W H Grenfell, 1st Viscount Desborough, the best known and most energetic chief of the Thames Conservancy, the cut runs for about half a mile, cutting across the convolutions of the old river through Shepperton and Lower Halliford. A cut was first proposed here in 1802, to assist the barge traffic, which was always being held up by shoals in the old course. In the end, the cut was decided upon to relieve danger of flooding in consequence of a drainage scheme that had been put into effect in the Wey valley. It was commenced in March, 1930, and completed in June, 1934. It is possible to moor at several places up the left bank, although the closeness of the road should be borne in mind and there are several more comfortable places within a short distance.

Unless you are in a hurry, the run round the old river is much more interesting, and Shepperton worth a visit. Where the river turns sharply to the right to follow this course is the site of one of the unanswered conundrums of Thames history, the Coway Stakes. Persistent rumour has it that they were a frieze planted by Cassivellaunus as an obstacle to the invading Julius Caesar. I suspect this of being an example of Victorian sensationalism, and find it regrettable that some modern authors continue to suggest it, without any real evidence.

What is certain is that Caesar crossed the Thames to attack Cassivellaunus. It is quite possible that he did it near here, since there are several ancient fords in the area. Halliford, the most infamous of the shallows in the vicinity is half a mile to the north. There was a ford at Coway too. Caesar *could* have used either; or he could have forded at Kingston, as some suggest he did. There seems no reason to connect Coway Stakes with his invasion however.

The stakes were in two rows, made of oak and shod with iron. Thacker saw several in the British Museum, one of which had a note: 'This stake was on 16 October 1777 drawn out of the bottom of the river Thames, in which at least five-sixths of its length was embedded; it stood with several others which (the water being uncommonly low) were then easily to be seen, about one-third of the river's breadth from its south bank, a quarter of a mile above Walton Bridge'.

There are several reasons why I do not think they have anything to do with Cassivellaunus. Firstly, there is no reason to expect the river was actually in the same place in 54 BC, and a good deal of evidence to suggest that this is unlikely. Secondly, preparation of oak stakes shod with iron suggests something far more permanent than a defensive hedge. There is a theory that they formed the piers of an eleventh-century bridge, which I find much more feasible. Thirdly, how would Cassivellaunus know early enough that Caesar was going to try this ford? As to the theory that the stakes marked the ford so that Caesar's troops would cross exactly where Cassivelaunus wanted them to, it does not bear examination. It would have been like manna from heaven to the Romans, who liked nothing better than marching in column of eight, straight at lightly armed enemy forces, protected by their overhead and flank shield screen from flying nasties.

Two more likely suggestions are of a double row of stakes to mark an awkward ford and prevent animals from straying off it into deep water, providing a sort of cow-way: and a fishing hedge, of which there were numerous local examples. Thacker thought the stakes he saw were too substantial for this purpose, but they could have been atypical to that extent. As to date, based on the movement of the river, this cannot be earlier than the eleventh century.

There is an official mooring on the left next to the end of the bridge across the cut (but in the old course). It is close to the road, but this is only a local road for the island. There is a gaunt stone building on the left, with 'North Surrey Water Board, 1905' written on it. The housing up the right bank starts as chalets, week-end stuff, but steadily improves. On the left, the island is not built on at all, and makes a pleasant counter to the opposite bank.

The river turns sharply left at Lower Halliford, which is really part of Shepperton these days. Halliford is 'Holy ford', but why holy is not known. Perhaps some long vanished religious cell stood by it.

Our course now describes an arc to the right. There are several potential looking moorings to the green and pleasant left bank, but these are all too shallow. However, round the right hander is a meadow with a screen of trees behind it, on the right, and this is the official Shepperton Mooring. It runs about 200 yards, beyond which is another 100 yards, exactly identical, with a 'Mooring Prohibited' notice. One can almost hear the reasoning of local bureaucracy: 'We must give but also take away, or the peasants will not understand their place'.

The mooring is nevertheless an excellent one, and gives access to Shepperton village in about five minutes' walk through the trees to the left, and diagonally across the green. The Three Horseshoes stands at the head of the village street, past which are grouped all the necessary shops, and Barclays Bank. If on the other hand, you keep left at the green, then in another five minutes you arrive at the old village centre, with its square, church, and the King's Head Hotel. Nothing much has changed here for at least a hundred years. I have a photograph taken that long ago which looks just the same. Shepperton is 'shepherds' farm'. I am surprised that keeping sheep was a specialised business at that time in this part of the world. Presumably that is what made it distinctive.

The river turns sharply to the left again, past Shepperton Manor, whose lawns run down to the river. The run back to the Desborough Cut is uneventful, and leads to another sharp turn which takes us to D'Oyly Carte Island, which once echoed to rehearsals for Gilbert and Sullivan operas.

There is a bewitching house on it, full of corners and galleries and dormer windows, all extravagance, but somehow it seems just right. You can pass either side of the island, although the more interesting channel is to the right.

Shepperton Lock is dead ahead. Observe the lock cottage on the island. It must have marvellous views. It was originally the Engineer's house. Shepperton is, for me, one of the loveliest locks on the river.

On the left, before the lock, the River Wey joins the Thames, and on the left bank is a Thames Water mooring. From here it is a short walk to the local pubs, ten minutes to a quite adequate village store, and ten minutes more to the start of any other shops. I gave up. There is a ferry between Nauticalia, the yard on the Shepperton bank, and the mooring. This is a good place to pause and consider.

Until the eighteenth century, the river went round a long meander of nearly half a mile to rejoin the present stream about fifty yards above the lock. It still does of course, only now it is the weir-stream. From the early 1700s however, the river started to break through the neck of the meander whenever there were flood conditions. The breakthrough channel came to be known as Stoner's Gut. (Gut = small channel or cut). Eventually, the river ran through it so frequently that it was found necessary to build a wall across the upper end of it to ensure that the river kept in its old bed. This was expedient here because of the important barge trade port at Weybridge.

In 1813, the lock was built where the Gut had been, or close to it. There is now an overflow weir, with a rather smart tiled roof, a short distance down the weir-stream from the lock, which is not shown by Taunt but seems to be on Thacker's map. This suggests the pressures were not entirely relieved by the building of the lock.

The waterways in the old channel are quite complicated, with the relief weir, main weir-

SHEPPERTON   1813

Fall 6'8" : 2.03m | Deep | Sanitary station

Upstream There is a nasty back-stream from the River Wey/weir-stream which curves into the lay-by area. It has a tendency to run you against the right hand lay-by and resist your leaving it. The left hand lay-by seems simple but there is a late attempt to push you back to the left close to the lock as you try to enter. Do not leave the lay-by until you are clear to enter and then steer into the middle of the approach channel and you should be safe enough. The Sanitary Station is on the right.

Downstream Get ready as you pass Pharaoh's Island. There is quite a sharp turn to the left into the lock. A strong stream will take you off to the right and this has to be overcome in addition to the need to counteract the left hand bend, if a satisfactory landing is to be made. The concrete hard-stand is on the left and is quite long, but do not approach unless you can see space to tie up. The width of the river above the lock is ample for standing by when the lay-by is full.

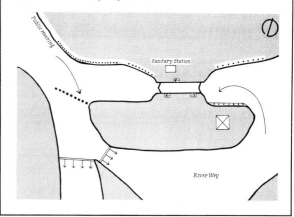

stream and then two arms of the River Wey issuing into it in quick succession. The Wey is the second from the left and is labelled. It can only be navigated by boats having a British Waterways licence, and penetrates to Godalming, a distance of about twenty miles. The point where the Wey meets the Thames weir-stream is the furthest south the Thames Navigation reaches.

The course is now north west by north all the way to Staines. Above the lock, the reach that greets us is well wooded and easy on the eye. The Thames Court Restaurant lies to the right, and has a mooring for customers. It looks a bit like a posh country house, but turns out to be one of the more relaxed and welcoming establishments on the river. If the mooring is full, double park.

Pharaoh's Island is the name of the large eyot above the lock. Why is not recorded. Thacker notes that it was often confused with Dog Ait, which used to lie half a mile up stream, but has now rejoined the left bank. I note that it still is so confused, as recently as 1983. The island is fully built up, with a road down the middle. It must be a most desirable place to live. There is no bridge, leading me to speculate about things like moving house, waste disposal, post and newspapers, to say nothing of daily commuting. I noticed a number of dinghies drawn up on the Middlesex bank, presumably left by the breadwinners on the way to the office. But if *he* has the dinghy, how does *she* do the shopping? Two dinghies presumably: but even then there is no way of calling in unexpectedly for coffee, especially if your friend lives on the other side of the island from the road. No doubt all this has been sorted out years ago. There is actually a notice giving instructions to visitors. As usual, all the houses have boats moored at the bottom of the garden, a happy sight.

A sharp bend to the right brings another change of scene. Both banks are built up, the right somewhat better than the left. Where the road leaves the river, on the right, there are two hundred yards of mooring to a concrete topped, sheathed bank. After this the mooring on the right appears to be private and lined with boats that seem to be lived in. The left bank is now heavily tree-lined, and there is no mooring until close to the top of the stretch, at 12 $\frac{1}{4}$. Here is a flight of ornamental steps, set in open country,

complete with nearby cows! An enigma, but I found 'no bottom' at three feet, and there is no reason to suppose one cannot moor, so why not?

Meanwhile the road reappears on the opposite bank and there is some good mooring below this point. After which there is nothing below Chertsey Bridge, except at Bates' yard, for a fee, when space is available.

The river turns sharply left and then commences a long, sweeping curve to the right. On the left, a public park, on the right, a field. It comes as a shock to realise that this, and the one by the steps, represent the only fields, as opposed to open spaces, we have passed since setting out. Furthermore, the next one is not until after Eton, thirteen miles away.

Chertsey Meads Marine are on the left, halfway round the bend. They hire cruisers and offer basic services. Above them, just below the bridge, W Bates and Son also hire cruisers, and offer all services.

Chertsey Bridge has good looks, symmetry and character. It is also an officially WEAK bridge, which is excellent news, for it means it does not carry heavy traffic. It has five arches. Going up, take the middle arch, or the one to its right. Coming down, take the middle. The bridge crosses a narrow part of the river at an awkward angle, tending to throw downcoming boats into Bates' yard, if there is a stream running.

Going up, it is necessary to keep quite well over to the left to open up the bridge. Funnily enough, the bridge is at exactly the opposite angle to that shown on Stanford's map, the only occasion I have found where the map is drawn incorrectly. In fact, it cannot be helped, because it is the out of scale width of the river, (which makes the map so readable) rather than faulty drawing that causes the problem.

The bridge was built between 1780 and '85. That is to say, it was started and finished in those years respectively. It has a plaque on the downstream side recording its partial rebuilding in 1894. Thacker quotes a report that the contractor of 1785, 'having completed the number of arches he had engaged for, and they not reaching the Surrey shore, that county was obliged at great expense, to supply the deficiency'! And another report states that the ends reached neither bank, involving both Surrey and Middlesex in expense, (cf. Datchet Bridge).

PREVIOUS PAGE. *College eight in training early at Oxford. (Chris Donaghue)*

Swans share a riverside picnic.

Rowing boats waiting for custom at Windsor. (Tony Page)

Cliveden House was once home to the Astor family; it is now owned by the National Trust.

Cliveden Woods provide a backdrop to Cookham Lock. (Raymond Blythe)

The cottage at Cliveden.
Rolling lawns at Shiplake.

You can moor to the left, at a wharf just above the bridge (in which case use the left-hand arch going up), although it is only just deep enough. There is a large bay above it, with a notice proclaiming mooring for customers of the Bridge Hotel, but take care. I was aground for 20 minutes trying to tie up there. You would be all right in a skiff.

Chertsey is a strange name. It stems from the Roman-British 'Cerotus' and the Saxon 'eyot', and is strange because you usually have one or the other, but not both. So, 'Cerotus' Island, (or well watered land)'.

The town is impossibly far away for shopping etc. It is chiefly famous for the great abbey that was founded in *c*666, and again in 964, and again in 1010. It covered four acres at its greatest power and is now razed as though it never was, like Osney at Oxford. It offered sanctuary to the body of that sad, inadequate and murdered king, Henry VI, until he was finally laid to rest at Windsor by Richard III.

A stream called the Abbey River runs into the Thames to the left of the lock. It starts at Penton Hook, and used to turn the abbey millwheel. The abbey stood on the island between this stream and the Thames.

Chertsey Lock was opened in 1813. Its proposed site was somewhat higher, above the junction with the Abbey River, but Lord Lucan, who lived at Laleham, objected that it would spoil his view. So the plans were redrawn to overcome this difficulty. It was also planned to cut through the top of the long bend we have just come round, but his lordship was not having that either. It is said that the lock cottage, a bungalow standing by the lock but no longer used, was one of Lord Lucan's lodges, which he gave to the City rather than that they should build another. Certainly it is unlike the other lock houses surviving from this period.

There is an infuriatingly enigmatic comment by Taunt: 'Traces are still in existence of the curved channel in which the Thames here ran, but on the lock being built the course of the stream was altered as at present.' The lock cottage was always in Surrey, when it should have been in Middlesex on this bank, suggesting that the river once passed to the east of it. But if this had been the case at the time the lock was built it could not have been one of Lord Lucan's lodges, for the opposite reason.

Further, if the river already flowed to the east of its present course, why would the engineer suggest the cut across the bend, just mentioned? One version of the theory about the change of bed has the bridge built on dry land and the river then diverted through it, which makes nonsense of the story about the arches not reaching the bank. That the course of the river *has* changed seems likely, the county boundary is sufficient evidence for that, and I am assured signs of the old bed are still to be seen. I think it must have done so much earlier than the present bridge, however, and am surprised that there seems to be no record of it in connection with earlier bridge building, for which there is documentary evidence back to 1530. I have also heard it said incidentally, that the reason why the present bridge is at an awkward angle is that it thus presented the best prospect to Lord Lucan, and this I *could* believe!

CHERTSEY 1813

Fall 4' 0" : 1.22 m | Marginally deep

Upstream The lock is on the right. Prepare before passing Chertsey Bridge. The main lay-by is to the right, but there is a short length on the left as well. I found no problem with the weir here.

Downstream The DANGER pilings, which are joined by chains, vary between 20 yards at the upstream end and zero at the lock end from the weir. The approach is not wide. So do not allow yourself to be squeezed to the right when coming down. There is plenty of width higher up. The main lay-by is to the left and there is a short length of piling to the right.

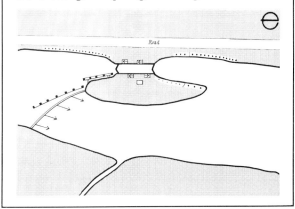

Above the lock, the M3 crosses on a miraculously slim bridge, with the merest hint of an arch. Shortly above the bridge there is a mooring to the right, to a grassy bank, close to the local road. A better looking position, where the road stands back a bit from the bank, I found to be too shallow.

The river now swings left and then right, past quite pleasant country, although the left bank looks most inhospitable in a tangle of trees, bushes and high undergrowth.

14 Laleham Sailing Club is somewhat curiously on the Chertsey bank, and 100 yards above it

there is a mooring on the right, followed by two more, either side of mile 14, each a little better than the last. There are moored boats and a reservoir opposite.

The open space on the right is now a public park, with the road rather further away. It does not seem a very busy road. When I passed there were large numbers of geese and other water fowl, the geese filling the river with great rafts of birds, or going ashore to dry and preen them-

Penton Hook with its elegant lock house built in 1814.

selves. No hope of mooring here, much too shallow.

There is a public mooring at Laleham, opposite Harris yard. Harris has been a name in these parts for many years. They hire cruisers and offer good facilities for the passing boater. Laleham, 'great bend where withies grow' (or perhaps 'village' rather than great bend, it is not clear), is on the site of a pre-historic ford and one of the principle shoal-waters that vexed bargemen down the centuries.

The left bank now fills with weekend cottages, but higher standards are maintained on the right. There is an ornate water-board extraction point on the right, a concrete erection of 1924. Shortly above is a white gate on the tow-path, which may be the successor to Laleham Upper Paygate. The paygates were a feature on the river from Datchet downwards. They were raised by the riparian owners, who imposed tolls for the use of the tow-paths over their land. We have passed the sites of several of them but this is the only one which still has a gate in roughly the right place. The tolls were eventually bought out by the City.

Penton Hook Lock is the highest and the second youngest of the City locks, being opened a little before Molesey, in 1815. The original, fine lock house is still in position. It is like that at Sunbury, complete with the arms of the City of London, and the date it was built, 1814.

Penton Hook seems to have been named in association with a local field, Pentyhoke, and is of fairly recent origin, 1535 being the first reference to it. It is descriptive of another extra-ordinary meander, similar to that at Shepperton, where the river takes half a mile to travel perhaps 50 yards. As at Shepperton, it kept breaking through the neck, and again as at Shepperton, a relief weir has been placed across the neck to counter the frequent flooding that continued after the lock was built. The neck is incredibly narrow now, it seemed to me to be as little as 20 yards. Strangely, and uniquely as far as I know, there was no weir put in the river until at least 40 years after the lock was built.

You can run down the Hook channel below the lock to Penton Hook Marina where there is mooring, on application to the office, and all services are offered. At the bottom of the stream, by the Yacht Club, is the start of the Abbey River.

Fred Thacker makes a beautiful thumb-nail sketch of 'old Myhill', the lock keeper in his day, who he had known at Hambleden: 'I thought he looked more than ever saturnine; having added to his natural air of admiralty a still profounder aspect of austerity with which not the most truculent bargemen of them all would successfully have trifled. Myhill; with whom royalty, they say, would once step ashore and converse.' Both would surely have approved of his present successor, Mr Arthur Cushing, a lovely man, full of lore about his beloved river, and one whose eye alone compels obedience.

PENTON HOOK   1815

Fall 4' 0" : 1.22 m | Marginally deep

Upstream The lay-by is on the right and there is a piling before this. There is also a short length of piling on the left. I found no back wash from the weir-stream. There are stanchions on the lock side in this lock, instead of bollards.

Downstream The lay-by is on the left, followed by a short length of piling. There is a strong pull to the right as you approach the lay-by, at which point there is a back-stream which will try to turn you broadside across the lock. In a strong stream this is one of the more difficult approaches on the river. The lock has offset doors and widens on the right after entry.

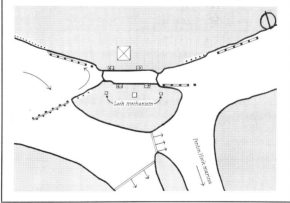

Above the lock, the river sweeps left again and then right. At the extreme of the right hand bend, you will observe a curious folly, a brick tower, upon the shore. This marks the site of an older structure, known as the Fishing Temple. It is also the site of Savory's Weir, of

15

which Thacker could find no evidence but the name. A short distance above this spot is Truss's Island, no longer an island, on which there is a mark stone of the City of London.

I have a feeling that all these things are connected to the Abbey River. There are a number of theories about this stream, of which little is actually known. Taunt states that it was cut by the monastery at Chertsey in the eleventh century, and this is a popular supposition. I understand there is nothing in the Abbey Chronicles to confirm it. In fact it seems most unlikely. Its length, two miles, would have presented an enormous task to people armed only with shovels. Even if they decided to try it, why did they meander all over the place when a straight line would have been much more practical? For working the mill, a much shorter, narrower and shallower cut would have sufficed. Certainly the monks would have improved the channel over the years, and this may be how the idea of their digging it arose.

Penton Hook has evolved over the years to its present shape. It would have started as a bend up near the present neck. (I discuss this process on page 118). Whilst it is perfectly reasonable to imagine that the Abbey River always ran out of this bend, there is some evidence to suggest that it ran on to issue from the River at the Fishing Temple until the enlargement of the Hook finally broke into it. If this was so, Savory's Weir could easily have stood at its head, as a fishing hedge or to deflect water into the Abbey stream. The 'Temple' might then have been a shelter or shed or even a cell for those having business there, who presumably would have been monks.

On the same basis, I think the stream may well have flowed behind Truss's Island until the bend at the Fishing Temple deepened to break into it and form the island. The island was named after the City of London's Clerk of Works, and the mark stone seems to have been placed in 1774, an indication that the City felt a need to claim it at that time. Could this be because it was then newly a separate entity?

As a side issue, there was an attempt by a certain General Scott to remove the stone and take over the island in 1827, but the City forbade it. I hear there was a recent attempt, by a development company, to remove it, but that this too has failed!

There are houses, of varying quality, on both sides up the next stretch, although those on the right stand back a reasonable distance. Staines is now coming up fast. J Tims' yard, on the left, hires cruisers and offers services but no casual mooring.

The railway bridge is a slab-sided, iron affair, with three arches, of which the centre is the navigation. The bridge is exceedingly popular among local pigeons, for there is a conveniently placed shelf, with roof over, close to the top. I have seen this shelf filled from end to end on a cold, damp day.

The old Pack Horse public house is now called the Thames Lodge Hotel, for some insensitive reason. It has a mooring. The Pack Horse had been a well-known inn for many years, and its name reflected the trade with which it was closely connected.

Above Staines Boat Club, on the left, there are 50 yards of Thames Water moorings, none too deep, and above that, mooring at the Swan Hotel. Opposite the Thames Water mooring is a short stay mooring for those wishing to shop.

Shopping in Staines is perfectly possible but not quick, since the sort of shops the boater needs are spread over a relatively large area. From the mooring you pass through a small, formal garden and thence to the road. Turn right and keep going.

The best of Staines seems to be the pubs on the Surrey bank. Within 100 yards of the Thames Water mooring there are three, including the Swan. There is an eye-catching modern development on the right, with a neat wooden bridge across the River Colne, which joins the Thames here. Just below Staines Bridge is the Riverside Carvery, a restaurant, with several battered-looking mooring rings for the use of customers.

Staines gets its name from 'Stan', meaning stone, and possibly referring to a Roman milestone at the crossing. There is speculation that the Romans may have bridged the river here. They called it Pontes, 'bridges'. This plural is a strange thing about Staines. By rights, Stan should have evolved to Stone, rather than Staine. As to why it became Staines, 'stones', nobody seems to know.

The present bridge, of classic design, has three arches, and the centre is the one to use.

Above the bridge, Biffens yard hires cruisers

The London Stone. 'God preferve ye CITY of LONDON'.

but has no facilities for the general public. Church Island has a good looking modern development to the right of it, followed by a public park, alongside which one can moor. It is quite shallow however. The other slight problem is that the park is locked at night, which could be embarrassing if one should go on a pub crawl.

Behind a hedge above the mooring, protected by iron railings and approachable only with the assistance of the park keeper, stands the London Stone. At least, an exact replica stands here, made of glassfibre. The actual stone is in Staines Library. The replica stands on four plinth stones, which *are* original, and on which are recorded a series of visits by Thames officials in the past.

The top pedestal stone records:

The ancient Stone above this infcription is raifed upon this Pedeftal exactly over the Spot where it formerly ftood Infcribed

God preferve ye CITY OF LONDON
AD 1285

S WATKIN LEWIS Kn LORD MAYOR was responsible for supplying this pedestal stone, in 1781. There are also records of the visit by:

The Right Honourable WILLIAM VENABLES LORD MAYOR of the CITY of LONDON and Conservator of the River of THAMES Viewed (?) the Western Boundary of the CITY'S Jurisdiction over the said River Marked by the ancient Stone Raised upon this Pedestal Erected AD 1285 On the 29th day of July AD 182(6 or 0).
God preferve the CITY of LONDON
CLAU^{DS} STEP HUNTER LORD MAYOR was here in 1812.

On the next pedestal stone below is recorded the change of control of the river:

THE CONSERVATORS OF THE RIVER THAMES 1857

The names of all the first conservators, many of which I could not decipher, are here, but the panel showing the last and least important is clear and preserves the following names:

JOSEPH TURNLEY Esqre
THOMAS HENRY FRY Esqre
THOMAS DAKIN Esqre DEPUTY
CAPTAIN HORATIO
THOMAS AUSTIN R.N. C.B.

There are several other recorded visits, but the last is the most poignant:

CONSERVATORS OF THE RIVER THAMES 1857–1974
PAID THEIR LAST VISIT IN JUNE 1973 WITH
ALDERMEN AND COMMON COUNCILLORS OF
THE CORPORATION OF LONDON

Truly this monument is an encapsulation of the history of this stretch of the river. That the Stone has been maintained here for 700 years is a remarkable tribute to the continuity of management of London City's river. That the stone has now had to be shut off behind railings and the original stone removed, is perhaps a less happy commentary on the behaviour of the present generations of Britons.

From here the first part of our journey comes rapidly to a close. Holm Island is a short distance above the Stone. It has a lovely house on it, nestling amid some amazing willows. Then follow the twin bridges of the M25, the confluence with the Colne Brook, and finally Bell Weir Lock.

BELL WEIR   1817

Fall 6′ 0″ : 1.82 m | Deep

Upstream You will see the lock before you pass under the M25 bridge. There is a short hard-stand on the left and 120 ft of piling on the right. The weir will try to push you off this as you slow down, so make sure you get your bow in and rope ashore. You can drive your stern in at leisure. If the lay-bys are full, there is plenty of room below the lock to manoeuvre. This lock has side sluices, in addition to those in the gates, so keep the ropes tight while the lock is filling, or the boat will move off across the lock.

Downstream The lock is on the right. So is the lay-by. There are pilings, followed by a walkway with bollards. The weir is all down the left of the lock cut and will tend to lift you off the lay-by. Do not attempt to enter the cut unless you can see that there is room to tie up. If there is any doubt about this, manoeuvre well above the weir.

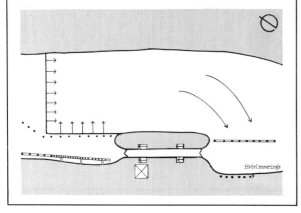

A cruising yacht with piggy-back dinghy passes Holm Island.

MAP 1

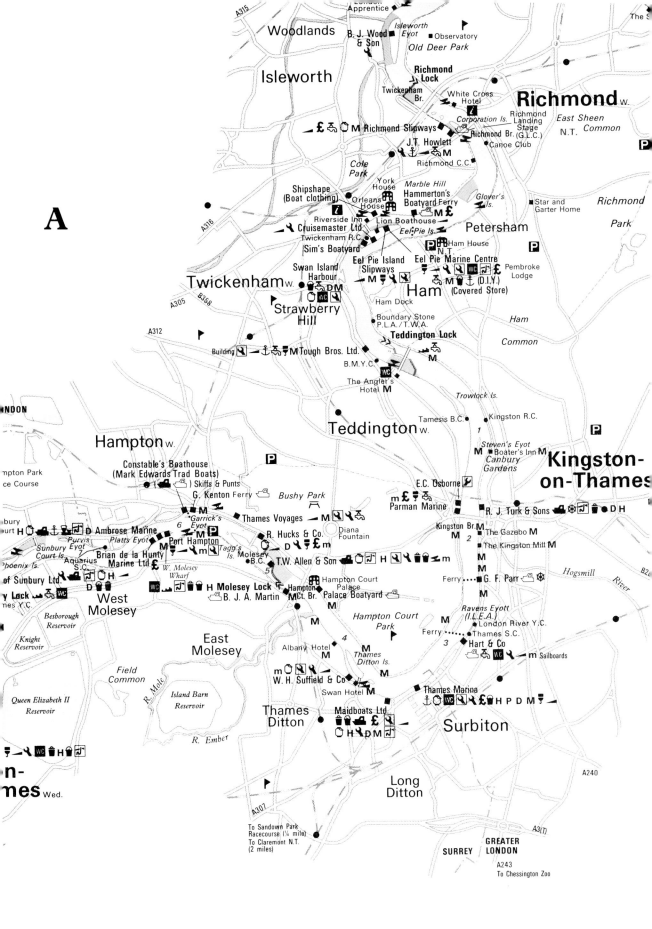

A

Woodlands

Isleworth

London
Apprentice

B. J. Wood & Son

Isleworth
Eyot

Observatory
Old Deer Park

Richmond
Lock

Twickenham
Br.

White Cross
Hotel

Richmond Landing
Stage

Richmond W.

Corporation Is.

Richmond
Slipways

Richmond Br. (G.L.C.)

East Sheen
N.T.

Common

J.T. Howlett

Canoe Club

Richmond C.C.

Cole
Park

York
House

Marble Hill

Glover's
Is.

Star and
Garter Home

Richmond

Park

Shipshape
(Boat clothing)

Orleans
House

Hammerton's
Boatyard Ferry

Riverside Inn

Cruisemaster Ltd

Lion Boathouse

Eel Pie Is.

Petersham

Twickenham R.C.

Ham House

Sim's Boatyard

Eel Pie Island
Slipways

Eel Pie Marine Centre

Ham

N.T.

Pembroke
Lodge

Twickenham W.

Swan Island
Harbour

(D.I.Y.)
(Covered Store)

A305 B358

**Strawberry
Hill**

Ham Dock

Ham

Common

A312

Boundary Stone
P.L.A./T.W.A.

Teddington Lock

Building

Tough Bros. Ltd.

B.M.Y.C.

The Angler's
Hotel

Trowlock Is.

Teddington W.

Tamesis B.C.

Kingston R.C.

1

Hampton W.

Steven's Eyot
Boater's Inn
Canbury
Gardens

**Kingston-
on-Thames**

Constable's Boathouse
(Mark Edwards Trad Boats)

G. Kenton Ferry

Bushy Park

E.C. Osborne

Parman Marine

R. J. Turk & Sons

D H

mpton Park
ce Course

Thames Voyages

Diana
Fountain

Kingston Br.

The Gazebo

The Kingston Mill

Garrick's
Eyot

R. Hucks & Co.

Port Hampton

Tagg's
Is.

Ferry

G. F. Parr

Ambrose Marine

Platts Eyot

D

bury
urt

Purvis

Sunbury
Court Is.

Brian de la Hunty
Marine Ltd

W. Molesey
Wharf

B.C.

T.W. Allen & Son

Hampton Court
Palace

Palace Boatyard

Ravens Eyott
(I.L.E.A.)

Hogsmill

River

Aquarius
S.C.

Molesey

Phoenix Is.

f Sunbury Ltd.

B. J. A. Martin

Hampton
Ct. Br.

London River Y.C.

Thames S.C.

y Lock
es Y.C.

**West
Molesey**

Molesey Lock

Hampton Court
Palace

Ferry

Hart & Co

Sailboards

**East
Molesey**

Albany Hotel

4

Thames
Ditton Is.

3

Queen Elizabeth II
Reservoir

Field
Common

Island Barn
Reservoir

R. Mole

W. H. Suffield & Co

Swan Hotel

Thames Marina

Knight
Reservoir

Thames Marina

H P D M

Surbiton

n-
mes Wed.

R. Ember

**Thames
Ditton**

Maidboats Ltd.

H D M

**Long
Ditton**

A240

A307

To Sandown Park
Racecourse (¼ mile)
To Claremont N.T.
(2 miles)

SURREY

**GREATER
LONDON**

A243
To Chessington Zoo

A3(T)

Part Two

BELL WEIR

TO

READING

17 THE splendidly ugly Victorian pumping station is the only item of note to strike the eye as you leave Bell Weir Lock. Bell Weir appears to take its name from the lock-keeper who was working the weir at the time the pound lock was built, and who became the first lock-keeper. I say appears, because there is no absolute evidence to prove it and we are sufficiently close to the legend of the Bells of Ouzely for that also to be a possibility, of which more anon.

You can moor to the left beyond Nicholes yard. It is not the most inspiring mooring on the river, but it is deep.

18 There is another mooring on the left as you swing right-handed into the Runnymede reach, close enough to the road to be more useful in emergency or for lunch, than for the night.

Runnymede probably had a track across it on that fateful day in June 1215, when the great barons of England gathered to force King John to sign their bill of rights. The name is not 'water-meadow', which is what you might reasonably expect, but 'council-field', which is presumably why it was used for the purpose. In that case, it would have looked very much as it does today.

In Saxon times, the councils of the nation were held in large open spaces, not because they did not have a building big enough, but because massacre was less likely out of doors. Deep suspicion was the order of the day and each eorl brought a small army with him and was prepared to fight his way out if things became awkward. Thus it would have been in 1215 also, for the only reason the barons were prepared to put up with John at all was that they could not agree on an alternative.

So you may picture each lord in his tent, literally surrounded by his men-at-arms. We know that John rode in from his castle at New Windsor, furiously angry and armed to the teeth. There is debate as to where the document was endorsed, one faction claiming it was in a cottage on Magna Carta Island, and pointing to a large stone which, it was said, was used to press against. A pretty story, but unlikely, if only because to boat over to the island would give all the opportunities for murder that meeting on the runi mede sought to avoid. Besides, as has been suggested*, it was surely possible to provide a table and chair in England on that day, without recourse to kneeling over a stone.

There is a simple monument now, on the field, in as likely a spot as any, and as luck would have it, you can moor almost exactly opposite it, on the left, and stroll over to look. The memorial to John F Kennedy is a little to the right of it and up the hill, well intentioned but an example of the wisdom of not raising monuments to people or events for at least a millenium. On the top of the hill, further to the left, is the Air Forces Memorial, from which the views are phenomenal and in which are recorded the names of 20,000 allied airmen who perished in World War II. But that is probably the subject of a separate journey. Magna Carta Island, which is on the right, hardly counts as an island any more. In fact you would not know it was one without careful inspection.

The island further up on the right is not 19 Magna Carta. You can moor on the left above it, beyond French Brothers boatyard. This is quite a pleasant spot, screened from the road, although still close to it. Two hundred yards further up, you can moor outside the Bells of Ouzely. There is a row of what appear to be mooring posts, but which are all that remains of a post and rail fence, so check that your post is sound.

The Bells of Ouzely used to stand on the river bank, with the road behind it. The present building is quite new, its predecessor having been bombed. This ancient pub is now chiefly called Harvester Steak House, although its genuine name can still be seen on close inspection. The legend, to which I referred above, is that the bells of the great monastery of Ouzely

* By Mr and Mrs Hall in *The Book of the Thames.*

were rescued by the monks when that abbey was dissolved by Henry VIII, and taken off down river in a barge. At this point in Old Windsor, pursuit growing hot, they threw the bells in the river for safety and fled. When everything calmed down, they returned to collect their precious treasure. Alas! There was no sign of them, and to this day they have never more been seen.

The truths and facts behind the story have proved elusive. I have not read a satisfactory explanation, the chief difficulty being that there is no record of Ouzely Abbey ever having existed. The river at that point has been considerably widened and deepened over the years, and it is inconceivable that anything as large as a church bell, let alone six of them, should have escaped detection.

I therefore humbly offer an explanation of my own, which is not to be regarded as anything but reasonable hypothesis. The abbey in question was not Ouzely but Oseney, at Oxford, which was suppressed and which did have a fine peal of bells. I think the confusion in names is nothing more than a mistake of dialect or a misreading of someone's scrawl. Whoever was pursuing quickly caught up with the fact that the bells had been abandoned. (It would have taken about two hours to discover they had passed Windsor and never arrived at Staines.) It seems to me quite likely the monks had moored at Old Windsor and gone to a rest house for the night. The King's men simply found the barge and the bells and went back with them to Oxford. They are now in Christ Church Cathedral. There is no record that they ever went missing but there is a story that the bells of Oseney were famous as far away as Windsor. Why Windsor, I ask myself?

Crevalds yard have a notice refusing service to hire craft. They are one of two yards with this prohibition. I did not ask why.

20   Just before Old Windsor Lock the weir-stream joins from the right. It runs for almost two miles up to the weir, and is fully navigable. There is no point in going up there except to say you have. The houses on the right bank are in general rather better than the ones you will have been passing for the last mile, but that is not particularly remarkable. Ham Fields, on the left of the stream have a large sewage works in the middle, but you cannot see, or usually

smell this. Thacker has it that this stream was that referred to as Colnbrook Churchyard, so called because of the habit of the local footpads of old to chuck the bodies of those they had slain into the river at this point. That may be so. Certainly the area must have been very lonely and marshy 200 and more years ago, and the river swift and deep. Taunt says a complete skeleton was found by some men working on the river bed.

It seems that the old flash-weir that preceded the present lock was placed slightly above the modern weir. I found no sign of it and did not expect to.

Old Windsor was, as the name implies, the original site of Windsor. Hall translates Windsor as 'windle sora', winding shore, and asks: 'Why not?' Well, one thing we shall discover on this journey is that the Saxons were most unwhimsical. When they named a place, the name made practical sense, at least to the local inhabitants, which meant almost everybody who would need to know. Winding shore would only make sense if the river wound particularly at this point, which it does not. Gelling has it 'windles ora', river bank with a windlass, which rings true and is most exciting. For it tells us that the Saxons found it necessary and practical to erect a windlass to haul boats up what must then have been rapids. In other words, the volume of traffic in the ninth century or earlier warranted such a device. The rapids were probably natural, since there is no record that I have found of flash-locks as early as this. The windlass may have looked like the Hurley winch.

Emerging from the Old Windsor lock cut, you are very soon at Albert Bridge, one of a pair built under the direction of the Prince Regent, to replace the defunct bridge at Datchet. The other is called Victoria Bridge, as you might expect. At the time of their building, the land between them was taken by the Crown, and the old road, whose successor still runs along the left bank, closed to the public.

The bridges at Datchet were among the most disreputable on the river, not for the usual reason that boats could not pass them, but because they had an alarming record of collapse. The last one was a classic piece of bureaucratic idiocy, in that the Councils of Berkshire and Buckinghamshire could not agree on whose

OLD WINDSOR 1822

Fall 5'9" : 1.74m | Deep

Upstream Start preparing as soon as you see the tail of the island. The lock appears suddenly and there is no room to manoeuvre if the lay-by is full. There is a hard-stand, on the left. There is no problem with the weir. After leaving the lock and travelling up the cut, take care to keep clear of the weir on the main river, which runs beside the cut for about 50 yards. There will be a tendency for downcoming craft to push you across, in the confined space of the cut. Resist this.

Downstream The lock cut is long, so you will have plenty of warning. But, be warned, the lock is just around a sharp bend. The pilings, on the right, curve round the bend and are therefore awkward to get on to. To add to the excitement, there is an overflow weir on the left, just before the lock, which will pull you off the pilings. Fortunately, it is only small, so the art here is to approach slowly but with good steerage way, get on to the pilings as soon as you can, to leave yourself time to rectify mistakes, and then 'walk' the boat up to the top. It is not very elegant, nor very brave, but it works! The weir above the lock-cut is rather threatening. It stretches across the river, runs beside the lock cut for about 50 yards, and it pulls. Stop well above the weir if there are boats coming up, and only proceed when you can see your way clear past it. Then keep going until you are into the cut. For guidance, there is a hump back bridge half way down the cut.

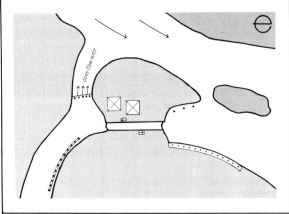

responsibility it was to build it, what it would cost and of what material to make it. So they built it in two halves, to two different designs, of totally different materials, iron and wood. In the middle, one half was three inches lower than the other! Fortunately, it only stood for 40 years before becoming dangerous which was when the Regent stepped in.

The park on the left, between the two bridges is therefore the Queen's garden and you should not moor there unless you wish to be cast into the dungeon at Windsor Castle.

There is a good mooring to be had at Datchet, supplied by the local council and Hicks yard will be happy to accommodate you, so long as there is space available. (This means anytime except Friday/Saturday, when they are changing their hire fleet. This applies to any yard with a hire fleet, even when they allow casual mooring in principle.) Hicks make a small charge, and offer most services.

Datchet is a pleasant little village, with most shops you will need. It is certainly easier shopping than Windsor, which is a nightmare. There are also three pubs, The Manor, The Royal Stag and the Morning Star. I moored for the night, an interesting experience that took me back 20 years to when I lived there, and reminded me why I left. The aircraft, inbound to Heathrow, appear to use Hicks yard as a fix. It is all right at night but I was fascinated in the morning, watching them coming in at one minute intervals from about 7 am. They all flew past the Queen's bedroom window too, which must be charming for her. 'Uneasy lies the head that wears the crown', wrote Shakespeare.

Once past Victoria Bridge, the left bank is public, and there are several moorings, just below the railway bridge on this side. After which, Romney Lock is just round the bend, and the long cut above this brings you almost up to Windsor Bridge, which is now part of a pedestrian precinct on the Windsor shore and very well done it is. There are several pubs close to Windsor Bridge, including The Swan, The William IV, The Thames Hotel and the Adam and Eve, which is by the Theatre Royal in Castle Hill. Just below the bridge, on the right, is the Eton Excelsior Rowing Club, one of the top clubs on the river, and immediately above the bridge are the Eton College boathouses. In the summer term the 'wet bobs' from the

ROMNEY 1797

Fall 6′7″ : 2.01 m | Deep

Upstream Start preparing after the railway bridge. The piling is on the right and curves left, so is easy to come on to. It stops 150 ft before the lock, although you can go ashore and walk up. This is a modern and, to the upper Thames man, massive lock, with side sluices, like Bell Weir, so be sure you have secured properly. There are two sets of steps on each side, and they all run the right way.

Downstream The approach to the lock can be difficult in strong stream conditions. Once in the cut there are few problems. There are overflow weirs on the left, halfway down the cut and outside the lock, but as long as you keep off them, they are not strong. The pilings, on the right, are not continuous. There is a long section, without access to shore, and a short section, opposite the overflow weir, with access. There is a boom across the old weir stream, at the top of the piling. It is not an additional lay-by, keep off.

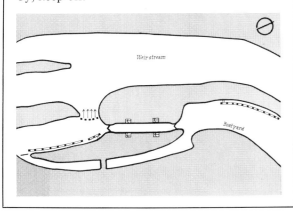

Weir stream

Boatyard

college are out in force, from here to Boveney.

Above and below the bridge on the Windsor bank, there are numbers of large passenger launches, which are employed running trips throughout the summer, mostly up to Boveney Lock. In fact, one way and another, the Windsor reach on a summer's afternoon can be about as busy as anywhere on the river.

You can moor immediately above the bridge on the left, each side of the mooring for the Wren House Hotel. Failing that, once you are clear of the college boathouses, there is reasonable if variable mooring up to and beyond the railway bridge, on the right bank for a fee collected by the water bailiff.

There is also an excellent public marina up on the left, beyond the island. The charge for 24 hours mooring at this mooring is almost the highest on the river, but depends on your being able to find the keeper of the miniature golf-course, in order to press your money into his hand, since he does not come looking for you. The miniature golf-course is either extremely small, or I keep looking the wrong way (there are no directions given), because I have yet to find it.

No doubt you will wish to visit Windsor. If you have not been before, the castle really is something. The views from the battlements, or from the Round Tower, if it is open and you are energetic enough; the exquisite dolls' house; the sumptuous State Apartments; the splendour of St George's Chapel; and of course the soldiers in their scarlet tunics and their bearskins; each of these singly is worth the visit. If you go along at about 10.30, they change the guard, complete with music, which is fun. If the Queen is there (Her standard will be flying from the Round Tower), there will be a brass band; if not, you will probably have to make do with fife and drum. When we lived in Datchet, we used to come and watch on most Saturdays.

Twenty years ago they had the shops sensibly placed. Now, unless you want souvenirs or teas, you will have a major problem. If you really must buy a bottle of milk or something, this is what you do. Walk up to the castle (half a mile minimum from the mooring), turn your back on Queen Victoria and walk down Peascod Street to the bottom (about half a mile). On the right you will find some brick steps, which lead to a shopping precinct. Afterwards, retrace your steps. On no account follow the signs in the precinct which say 'To the River'. They only lead to a dual carriageway with a metal fence on both sides and in the middle. Hurdling that lot with a couple of carrier-bags is simply not practical. Furthermore, I am pretty sure it is not in the right direction. If you want money, you will pass the banks on your way to the precinct, and the Post Office is down that way too.

You would think some genius in Eton would open up a grocery and save us all that trouble but if he has, it is very well hidden, for I found no sensible shops there either. The chief characteristic of Eton pubs is that none have any provision for children. The Eton Buttery does, is reasonably priced, informal, and faces the river. Otherwise there are The George, The Crown and Cushion, the College Arms and the Donkey House, all within easy reach.

25 The run up to Boveney Lock passes Windsor Racecourse on the left but otherwise is not of any note. It was as they passed down this reach in 1859, that Mr and Mrs Hall discovered that the rule of the road was to keep right. Not bad, having come all the way down from the source! The information was imparted, somewhat forcefully, by some Eton boys whose progress they had presumably hampered.

I met three lovely ladies in a camping skiff, dressed in crinolines and mob caps, displaying a notice: 'Three Women in a Boat in aid of Cystic Fibrosis.'

26 Boveney means above island, which exactly describes the situation of the village. Above the lock, there is a mooring on the right at the first

Swans at Windsor in the shadow of the Castle.

left-hand bend. From here you might visit the strange little church, lost in the trees and undergrowth. The Halls tell a harrowing story of meeting a woman here who was quite distraught at being unable to find her husband's grave. She was convinced someone had moved it. Apparently, so her father said, the man had died and been buried overseas but the poor widow could not be convinced that this was so.

The entrance to the Racecourse Yacht Basin is on the left, the channel being round the top of the small island. Further up on the left is PHM Windsor Marina, where you may moor overnight and which has good facilities. Immediately above the marina, there is a mooring on the left, alongside some new piling, otherwise nothing before Queen's Eyot except at the landing-stage of Oakley Court Hotel, the rest of whose frontage is full of dangerous obstructions. There is a fine view of Windsor Castle's Round Tower to be had from this reach, your last or first, depending which way you are going.

You will pass Bray Studios on the left, once a lively part of the British film industry but now looking very sad, and with a rather unsightly lot alongside, full of rusting junk.

BOVENEY 1838

Fall 4′10″ : 1.47 m | Deep | Sanitary station

Upstream You will see the lock in plenty of time. The weir is on the left, and the Sanitary Station is in the weir-stream. There is room for only two boats at a time at the Station. The pilings are on the left. You will usually find the lock approaches congested in the season, especially as there are a number of large pleasure boats both turning at the lock and passing through. These are given some priority at the lock, so you may have quite a long wait here. There is plenty of room for manoeuvre in the approach, fortunately.

The main difficulty is the tendency of any wind blowing from the racecourse to blow you off the pilings, since the lock is somewhat exposed. This is not helped by the shortness of the pilings, which means that you have to be accurate.

Downstream The weir is on the right, so keep as close to the left as upcoming boats will let you. Pilings on the right, and they are short and subject to cross-winds trying to blow you off them. Manoeuvre well above the lock if you are not sure of coming alongside the pilings. There is plenty of room.

Boveney is one of the few locks still possessing boat-rollers, and the only one to have double ones in fact although only one is now in working order.

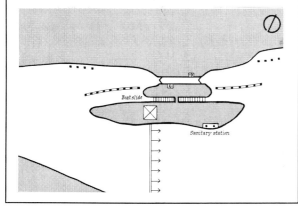

in situ, is immediately above the island. In fact, if you are going to stop there, you are better off going up the left side of the island. If you do so, you will notice a curious pavilion on the island. I am not going to tell you what brings it there, because I do not know, but I suspect croquet. The island is too small for cricket and the turf too rough for bowls. In any case, I think whatever it was for no longer happens.

Which brings us to Monkey Island. This used to be a very relaxed place, with a good restaurant, pleasant surroundings and moorings. Now a notice proclaims mooring for patrons with reservations only, no dogs and the island is closed in the afternoon. All of which is a pity, for the old hunting lodge at the core of the present complex is quite singular. It has wall paintings of monkeys fishing, shooting etc., and is all rather jolly. Naturally this inference is misleading. The name comes from Monks' Eyot, there being a monastic cell there at one time. You can moor opposite the island, on the right.

It looks as though there ought to be a mooring just before the Motorway bridge, on the right, but it does not work out in fact. Immediately above the lock there is a mooring on the right, which is the last before Maidenhead.

So you will have to sail past Bray, which is a pity, because it is a pleasant little village. The Waterside Inn has a notice: 'Waterside Inn—Restaurant only'!

You can see Bray Church quite clearly, poking its tower above the village. Bray apparently means mud, a low marshy place. The celebrated vicar did exist but a hundred years earlier than the song would have it. He therefore found himself in the rather nasty time from the Dissolution under Henry VIII, through 'bloody' Mary to protestant Elizabeth. He apparently once witnessed a burning, which had a profound effect on his thinking thereafter. Seeing his duty, rightly, as to his parishioners first and the vicious political manoeuvring of religious faction a poor third, he behaved with great sense and happily espoused whatever happened to be the 'true word of God' at any given time.

With one notable and recent exception, the houses in the Bray reach up to Maidenhead are quite attractive. They are filled with 'top people', who apparently never venture forth

There is a mooring on the right at the tail of Queens Eyot. Bray Marina, which has a sandwich bar, apart from other essential services, including overnight mooring and sign-writing

BRAY 1845

Fall 4'9" : 1.46 m | Deep | Refuse disposal

Upstream The lock is visible from a good way off. There is a long lay-by to the right and no problem with the weir on the left. There is a refuse disposal point at the lower end of the lay-by.

Downstream The river curves to the right on its approach to the lock, and the weir lies to the right. This results in a cross-current close to the lock. Keep left as far as possible. The pilings are on the left and curve towards you at the end by the lock, which is helpful if you overshoot a bit. There should be no major problem here unless you fail to keep way on while still in the weir-stream. Do your waiting well above the lock.

Note This lock is due for enlargement, which will alter the landing arrangements.

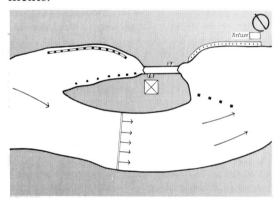

into their gardens, perhaps for fear of being hailed by the passing mob on the river. One thing that struck me particularly here is how few of them seem to keep a boat. Perhaps the residents' association discourages it?

The approach to Maidenhead is heralded by the sight of Brunel's masterpiece in brick, the crossing made for the Great Western Railway on the longest, flattest brick arches in the world. Each one spans 128 ft and rises only 24 ft. Presumably such perfection will never be surpassed now that we have steel and concrete to achieve the same results more cheaply. What actually happened was that the Thames Commissioners, threatened with the loss of revenue

from barge traffic with the coming of the railways, found the original design, for a perfectly standard bridge which created an additional hazard to be negotiated, as just about the last straw. They protested and asked Brunel to enlarge his arches. It was the sort of challenge the great man was never able to resist and he responded by throwing his bridge across to the island in mid-stream and thence to the far bank in two, glorious strides that cleared the channel.

You can moor along the right for 150 yards before the bridge. It is not quiet, but no worse than the aircraft. The wall slopes away from the river, so is a little awkward to come alongside. I used a spring here to overcome the problem of bumping. It is a short quarter mile from the mooring to Maidenhead Bridge, on the other side of which is a useful shop at the petrol station. Alternatively, there is a parade of shops including a bank and Post Office about five minutes' walk towards the town.

On the way back to your boat, take the towpath under the railway bridge and try the echo. It is called a sounding arch. Whatever you say, sing, shout or whistle, it will repeat perfectly. It only does this from the side incidentally, driving underneath and shouting does not work.

Between the two bridges is Maidenhead Boat Centre, HQ of the Waterline Cruisers hire fleet. It is also the workshop of Evans Marine, who rebuilt my exhaust system inexpensively, efficiently and with great good cheer. He is a useful man for the private boater to know, for he is one of a handful of engineers who will come out to you if you are stricken far from home.

Maidenhead Bridge is also well known, mainly because of where it is, rather than for any special architectural merit, although it is an attractive stone structure. It has no navigational vices. There are three main and three subsidiary arches. Use the main arches, centre or right both ways.

The derivation of the name of the town has caused a great many headaches. It was generally agreed that the 'head' was a corruption of hythe = wharf. One suggestion seriously put forward was that it was a wharf where maidens were wont to disembark! Another medieval explanation was that it was the hythe to which

PREVIOUS PAGE.
*Morning mists at the
foot of Winter Hill, near
Marlow. (Raymond
Blythe)*

A typical Thames bridge.

*Backwater islands above
Marsh Lock.*

OPPOSITE. *The Thames
on a still winter's day
near Marlow.
(Raymond Blythe)*

The River below Winter Hill, Cookham Dean.
(Raymond Blythe)

Horses in the water-meadows above
Mapledurham.

Busy time at Bray as the Lock fills up with 'wet bobs' from Eton.

were brought the relics of one of 20,000 Christian virgins martyred by the heathen hordes. This was later modified on the grounds of difficulty in finding 20,000 virgins in Germany and then abandoned on the grounds that heathens do not generally massacre virgins. It is worth recording as an example of the sort of rubbish put out by the Church.

Thacker suggested 'Mai dun hythe', wharf by the great hill, which made good sense, although it seemed strange to name Maidenhead after a hill on the other bank. A new and well researched little book* seems to have cracked the problem. It records that Maidenhead was called Southelyngton in Domesday Book, Elyntone in 1277 and not Maidenhead until 1324 (Maidenheth or Maydenhuth). So it could not derive from the OE mai dun hythe. Furthermore, it did not exist as a town until after the bridge was built in 1280; nor was there a wharf until then either, the one led to the other.

It appears the name comes from the town seal, which was brought to the area by a monk, it being the seal of the monastery of John the Baptist at Thiers and used without permission by the Borough. The seal depicts the head and shoulders of the saint, but his hairstyle and

* *Maidenhead and its Name*, by E A S Brooks.

pretty looks, done in the prevailing chivalric style, make him look like a woman. Further, the crest of the Norreys family, who virtually controlled the area at the time, was the bust of a woman. Thus, Maidenhead means exactly what it says!

Maidenhead is a used to town. It used to attract hordes of visitors from London, on the train at the dawn of the modern habit of ordinary people taking to boating in their leisure time. It used to be the place for the flappers to meet in the twenties, when Skindles Hotel was at its height of elegance and fashion and when a weekend at the Riviera was regarded as too, too daring for a nice young gell.

Now all that has gone. Maidenhead is not really a riverside town. It is set over a mile away actually, so that the boater has no incentive to stop as he does at, say, Windsor, Henley or Marlow. You can hire your boat from here and it is certainly a good place to start from.

The river races past the islands as you pass Bushnells Yard. Keep going here whatever you do. Bushnells is one of the old Thames names and this is one of the largest hire fleets. Because of the stream, they have a notice requesting boats always to moor facing upstream. It is more than usually important to do so here. If you have to turn round, go up or down to a wide section before attempting to. You can pass to the right of the island if you prefer.

There are rings in the left wall from above Bray Boats to Boulter's Lock. You can moor

31

there if you like, although the road is right above you. Boulter's is another lock, like Bell Weir, named after an ancient lock-keeper rather than the place in which it is. There are very few of these left, as we shall see, whereas, in the past, almost all the locks were so named. Furthermore, they used to change names as the keepers changed, and this causes great excitment when trying to trace their histories. There is a caveat in this case. Boulter or bolter is also a sifter of meal, says the *OED*, so the reference could be to such workers at the great Ray Mill which stood here from the early fourteenth century, at least. On balance I think it was more likely named after one who had taken this surname.

Boulter's is the most famous of the locks on the Thames. Until very recently it was about the largest also. The reason for both these things was the popularity of Maidenhead, just discussed, combined with the popularity of Cliveden, which is to come. Some of the famous pictures of this lock in the '90s show it completely packed with boats of all types. It must have needed much skill on the part of the lock-keeper to fill and empty without catastrophe, and how the great press of boats disentangled itself without mishap remains a mystery.

Above the lock, the cut runs up for about 300 yards, before issuing into the glory that is Cliveden Reach. On the left, open meadowland, complete with cows. On the right, the great cliff that gives the place its name, hung with woodland. It is the only really splendid bit of scenery on the river, though none the worse for that. To see it late on a summer's evening, when the river has gone still and the soft light plays among a million leaves; or to come on deck on an autumn morning, when the mists are hanging like lace in the trees, sparkling with the new day; these things will bring deep contentment to the heart.

32   I only found one mooring on the left, right up near My Lady Ferry. On the right, there are a number of good moorings and an equal number of shallow moorings, for boats drawing just over a foot. They start below mile 32 and run up to a little above the top island. There are several on the right hand island and a couple more at the top of the left hand islands.

I spent a good deal of time sculling about in my dinghy while doing this survey. It is the

BOULTER'S 1772

Fall 7'10" : 2.39 m | Deep

Upstream The approach is not particularly wide, and there is a strong stream normally. You will see the footbridge and the Boulter's Inn in good time, but it may be wise to start preparing as you pass Bushnells.

There is a short piling on the right, primarily for steamers, and a short lay-by on the left. On a busy day, it is most unlikely you will get on either. In that case, you will find it difficult to manoeuvre. Fortunately, it is possible to come alongside the wall on the left for some way before the lock, and this is the best practice.

The lock is third deepest on the river, so if you have any option, it is a good idea to come alongside on the right in the lock, where the steps, 80' up it, are going the same way as you are.

Downstream The weir is on the left and does not interfere. Start preparing as you enter the cut. You will find 200 yards of bollarded lay-by on the right, making this now one of the easiest approaches on the river.

Notes

1 There used to be boat-rollers here. You can still see the bed in which they ran. At one time they were steam driven, but this proved to be one of the less successful of Victorian inventions, and the system was soon abandoned.

2 Just behind the lock is the Headquarters of Thames Water Navigation Service for this section of the river.

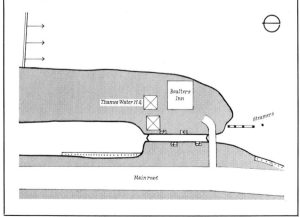

only real way to appreciate the river. So much is lost in the noise and size of a cruiser, to say nothing of the speed. There is a definite upsurge in the number of camping skiffs and punts to be seen, which is very heartwarming, especially as most of the campers seem to be young.

When you are in a vulnerable position, bobbing about in a small boat, there is great opportunity for studying the manners of the cruiser skippers. I made a habit of observing the degree of courtesy accorded to me on these occasions. I have to report that one is three times more likely to be swamped by the private owner than by the driver of a hire-boat. This is of course disgraceful, though it has apparently always been true.

I met a strange duck in Cliveden Reach. It turned out to be a Mandarin. In the following year there were over half a dozen around our mooring on one of the islands. They were remarkably daring and inquisitive, petite and pretty. There is apparently a feral group at Iver, a few miles away.

The word Cliveden means 'steeply sloping valley'. Its pronunciation causes difficulty. I was always taught 'Cleeveden' and you will often hear that still. The officer of Thames Water who I asked said it was the posh way. Nevertheless 'Clivden' is almost certainly better. (It is what he called it.) 'Clive den' is certainly wrong. The Clive part is Cliff or Clief in early records, the second explaining why the long ee has crept in.

Shortly after you enter the reach, you will see Cliveden House above the woods at the top end. It was totally enveloped in plastic when I was there. The whole area is now owned by the National Trust, who have leased the house itself to a Hotel Group, to become a rather different, if expensive, place to stay. It was most famous as the home of the Astor family and the 'Cliveden set' associated with them. There are several attractive cottages along the river front, one quite a large house in fact, and above it the cottage marking the site of My Lady Ferry.

This ferry was specifically for the use of the towing teams for the barges, which had to be transferred here from the Cookham to Hedsor bank. It was not a public ferry. There were several ferries like this. They were called accommodation ferries, and one caused a famous legal battle, as we shall see at Medmenham.

The entrance to Cookham Lock is at the top of the reach, up a short approach to the left. Dead ahead is the Hedsor stream, which is private. However, you can cruise up it for about 100 yards, and there are some shallow moorings on the left bank, from which you can explore the island and be out of the madding crowd. There is a weir-stream on the left, immediately before the lock cut, where you can moor at two places on the right. At both these sets of moorings it would be a courtesy to ask the lock-keeper's permission, since they are on Thames Water land. You should also note that there is no access to Cookham village from either place.

COOKHAM 1830

Fall 4'3" : 1.30 m / Deep

Upstream The lock cut turns sharply left off the river, and the lock is immediately upon you. You will be warned by the prohibition notice in the Hedsor Stream, which is about 100 yards above the lock cut. The secondary weir-stream runs in from the left immediately before the cut, but presents no problem. There are pilings on the right, followed by a short lay-by. There is also a short set of pilings on the left.

This lock is unique in two respects. It is the only double lock you will pass (Boulter's and Goring used to be), and the only lock in which *all* the steps are set back to front! Try and avoid coming alongside against the middle gates. These are so high, you cannot get ashore, even in a full lock.

Downstream Prepare as you pass under the footbridge. The pilings are on the right, but there is an excellent lay-by on the left. There is no problem.

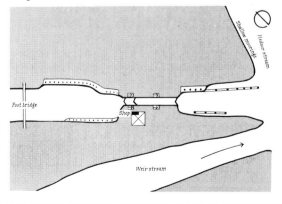

There is a well stocked shop at Cookham Lock, run by the lock-keeper's wife. You can even order newspapers. Since there are no food shops in Cookham, this facility is a great boon.

The cut above Cookham Lock is probably the prettiest on the river. It runs for nearly half a mile, between wood and meadow. If you double back to the left at the top, (right hand going downstream) there are two moorings on the left of the secondary weir-stream.

Just below the Ferry Inn is the Odney Stream, which is only navigable by dinghy but well worth the trouble. It is only about half a mile down to the old mill house, which you cannot pass and which is private anyway, but it is quiet and peaceful in the stream. I picked a soft morning in mid-August and simply floated down on the current, among the lilies. There was a cricket match in progress nearby; white figures through the trees, now languid, now energetic, with the occasional punctuation of bat making contact with ball. It made a pleasant interlude.

Tranquility in the Hedsor Stream, one of the River's 'secret places'.

Cookham is also worth visiting. It has excellent moorings for 200–300 yards above the bridge on the left. From here it is a short walk into the village, where there is a permanent exhibition of the work of Stanley Spencer, the artist, who lived here. Pubs in the village include Bel and the Dragon, The Kings Arms and the Royal Exchange, which is up on the common and the village is an attractive old place to poke about in. The flint church, which is near the river, is almost 900 years old.

The name is said to derive from Cook or Cocc: cook, and Ham : village. So, 'cook village', or 'cook village'. I do not believe either. There would be no market for cocks, because everyone who breeds chickens has more than enough. Anyway, a cock village would run out of chickens in quick time, would it not. And who would a village of cooks cook for? Surely the word would get round that: 'Young Bora at Cookham makes a mean *coq au vin*'. At which the local gentry would bear down at a great pace and bear him off to their castle. Cocc also means hill: hill village. This is discounted because Cookham is only just above the flood line, as I remember well from 1947, when I lived there.

But if the place now known as Cookham Dean was the original Cookham there would be no problem, since it is on the side of the largest hill for miles around. It sounds more likely that this was the case.

The bridge at Cookham was a toll-bridge until about 1950. Its chief claim to fame is that it is said to be the cheapest road bridge on the river, at which the purists tend to raise a sneer. It certainly has no pretensions to be anything but functional, but it does not cause navigational difficulty and I have always rather liked it myself. It is a homely little bridge. They have painted it a pleasant shade of blue at present, which suits it. Take the extreme right arch coming down, second from the left going up.

Almost under the bridge, on the left, is Turk's boatyard. There was a splendid old black boat-shed there until a few years ago. Now it has gone. You can still hire rowing-boats from Mr Turk. He is one of those great characters who have passed across the history of the Thames over the centuries. A fine figure of a man in the twilight of his years and at peace with the world. He is the Queen's Swan Keeper and so was his father.

The annual swan-upping ceremony takes place in July. The idea is to establish which swans are owned by the Queen or the Dyers and Vintners Companies, severally. The Dyers' cygnets are given a nick in the beak and the Vintners' two nicks. The cygnets thus nicked are of course those whose parents have been nicked. I forgot to ask what happens when the cob belongs to one faction and the pen to the other. Perhaps that is just as well in these days of violent sexism. I did ask what the Dyers and Vintners did with their swans (they used to eat some of them), but Mr Turk assures me they do not *do* anything with them, just own them. You will probably only understand the point of this if you are English.

Cookham Reach is broad and open. For this reason it is one of the relatively few places where you will come across sailing-boats. You pass Cookham Reach Sailing Club at the bend above the bridge, and can expect to find dinghies racing at weekends. It can blow a bit here too. Coming down in the teeth of an August gale, I was surrounded by white horses and actually buffeted by waves, not a usual experience on the river. Nor was the mooring at Cookham. I

turned above the bridge in good order and slid into the bank, where there was not a lot of room. I found that, single-handed, there was no way I could get both ends of the boat to go ashore against the gale. I finally decided to moor the bows and worry about the stern later. By the time I had achieved this, the stern was pointing at Bourne End again. So I moored 'downstream', in only apparent contradiction of the rule.

The houses up the right bank are mainly attractive and usually large. On the left, the river meadows give way to rising ground, a golf course and the sweep of the hill which I think gave Cookham its name. The reach is absolutely different from Cliveden, which is quite unlike Bray. Perhaps this is the essence of the attractiveness of the Thames. The scale is small enough to make one feel comfortable and the scene changes dramatically, mile by mile.

There is no mooring before Bourne End railway bridge, where you can take any of the three spans. Above it, there is a sort of pub, called The Moorings, where you can moor as a customer, while on the right bank is Bourne End Marina, which offers every facility, including mooring overnight where space allows. Peter Naylor Marine are here too. This is another engineer who will come out to your aid. (If you are hiring, contact your home yard in case of trouble.) The Marina is the only mooring at Bourne End, so if you wish to visit that township, here is where you stop.

The Bourne End reach is also a fine sailing reach. The Upper Thames Sailing Club is on the right, and again you may expect to run into dinghy racing. There is a public mooring on the right, just past the crown of the bend, which I discovered by accident while trying to avoid three Merlin Rockets who were having a bit of a ding-dong. It has a sand bank at its upstream end, which is a little disconcerting when setting off against an onshore wind.

The river now passes a sort of shanty town, a host of perfectly dreadful weekend cottages, made chiefly of corrugated iron. At the same time, the great hill known as Winter Hill starts to press in from the left. The views from the top of this hill are marvellous but from the river the right bank is flat and featureless, gravel-pits in fact. The main interest is the little train that rattles along from time to time. It used to be called the Bourne End Donkey when I lived in the area, and comprised a lovely little steam engine and two coaches. It is now diesel, but I was happy to see it still running along.

36 The first island in this reach has a notice: 'Please leave no rubbish'. There are two or three moorings here, quiet and pleasantly wooded. They are the only attractive moorings between Cookham and Marlow. Do not try to moor opposite, on the right bank. I was aground for twenty minutes finding this out for you! It is sand-bank.

37 There are some much better houses up the left, behind the islands, nestling under the hill. So, if you are not stopping, the more interesting channel is to the left. The upper island is private. It is somebody's garden. Beyond the islands and Wootten's boatyard and past some more interesting houses, including one of my favourite 'horrids', the river sweeps sharply right, under the lee of the splendid Quarry Woods, whose true glory can best be enjoyed when running downstream.

On the left is the National Scout Boating Activity Centre, and there is likely to be a good deal of boating activity going on. Above it, on the right, above and below the by-pass bridge, there are moorings alongside fields. They are against a wall, which slopes away, so you should exercise care.

Marlow's suspension bridge has the greatest visual appeal of all. It is the work of William Tierney Clark, and was built in the 1830s. It has had a poor time since the war and was in grave danger of being pulled down at one time. Happily, it was decided to improve it.

Marlow is 'Mere shore', after the lakes that lay close to it. It boasts moorings as good as any on the Thames. They run from shortly above the bridge for 250 yards or so, up the right bank, alongside a riverside open space. In 1951, L T C Rolt wrote: 'The lack of facilities for visitors arriving by water at Marlow is remarkable. We could discover no reasonable moorings whatever.'

The town of Marlow and weir seen from the entrance to the lock.

MARLOW 1773

Fall 7′1″ : 2.16 m | Deep

Upstream Start preparing as you enter the cut. The weir stream runs in on the left some distance before the lock, and is not a problem. The pilings are on the right, with a very short lay-by on the left.

Downstream The weir curves round in a great arc. It is a spectacular sight when the river is running, but does represent potential difficulty. There is a new, unique piling on the left. While fairly short, it is double-sided, giving twice its previous capacity. Boats to the right of it should note that boats on the left have priority if they were there first, just as they would if they were in front of you. If both lay-bys are full, do not attempt to run down below the bridge. There is no room for manoeuvre, and the weir is then a positive threat. Take care also if there are boats coming up. They will tend to push you right, towards the weir.

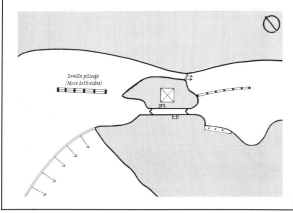

Double pilings
(Moor both sides)

38   How pleasant to note the excellence of the present ones. It is almost a duty to go ashore and spend money in the town as a token of appreciation. The shops are excellent anyway, and the hostelries, The Chequers and the George and Dragon, worth the trouble. I once had to spend three days here because of a strong stream. It was no burden, I walked in Quarry Woods and explored Bisham Church and lived well.

The only real disappointment here is the Compleat Angler. This is on the site of one of the most famous pubs on the river, the Anglers. Alas, it is now a very commercial restaurant,

excellent in its own way, I am sure, but retaining none of the magic of old.

There is no mooring from Marlow to Temple Lock, except at Bisham Church, for boats of shallow draft. If you can come alongside here, do try and make time. This lovely old building is the only church which actually fronts on the river. There is a memorial to Lady Hoby, a sixteenth and seventeenth-century lady of the manor, who killed her little son, so the story goes, for blotting his copy-book. Legal retribution did not catch up with her but it is said her ghost still walks, wringing her hands in guilty despair. All we know for sure is that she did have a little son who died in infancy. He is depicted lying at her feet, on the memorial.

Bisham Abbey, once belonging to the Knights Templars, was acquired by the Sports Council as the National Sports Centre. The last heirs to the Vansittart-Neale family, who formerly owned it, were both killed in action in the Second World War. All kinds of sport are practised here, of which the one which most interests the boater is sailing. You may well find dinghies in this reach.

You will by now have become aware of a considerable reduction in the aircraft noise, and consequent increase in peace and pleasure. From here to Cleeve is mostly lovely countryside, identifiable as 'Middle Thames'. Typically, this comprises lush meadows, running up to gentle, rolling hills, often spectacularly clad in natural woodland.

As you run up towards Temple Lock, you 39 pass a spot that will always remain close to my heart. It was here, in 1946, that my sister decided to teach little brother to swim. My reaction was to clasp her very firmly round the neck, thus almost managing to rid my mother of her entire family at one stroke. Who it was that dived off the bank to bring me ashore, I shall never know, but I have been grateful to him all these years. It is true, incidentally, that drowning becomes easier as it progresses. I had quite lost interest in the process by the time my rescuer arrived.

The reach between Temple and Hurley is the second shortest on the river, at just over half a mile. On the right is Harleyford Marina. There is a pontoon to which you can moor, overnight if you wish, and from which a 150 yard walk takes you to the grocery shop. Further up, on

TEMPLE 1773

Fall 4′1″ : 1.23 m | Marginally deep

Upstream The lock is in sight for plenty of time. The weir runs along the left as you run up, but the pilings on the left are shuttered, and this protects the approach to the lay-by, which is on the right.

Downstream The weir is to the right and there are pilings to the right of the cut and a lay-by on the left. The river bends to the left on the approach to the lock, which takes the stream away from the lock cut. Start to prepare as you pass Harleyford Marina landing stage.

Note This lock has a boat-slide for small craft, not rollers. It is unique in this respect.

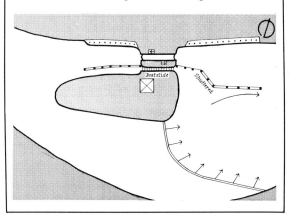

HURLEY 1773

*Fall 3′5″ : 1.05 m | Shallow |
Sanitary station*

Upstream The lock cut is to the left. Start preparing as you enter it. The tail of the old mill-stream is on the left, but no stream runs now. Peter Freebody's yard is in that stream. He builds old-fashioned boats superbly well. There are pilings on the right and a short lay-by on the left, but not a lot of room if times are busy.

Downstream Hurley weir is one of the most awe-inspiring on the river. The cut is to the right of it, and runs alongside it for the first section. There is also a small overflow weir just by the foot-bridge. So keep going.

The Sanitary Station is just beyond the foot-bridge on the left, at the start of the lay-by, which is plenty long enough. The old mill-stream goes off to the right, by the lock, but there is no pull from it.

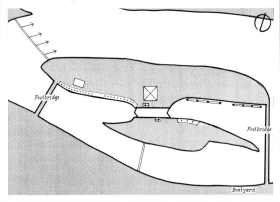

the left, you can moor to the field, although the fee is as high as anywhere on the river. If you want to visit Hurley village however it is the only mooring. The village is outrageously pretty, providing you avoid the caravan park, which is well hidden. There is a little shop, and a pub, the Rising Sun. Hurley means 'wood or clearing in a recess in the hills'! They did not waste words in olden days, did they? In view of the amount of woodland around even today, clearing seems the most likely to me.

The lock cut at Hurley is crossed by two attractive footbridges, above and below the lock.

40   At the top of the cut is the huge majesty of Hurley Weir, from which you should keep well clear. The old flash-lock must have been on the same site as the present weir. They used a winch for hauling the barges up over the lock, which

must have been a dreadfully difficult job, even with its help. The winch is still in position, in the woods on the right, although you cannot esily get to it from the river any more. Its very inaccessibility is undoubtedly the reason that it has survived for 200 years since the pound lock was opened in 1773.

The winch worked on the same principle as a capstan, the rope from the boat being passed round it a few times to obtain leverage, after which up to six men could insert poles between the iron bars and the upright and heave them round. The rope ran up a channel from the river, and passed round the upright underneath

Well-marked warning at the entrance to Hurley cut.

The last surviving flash-lock winch close to the bank at Hurley, 1987.

the horizontal bar supports. So you did not have to worry about tripping over it. The channel is still there too. Presumably, the tension was kept on the free end by attaching this to a horse, which simply walked up the towpath.

The next mile is another of those reaches best appreciated going downstream. From this aspect, the river sweeps right-handed round one of those splendid bends dictated by a great hill, which is dominated by a great house, Danesfield. The view as you go round the bend, going down, is a perfect picture of forest beyond the lock.

The RAF have a boat club at the foot of Danesfield. From the look of the ladies' eight that passed me here, they appear to cater for complete beginners. From the amount of spray flying, I at first mistook it for a paddle steamer coming up (the sun was in my eyes). By the time they passed I was quite relieved to find they were all facing the back of the boat! Well, we all have to start somewhere. No doubt by the time this is printed, the same crew will be carrying all before them.

41   There are now three islands, one on the right, the other two on the left. You can circumnavigate the lower one on the left but not the other two. There is a mooring on the right bank of the lower island, near the top, and there is a shallow mooring on the second one, about halfway up. Thacker reports a fish-weir here in 1775, on the lower island, which is known as Frog Mill Ait, a title which suggests other activity at an earlier date. In those days the channel would have been up the left, along the towpath, so the fish-weir was presumably across what is now the main stream.

Keep off the inside of the next bend, it is shallow. The following short stretch runs up to Medmenham (Medmnum). Here is a wealth of yew, clipped like an abbey cloister, which is

Medmenham Abbey. The days of the Hell Fire Club clearly long gone.

what it once was. Medmenham Abbey is chiefly remembered as the home of Sir Francis Dashwood, and thus the headquarters of the Hellfire Club, which got up to all manner of naughty behaviour, involving virgins and satanic rites, in the middle of the eighteenth century. It was thus an infinitely more wicked precursor of the Cliveden Set, and attracted all the 'top' people.

Alas, all that is left of this excitement is a comfortable looking country house, with what is apparently a nineteenth-century folly, a ruinous tower, at one end. It is one of the most attractive settings on the river.

Immediately above it is the site of an old ferry. The road from Medmenham village runs down to the river. Here there is an obelisk, which proclaims:

This monument was erected to commemorate the successful action fought by Hudson Ewebank Kearley, first Viscount Davenport P.C. which resulted in the Court of Appeal deciding on the 28th March, 1899 that Medmenham Ferry is public.

At this point, the towpath crosses the river. What was under discussion was the right of the public, as opposed to men or horse towing barges, to pass over and therefore up and down the river. The landowner claimed that it was an 'accommodation ferry', for the use of commercial traffic alone. Sadly, the ferry now being closed for economic reasons, the victory for the common man is presently only of academic interest. On the other hand, times have a habit of changing and yet remaining unchanged, and any future ferry would still have the legal right to pass anyone from bank to bank.

There is a good mooring immediately above the ferry, on the right, and a few isolated moorings, often for fairly short boats, up the right bank of the reach above. From here you can walk up the road for half a mile to the main road and the pub, the Dog and Badger. Medmenham means, apparently, medium sized or small village, and was so recorded in Domesday. One is left wondering whether it only received its name at that time. The King's Commissioners, seated at their table interviewing the locals, perhaps received no satisfactory answer to their

question about how the village was styled and made the best of a bad job by simply describing it.

Shortly above mile 42, on the left, is a notice inviting boaters to pick their own fruit and vegetables, advertising the farm shop and offering temporary mooring while they avail themselves of these benefits.

Above this there is a large island and a little one. There is a passage to the left of them, although the main channel is to the right. If you have pirates aboard, there is an inviting, though not easy, mooring up the left channel, on the larger island, with secret inlets and hidden coves to explore in the jolly-boat. Thacker reports eel bucks here in 1919. It is called Magpie Island, though I did not see one. I did pass here a camping Randan, a species I had thought to be extinct. It is a sort of treble skiff.

Towering high above the islands, on the left, is Culham Court, a Georgian mansion whose owners must be blessed with magnificent views but who must get greatly puffed climbing back up from the river bank.

Basket-work eel-bucks at Magpie Island 1875.
Henry Taunt.

Culham Court towers above the River below Hambleden Lock.

We lesser mortals are hardly less blessed and certainly less puffed, as the view up to Hambleden Lock from here is quite marvellous (and this time best seen going up). There is no mooring below Hambleden, except at the Flower Pot Hotel jetty at Aston, on the left. Unfortunately, this is too small for my boat to

---

HAMBLEDEN 1773

Fall 4′9″ : 1.44 m / Deep

Upstream The weir-stream is baffled by two islands. You should therefore beware of cross-currents as you approach the tail of the island before the lock. There are pilings on the right and these are shuttered to keep the main stream away. However, this causes the stream to run back up, wickedly, and you should be specially careful to secure your stern, or it will be whisked round. There is also a lay-by on the left, to which the same note of caution applies.

When filling, this lock has a marked tendency to hurl you at the top gates, so be sure you are properly secured and the ropes held by someone strong. It is a curious phenomenon, unique to Hambleden, and most disconcerting if you are not ready for it.

Downstream The weir is down to the left and is no problem. There is plenty of room to manoeuvre above the lock, and this will often be necessary in the summer. The pilings are on the right. When they are full, there are landfalls to be made above them. The only problem you may have here is if there is an off-shore wind, for the tie-up is very exposed. In such conditions, you may have great difficulty clawing on to the pilings.

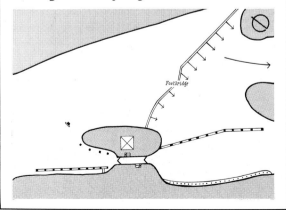

Footbridge

---

try but I noticed 25 footers moored there and it is a popular pub.

Just before Hambleden Lock, is Hambleden Marina, on the right, in what used to be the mill-stream. Hambleden Mill is now very select private apartments, preserving the look of this famous but disused old mill as one of the best known Thames landmarks.

There is a mooring on the left, above the lock, from which a footpath leads across the weir and past the mill, from where there is a pleasant walk of a mile or more to Hambleden village, which lies at the head of a lovely valley, nestling amidst wooded hills. The Stag and Huntsman alone makes this a worthwhile excursion.

A little above the lock, the river bends sharply left at the start of a ten mile stretch to the south west. Temple Island is now in sight. The bank on the left has been recently piled and makes a good mooring, from a short distance below the island to a point about level with the top of it. The depth varies a bit, and the best mooring is at the downstream end. There is about half a mile in total. You can also moor on the right bank, opposite the island.

Shortly before Temple Island, is my favourite house on the river. White, colonial, low and rambling, with beautifully kept gardens down to a long, gentle river frontage.

This was once the home of W H Smith, the bookseller, which speaks well of his taste.

Temple Island is called after the folly built at its upstream end, facing what is arguably the most famous reach of any river in the world, the Henley Regatta Course. The river runs absolutely straight for $1\frac{1}{4}$ miles, ideal for rowing. Although it will only allow two crews abreast, as opposed to the eight lane international regatta courses now specially built, it has many advantages: the setting, the space for water-borne spectators, the meadows on both banks for watchers and socialites alike. The Henley Royal Regatta takes place during the first week of July. If you are on the river then, do not expect to find a mooring between Hambleden and Marsh locks. You will be able to pass up or down the course, though slowly, and the delays at both locks will be appreciable.

At other times, there are moorings under

Temple Island's famous folly at the start of Henley's regatta course.

some horse chestnut trees, 200 yards above, and opposite Remenham. That is, on the right. Their upper limit is marked by two metal posts in the river which actually serve as an anchorage for a floating grandstand during the regatta. There is no mooring at Remenham, the bank is dangerous, due to rotten pilings.

45   From above Upper Thames Rowing Club, there is mooring on both banks, for a fee. The right bank is prettier but much shallower and further on foot from the town centre. On the left, from about a quartert of a mile above Upper Thames, you can moor almost to Leander, which is just short of the bridge. Do not ignore the notice about the 100 ft hotel boat on Tuesdays, unless you want to be turfed off your mooring when all other places are taken!

From the left bank mooring, it is about half a mile down the towpath to Remenham, 'village by the river bank', a pleasant way to spend an hour of a summer's evening. The church has a carved lych-gate, presented by a couple in memory of their 14-year-old daughter. In the churchyard is the grave of Caleb Gould, one of the great characters in Thames folklore. He was the lock-keeper at Hambleden for many years, in the eighteenth and nineteenth centuries. He always dressed in a long coat with silver buttons, like some character from Treasure Island, having no liking for the new fashions of the nineteenth century. His gravestone bears the epitaph John Gay wrote for himself:

CALEB GOULD
WHO DIED MAY 30TH, 1836
AGED 92 YEARS

The world's a jest
And all things show it
I thought so once
And now I know it

On the opposite bank the County Boundary changes from Buckinghamshire to Oxfordshire, where it remains, apart from a bureaucratic lapse into Berkshire at Caversham, until Eaton Hastings, a few miles from Lechlade. The left bank has been Berkshire from Bell Weir, and will remain so for some time yet.

The setting of Henley is full of romance, especially as you approach up river. The stone bridge appears to dominate the scene, with the houses and church to the right. Closer inspection reveals the Phyllis Court club, opposite the regatta finish, some delightful houses with the ground floor given over to boathouses, and then the waterfront. On the left before the bridge is Leander, the premier English rowing club in terms of status and not infrequently by results as well. If you see a racing shell with pink blades, that is a Leander boat.

Immediately above the bridge, on the left, is the new building of the headquarters of the

46

White posts mark the 1 1/4-mile regatta course at Henley.

Henley Royal Regatta. On the right, Hobbs boatyard, by appointment Waterman to HM the Queen, where fuel, water and chandlery are to be had. They have a public slip too. This is on the other side of the river, but you have to collect a key from the main yard office.

Henley is said to mean 'at the high wood', which is fair enough. The town nestles at the foot of hills on both sides of the river, and both are still largely forested. The bridge is pleasing to look at, if unremarkable. All the arches are navigable but the right one is very close to the mooring at the Angel Inn, which is so close to the bridge that the two appear to be jostling for position, while the arch at the other end should be avoided, going down, because boats are likely to be moored immediately below it. However, that still leaves three fine arches to choose from. The bridge was built in 1786, by William Hayward. There are two masks sculpted over the centre arch. They were done by a Mrs Damer, a relative of Horace Walpole, to represent Father Thames, facing down to Temple Island, and Isis, facing upstream.

Of more interest to me is the notice to be found at each end of the bridge, facing the road:

WARNING
ENGINE DRIVERS MUST ONLY TAKE
ONE LOADED TRUCK AT ONE TIME
OVER THIS BRIDGE. DRIVERS AND
OWNERS ARE RESPONSIBLE FOR
DAMAGE

Henley is a pleasant town to visit or in which to shop. Walk up Hart Street from the bridge to the traffic lights. The shops are to left and

The distinctive sterns of four slipper-launches moored at Henley.

right at the lights. To the left is a good baker, and there is an excellent grocery/delicatessen, about 300 yards down to the right is a Waitrose supermarket. There are said to be 21 pubs in Henley, which I can believe, although I have not found them all. I have not found a bad one either, so I suggest you take your pick.

MARSH 1773
Fall 4'4" : 1.33 m | Deep

Upstream You will have plenty of time to prepare. The lock is to the left, and the pilings are also on the left. There is shuttering to keep off the worst of the weir-stream, but this has a nasty tendency to run back up and push you off the pilings. So, do not approach too slowly and go against them with determination.

Downstream The weir is on the left, with the lock tucked into the right. Even further to the right is the old mill-stream, which is now blocked off. The pilings are to the right and the left side is shuttered, so there is no problem coming alongside. Incidentally, what appears to be the weir, as you approach, is actually the footbridge/walkway for the towpath. The weir is some way below it and does not interfere.

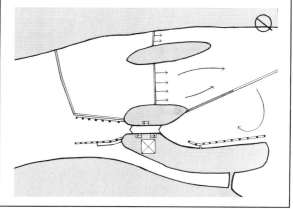

There is some mooring to be had on the right above the bridge, opposite the islands, and then nothing before Marsh Lock. I find no comments on where this lock got its name. Wargrave marsh is half a mile above it, so it could be that. The lock is remarkable for the amazing walkway, which carries the towpath out across the weir-stream to the lock island, and then back again to the right bank, a total of some 200–300 yards. The reason for this extravagance was

The tow-path and wooden bridge spanning the weir-stream at Marsh.

the establishment of a mill on the right bank, which blocked the towpath. This mill was unique for a Thames mill, in that it powered a brass foundry. You can still see the Victorian remains of a workshop or warehouse, as you run up to the lock. Not that they went without bread at Henley. The corn mill was on the other bank, by the lock.

47 Some charming private property lines the left bank above the lock, including a pretty converted boathouse, quite possibly the most photographed house on the river! In half a mile, Hennerton Backwater is passed on the left. It is over a mile long, but reputed to be unnavigable. I was unable to try it, because I could not find anywhere close enough to moor, so that I could launch the dinghy.

Opposite the backwater, is the first of three islands, Ferry Eyot, named after a ferry which carried the towpath across from right to left banks at this point. The stream to the right of Ferry Eyot is navigable, with care, and passes the first of several grand, modern country houses on this reach.

48 Poplar and Hardbuck Eyots follow in quick succession. Halfway up the left of Hardbuck, there is a mooring on the left bank, after which they occur regularly for the next few hundred yards, ending in 150 yards of Thames Water moorings, which run up to Henley Sailing Club, after which there are none until half a mile above Shiplake Lock. ($1\frac{1}{2}$ miles)

'Quintessential middle Thames' has changed little, if at all, over the years.

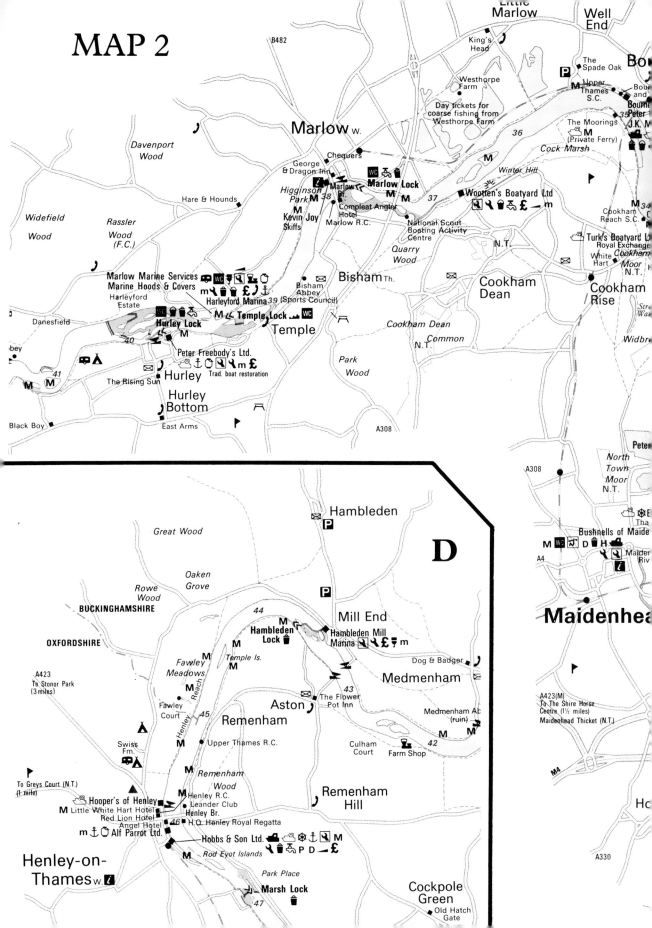

MAP 2

D

Little Marlow

Well End

Bo

King's Head

The Spade Oak

P

M Upper Thames S.C.

Bour and

35 Peter

J.K. M

B482

Westhorpe Farm

Day tickets for coarse fishing from Westhorpe Farm

36

The Moorings (Private Ferry)

Marlow w.

Cock Marsh

Davenport Wood

Chequers

M

Winter Hill

Cookham Reach S.C.

M 34

George & Dragon Inn

WC

Marlow Lock

37

Wootten's Boatyard Ltd

Hare & Hounds

Higginson Park M 38

Marlow Br.

M

Compleat Angler Hotel

M

National Scout Boating Activity Centre

N.T.

Turk's Boatyard L Royal Exchange

White Hart

Widefield Wood

Rassler Wood (F.C.)

Kevin Joy Skiffs

Marlow R.C.

Cookham

M

Moor N.T.

Cookham Rise

Marlow Marine Services Marine Hoods & Covers

WC

Bisham Abbey (Sports Council)

Bisham Th.

Cookham Dean

Stre Wa

Harleyford Estate

m

£

Harleyford Marina 39

Cookham Dean Common

Widbre

Danesfield

M

Temple Lock

WC

Temple

N.T.

bey

40

Hurley Lock

M

Peter Freebody's Ltd.

Quarry Wood

Park Wood

41

m £

M

M

Hurley

Trad. boat restoration

A308

The Rising Sun

Hurley Bottom

Black Boy

East Arms

Hambleden

P

A308

North Town Moor N.T.

Great Wood

E

Bushnells of Maide

M WC D H

Maidenhead Riv

D

A4

Oaken Grove

Rowe Wood

44

M

Mill End

Hambleden Mill Marina

M

m

Maidenhea

BUCKINGHAMSHIRE

Hambleden Lock

OXFORDSHIRE

Fawley Meadows

Temple Is.

M

Dog & Badger

A423 To Stonor Park (3 miles)

M

Henley Reach

Fawley Court

45

Medmenham

43

The Flower Pot Inn

A423(M) To The Shire Horse Centre (1½ miles) Maidenhead Thicket (N.T.)

Aston

Remenham

Medmenham Ab (ruin)

M

Swiss Fm.

Upper Thames R.C.

Culham Court

Farm Shop

42

M

To Greys Court (N.T.) (1 mile)

Remenham Wood

M4

Hooper's of Henley

M

Little White Hart Hotel

Red Lion Hotel

Angel Hotel

Remenham Hill

M

Henley R.C.

Leander Club

Henley Br.

46 H.Q. Henley Royal Regatta

m

Alf Parrot Ltd.

Hobbs & Son Ltd.

M

A330

Ho

P D £

Henley-on-Thames w.

M

Rod Eyot Islands

Park Place

Cockpole Green

Marsh Lock

47

Old Hatch Gate

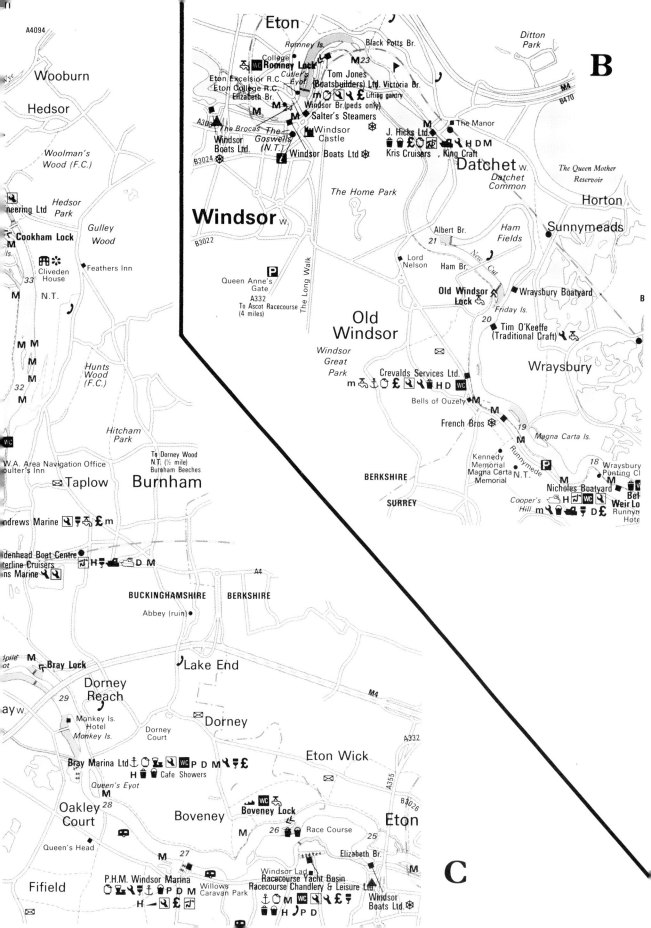

Unless you are stopping, it is a good idea to continue up the right of the islands. The houses are well worth staring at. Unlike Maidenhead, it is noticeable that everyone has a boat, some of them superb examples of launches, embodying good taste as a first essential. Not all the houses from here to Shiplake Lock are grand, some of them are better described as quaint, and some simply lovely. This reach is very easy on the eye. It is quintessential middle Thames; lovely countryside, tree covered islands, and marvellously soft.

49   There are three yards at Wargrave; Val Wyatt, from where you can obtain fuel, chandlery and water; Swancraft, who have a pump-out, and Bushnell's, who have a pump-out, fuel and water. Swancraft are busy with their own cruisers at hire change times, and Bushnell's is difficult to get into and out of, since it is up a creek. The Hennerton Backwater comes out behind Val Wyatt, and you can run behind the island between his yard and Swancraft, if it amuses you to do so. There is mooring at the St George and Dragon.

There is no access, in the ordinary way, to Wargrave, since none of the yards has room for casual mooring, and there is no public frontage to the river. This is a pity, since it is an attractive village. The name means 'grove by the weir', which indicates perhaps that there was a flash-lock here in very early times, before it was moved up to Shiplake. It seems to me that there are two possible historical references to this.

I have seen boats moored up the right bank towards the railway bridge, but it is shallow and very knobbly and uncomfortable. On my way down in 1985, there was a regatta in this reach, nothing smart, just good family fun. Such things are a feature of the Thames in the summer. They are no problem, so long as one does not try to hurry, and obeys the instructions of the marshals.

The railway bridge is one of the less remarkable of the Thames bridges, and serves mainly to warn you of the approach to Shiplake Lock, which is a quarter of a mile above it. Immediately before the lock island, the River Loddon flows into the weir-stream (left). This is a strange little river, of which it is said that he who rows against its stream will feel sick. Much as I would have liked to test this theory, there was again no convenient place to launch the dinghy.

SHIPLAKE   1773

Fall 5'1":1.55 m | Deep | Sanitary station

Upstream You will see the lock in good time. Start preparing above the railway bridge. The lock is on the right, with the weir-stream, a wide channel full of moored boats, running up the left, past Loddon mouth. Lay-by on the left. There is no problem.

Downstream Prepare as you pass Phillimore's Island. The weir is on the right. Do not steer too far right. The Sanitary Station is halfway down the cut, on the right. Below it is an overflow weir. Look out for this, and keep off it. There are pilings on the left and a lay-by on the right. There should be no problem with either.

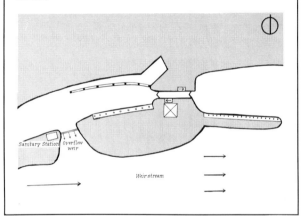

Shortly above the lock lies Phillimore's Island, where there is mooring for several boats, but which is open and not very large, and can therefore be a bit crowded when all the places are taken. Opposite the island is Borough Marsh Stream, which joins up with St Patrick's Stream, which leaves the Thames at Buck Eyot, $1\frac{1}{2}$ miles further up. St Patrick's Stream runs into the Loddon and these two streams are very unusual indeed, because they both run *out* of the Thames, which should not happen if you consider that a river is supposed to run at the lowest point of its valley. The answer is possibly that the raising of the level by the weir at Shiplake reversed the flow of the Loddon, which then cut its present bed, to come out below the lock. Furthermore, this process has probably been repeated twice, because there was an early weir at Buck Eyot, as we shall see,

Shiplake's earth-sided Lock and Mill in the last century. Henry Taunt, 1870.

which could have caused a change in the stream, making the present Phillimore's Island arm, and perhaps causing Phillimore's Island in the process.

I determined to navigate Borough Marsh Stream in the dinghy, and perhaps link up with the Loddon in this way. It is not something I advise anyone to attempt! The stream runs fast for $\frac{1}{2}$ mile and then falls over a weir. I decided to abandon the Loddon, portaged round the weir, and set off up the other arm. An hour and a quarter of hard rowing took me a mile up this tortuous and swift little stream, at which point an oar broke and lost me 50 yards in three seconds, before I could grasp a passing tree. I then portaged past another weir, and paddled in a series of circles, ridiculously, back to Phillimore's Island, in constant peril from shipping. The stream is pleasantly wild and full of interesting (and surprised) animal and bird life, for all that.

Above the island, the river turns due south as it passes Shiplake, which is high on the hill above. Shiplake is said to be 'stream where sheep are washed', which is not very satis-

factory. Funnily enough, there is a stream, a drain really, which runs along the bottom of the hill and into the river at the bend. But surely, in medieval times, one would not go driving one's sheep for miles to a special washing stream?

There follows another group of islands, on the lower two of which, The Lynch and Hallsmead Eyot, there are good moorings to be had. Unfortunately, the locals know about them too, so that they are usually taken at weekends, but they are excellent for a quiet stay, or for pirates, for that matter. It can use up a great deal of imagination though, when one is approaching a tropical island, hitherto undiscovered, only to have to hang about and wait for the local head-hunters to leave, before finding a mooring!

There are also a couple of short moorings on the right by Hallsmead. Both large islands are circumnavigable, but Buck Eyot, the top island in the group, is not. Thacker reports Hall's Weir here in 1632. There is no real sign of it. I should think the flash-lock would have been in the channel that is no longer navigable, which shows signs of having been dug and of now reverting to nature. In that case the fish-bucks would have been in what is now the channel.

51   There are moorings on the right above Buck Eyot, at mile 51. The reach is unremarkable, the country noticeably flatter than it has been for the last few miles.

52   However, in a mile, a sweeping bend reveals Sonning Bridge, and one of the prettiest villages on the river. There are moorings, for a fee, to the left bank below the bridge, which is owned by the White Hart, and to the right bank along the concrete wall.

Sonning is pronounced 'Sunning', although fewer and fewer people seem to know that, even locally. It is the first of several places we shall come to named after a Saxon chief. If a place on the Thames ends in 'ing', it is almost certainly so named, 'ing' being short for inga(s): of the family, clan, tribe of.

So, Sonning was held by the people of Sunna, presumably as a ford or crossing place, or even as a trading post/port. I have always had a marvellous picture of Sunna's longships moored where the White Hart now is, one June day in 700 and something, while the crews repaired to the Bull for a few jugs. Naturally, it all got out of hand and turned into a major party, from which Sunna awoke the following morning with the most fundamental hangover, decided he was getting too old to be a pirate, that he had found a spot where one could grow old peacefully, that he would stay. It seems they were quite a powerful tribe, for it is thought that Sunninghill, fifteen miles away, near Ascot, was also named after them. The tribe, if not its founder, would certainly have served as one of Alfred's bulwarks against the Danes.

There is a dear old brick bridge at Sonning, built in 1604, of which only the centre arch is large enough for cruisers. It is awkwardly placed, coming down, especially in any stream, since you have to keep left until the last moment, and then turn right quite sharply, to pass the bridge. Make sure, when you are going up, that the bridge approaches are clear before you proceed, and if in any doubt, wait below. There is plenty of room in the pool below the bridge. Since the lock is only 300 yards above the bridge, you will find boats coming down in lockfulls, i.e., four to eight at a time, and you will have to give way to all of them and miss the lock as a result. There really is no safe alternative to this, because there is very little room to manoeuvre above the bridge, even if

Sonning Bridge is awkwardly placed, coming down River.

stopping is a practical possibility.

While you are waiting, the backwater to the right under the footbridge is worth observing. The French Horn Restaurant is at the head of the pool and you can see Sonning Mill through the trees. This is another of the well known Thames mills, which ground corn until quite recently. It is now being used as a theatre restaurant, where your theatre ticket buys your dinner as well. As such, it is certainly not expensive, but whether you could obtain entrance casually depends presumably on the day and what they are playing. In any case, it is good to see the mill still there. I have seen no shops in the village, and the Bull is the only serious pub.

The approach to Sonning Lock is heavily wooded and attractive, with a large, well kept, private garden on the island to the right, and the church peeping through the trees to the left. You can pass directly into the churchyard from the towpath, and from there to the garden of the Bull.

There is an official Thames Water mooring on the left, above the lock, which runs right up to the start of the island (about 400 yards). It is in need of deepening; my boat was two ft off the bank at the stern.

53   There was once a flash-lock at the island on the bend at 53. It was known as Breach's Weir, and was there until 1793. It was one of the more unpopular locks on the river, being too near the bend for comfort in a strong stream. I found no sign.

Shortly above the island, the river turns left and the boater is faced with six miles of Reading and its effects. The visitor for the first time will be not much encouraged to learn that it used to be worse. Now it is dismal and bleak. I did not look for moorings up this reach, since I cannot imagine anyone would wish to stop.

54 A quarter of a mile above the bend, the Thames and Kennet Marina lies in the ex-gravel-pit on the right. It offers overnight mooring and full services but has a notice saying 'No Hire-boats'. It is quite pleasant inside, and screened by trees from the Reading scene.

At the next right-hander, the River Kennet enters from the left. A little way up this river is the only lock run by Thames Water which is not on the Thames. It is called Blake's, and will not concern you unless you hire a boat from Reading Marine Co, who live about a quarter mile up the Kennet.

In another half mile, Better Boating Co, on the right, offer all facilities except overnight mooring, and were noticeably obliging into the bargain, when I called. They have a shop for

Ship-shape fend-offs kiss the water at Sonning Lock.

SONNING 1773

Fall 5'4" : 1.55 m | Deep

Upstream The lock is a good quarter mile above the bridge, but be prepared. The pilings are on the right. There is unlikely to be any problem with the weir, which runs quite straight at this lock.

Downstream Prepare after the island. The lock is on the right. There is a lay-by on the right and pilings on the left. The weir is well down the stream and presents no difficulty.

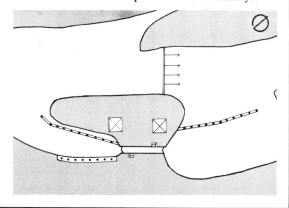

basic necessities. Caversham Marina is just above them, on the right of the left-hand bend before the lock. On the left bank, there are one or two possible moorings against a public open space, which would do in an emergency.

55   Caversham Lock is now in full sight. I hope the lock-keeper does not mind me quoting his comment, which sticks in my memory because it is so close to my own view. 'There is not a lot to be said for Reading', he said. To be fair, he had spent most of his career at Goring, for which there is a great deal to be said, and asked to be moved to Reading for personal reasons.

Above the lock is Reading Bridge, which is modern and functional and spans the whole river, so that it presents no problems. On the

---

CAVERSHAM 1778

Fall 4'9" : 1.44 m | Deep

Upstream Start preparing as you pass Better Boating Co. This lock has been the subject of major, much-needed, improvements during 1987. There is now a sensible lay-by on the left, and the notorious shallows have been dredged. There is a fair amount of space for manoeuvre and the weir creates no difficulty.

Downstream The lock is shortly below Reading Bridge. It lies to the right. The weir-stream does not threaten. There is a lay-by on the right, of good length. Even so, the lock is so small (it only holds three boats of any size) that there are usually queues here.

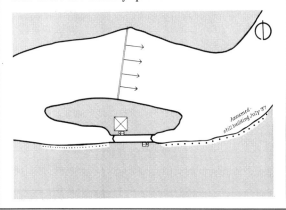

---

right is a public mooring, for a fee, provided by Reading Council, at the nearest point you will get to the main shopping centre. The alternative is to run up to Caversham.

Opposite the mooring is a new housing development, which looks perfectly suitable and is a welcome improvement to the riverside. Let us hope it is the start of a riverside renaissance, such as is taking place at that other blot on the river landscape, Oxford.

You can pass both sides of Fry's Island. On the left of the island are Caversham Boat Services, and Bridge Boats, both of whom hire cruisers and have service facilities, with the usual caveat concerning their busy days.

Shortly above the island lies Caversham Bridge, another modern structure, and quite handsome in its way. You can moor below the bridge, on the left, which gives access to The Moderation and The Crown on the Reading and Caversham ends of the Bridge respectively, and to the shops (including Waitrose) in Caversham. After crossing the bridge, bear right at the lights and you should be able to buy all you need within about 200 yards.

Reading was indeed founded by Reada, who was presumably impressed by the defensive possibilities of having the rivers Thames and Kennet guarding three flanks of his settlement. The town that grew up here was much admired by visitors. A great abbey was founded and the area prospered. The rot set in with the coming of the industrial revolution and the railway, and since then the town has sprawled amorphously and lost any real identity. For my sins, I have been a long distance supporter of Reading Football Club for 40 years, during which they sat ingloriously in the middle of the Third Division, seemingly without any desire to be anywhere else. Their recent promotion to the Second Division and the recent rebuilding work that makes the town so much more pleasant for the boater, are perhaps both indicators of a burgeoning new confidence in the town.

At the same time, Reading does provide an excellent place to start a holiday, for it is perfectly feasible to run down to Windsor or up to Oxford. I have done both, thirty years apart.

Part Three

CAVERSHAM BRIDGE
TO
OXFORD

IF YOU ARE starting a cruise from Reading and you are a beginner, it is more important than usual to start downstream. The reason for this offer of advice lies $3\frac{1}{2}$ miles upstream.

Use the left hand arch of Caversham Bridge, the other one is too cluttered. The arch is plenty wide enough for boats to pass each other beneath it but you should avoid trying to overtake as you approach.

'Caphere's village' is where you live if you have to be near Reading but can afford to settle across the river. Caversham runs back up the hill, which suggests that it was a desire to have dry feet rather than a defensive situation that caused Caphere to choose it in the first place. Perhaps he was a Roman-Briton, in which case the greatest danger would be from Saxon warbands coming up river or from the south, and a hill fronting the river would then be the best position.

For river users, the Caversham bank is easily the best bit of Reading. There are some most attractive houses up the right bank. My favourite is a splendid turreted extravagance over a boat-house, probably Edwardian, and I am also intrigued by the modern house which appears to have given birth to a small replica which stands next to it. The woods on Caversham Heights are also a fine sight, especially if you are coming down river.

There are about four moorings on the left-hander opposite St Mary's Island. There were once eel bucks here and Thacker suggests it as the probable site of Chawsey Weir, of which the last written record was 1585. The water behind the island appears to be private, and I notice five Thames Water pilings and a boom a short distance back from the top of the island.

The inference is that there are the remains of a weir at this point. It would be the old eel buck weir but this would most likely be on the site of the earlier structure. The flash-lock itself would have been in the main channel, unless this was dug when the lock was abandoned, to avoid the need to extract the old pilings and to straighten the navigation.

In half a mile you can obtain chandlery, fuel and water at Reading Marine Services, on the left. After this the railway closes noisily in at high level for $1\frac{1}{2}$ miles up the left bank. The only thing to do is to press on grimly.

If you run up the right of Appletree Eyot and Poplar Island, there is some relief to be had. Indeed, there is a right bank mooring opposite Appletree, against open fields; a little oasis from which, in summer, you cannot see the railway.

It was as I ran down to Appletree Eyot that I saw my first Great Crested Grebe chick; the first that is that I ever saw. I have no early memories of this bird on the Thames, having first seen it on the Norfolk Broads. I think they must be relative new-comers, like that other bird which is now such a lovely feature of the River, the Canada goose. Can the Grebe fly? I have never seen one try. They are the most timid of water birds, making that shy, retiring little character the moorhen seem almost brazenly confident by comparison.

The Thames has now begun a thirty mile run to the north, with only occasional westward leanings. For a little while it seems as if the railway is not going to let go. Just above 58 miles, the line runs along the top of a high brick wall, directly above the river bank. On a dull day it is almost too much to bear. 'The deepest darkness comes before the dawn' is fortunately very true here, for the river turns sharply to the right and runs up to Mapledurham and some of the loveliest countryside it passes between source and sea.

At the tail of the island below 59, there were a few birds standing on a mud-bank; a pair of coots, several assorted ducks and a brown cormorant. If you should be cruising on the river and come across a pilotless narrow-boat, ploughing resolutely on, like the *Marie Celeste*, it is quite likely I, with an urgent need for my bird book. This is always to be found at the far end of the boat from where it is needed. Such was the case on this occasion, for I have always

Mapledurham Mill 1888; almost as it is today.
Henry Taunt.

thought of cormorants as exclusively sea birds. I heard later, on the wireless, that young, unattached cormorants frequently travel inland and live for long periods, quite happily. This one was still sitting there in '86 and in '87, so he seems to have found it to his liking. We shall meet some more cormorants above Oxford.

This island has to be passed on the right (left coming down), and the channel is quite narrow. For this and other reasons, slow down and summon your crew on deck. As you pass the head of the island you will have a fine view of Mapledurham House, a marvellously mellow brick Elizabethan mansion, set in farmland and park in a manner that would have given 'Capability' Brown great satisfaction. Indeed it may have done, although it was actually landscaped by Alexander Pope.

'The village by the maple tree' was called Mapledre-ham in Domesday. How lovely: perhaps again nobody had thought of a name and so it was a simple description. If so it was a happy thought. It is a most singular place to this day. The village is small, off the main road

and without pub or shop, dominated by the great house with its little church. There is a venerable mill, grinding corn again after ceasing to do so for a time and otherwise having done so since before the Norman Conquest. Here is a place that can have changed little in the last few centuries.

The village church, serving the Anglican community, has attached to it a chantry chapel, built by Bardolph in 1390 and the property of the owners of Mapledurham House, staunch Catholics. It is not used for worship, but as a chapel of rest, since it is not consecrated.

The house has been in the hands of one family, the Blounts, since it was built, until the present generation and is still occupied by a relative. It is possible to tour all this during summer weekends, starting from Caversham Bridge with a firm called D&T Scenics. The owner assures me he allows visitors to moor in the weir-stream, above the lock.

The chief reason for slowing down is Mapledurham Lock, which is now dead ahead. The general opinion amongst Rivermen is that Mapledurham upstream is as stern a test of watermanship, if any sort of stream is running, as you will meet. Even the lock-keeper has trouble with it, as he ruefully admits. Do not be too worried, particularly if there is little water coming down. This lock may have smashed lifetime reputations in seconds, but at least nobody will be surprised if you make a nonsense. It is also a fact that I, who have spread mayhem and paint over the least offensive of locks, up and down the river, have never had a moment's bother here! Actually, I can only remember going up it half a dozen times in my life, which may have assisted my good fortune. It is not, however, the ideal place to start learning about locks and locking, hence my comment at the start of this section.

Above the lock there are two, shallow, moorings on the left, beyond the lock pilings. There are also a couple in the next field and one opposite these, all shallow. Just before the little island there is a mooring on the right, and three more on the left, slightly above mile 60. These last were occupied when I passed but I doubt they are deep enough for a narrow-boat.

Take your fill of the view on the right above Mapledurham. There is lush watermeadow,

The weir stream races past Mapledurham Lock.

MAPLEDURHAM 1777

Fall 6′ 9″ : 2.05m | Deep

Upstream Slow down and prepare as you pass the top of the island below Mapledurham House. The best approach is to try to go straight into the lock, if at all possible. A dead slow approach up the last 200 yards will help to achieve this. It will also help counteract one of the lock's foibles. This is the sudden change between forcing up against the current, and rushing uncontrollably forward when you hit the weir backwash.

There are 150 ft of pilings on the left, followed by 100 ft of lay-by. The pilings are better to get on to, because the stream will push you, but correspondingly difficult to get off again. The lay-by has the opposite characteristics.

The last approach to the lock involves avoiding being dashed against the right hand wall by the combined forces of the backwash and the small stream that runs in on the left, by the lock. The further away you can be, the more easily you can deal with this problem, which is why the pilings are the better place to start. Mercifully, if you are feeling shell-shocked by the time you reach the haven of the lock, this has four sensibly placed sets of steps, all running the right way!

Downstream The lock is on the right. You will see it in plenty of time. There are pilings on the right, which curve at the end nearer to you. This creates the only small difficulty you may have. Beyond the pilings, there are three bollards on the bank.

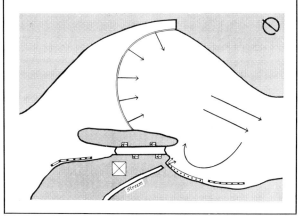

Mapledurham House and Church, well hidden by trees.

gently sloping pasture, steep field and then woodland, the whole rising in a sort of natural crescendo from the river, with a little rustic hut as a counter point; woods and rolling hills, as far as the eye can see. There is also a single, magnificent cedar.

A short distance below mile 60 is a sad little island, which looks just about on its last legs. In times past it was a well known spot, boasting a summer-house and used by parties from Hardwick house. Now there is not enough of it to moor against.

60   Hardwick House is on the right, another Elizabethan manor house, with later additions, standing back at the end of a rather narrow-looking avenue of garden and paddock. It is a discreet sort of house that wishes to keep itself to itself. Queen Elizabeth absolutely did sleep here and King Charles I played bowls here by

all accounts, and with that sort of pedigree one does not need to be pushy. All the same, we on the river are allowed to look upon it and can be glad of that.

Here the river makes a brief sweep to the south-west, past a lovely, low house with wooden post and rail fencing around its paddocks; a stud farm. After that a road runs down to the right bank for no very obvious reason, except that there is a splendid boat-house there.

Elizabethan elegance. Hardwick House emerges from the background.

Whitchurch viewed here from the toll bridge, showing the mill scout.

There is now a mooring prohibition notice on the left, but an invitation to moor on the right, for a fee. I found one good mooring there and two 25 footers, but the bank is a bit knobbly with tree roots. After this there is nothing until the official moorings up the left bank below Whitchurch Bridge. These are very popular and usually crowded. You cannot moor for about 200 yards below the bridge, but there is perhaps a quarter mile of bank below that. These moorings are the only ones giving access to the shops at Pangbourne and to Whitchurch.

Whitchurch Bridge is one of only two toll-bridges remaining on the Thames. It is somewhat similar to Cookham Bridge in design, a simple iron structure. There is no charge for pedestrians, so it is pleasant to walk across and look at the picturesque old mill and the houses and church that nestle around its pool.

There is a definite feeling that the residents rather wish you would not wander about. Things are not actually as private as they would like you to think, as is indicated by the signpost just past the toll house. 'To the slip', it reads. Sure enough, there is one, although it does not look as though many people have been

brave enough to use it recently. There is also a wharf indicated, but it is difficult to define which of the fenced off bits enclose it!

Whitchurch is said to mean 'white church', perhaps because the church is built of stone. Actually, it is flint faced, like most of the other churches for miles around. Could it rather be 'wich church' or 'wyck church', a church where salt can be had?

Pangbourne, 'stream of Paega's people', indicating perhaps another settlement using the flank protection of a tributary (the River Pang), at its junction with the Thames, as well as crossing point. Famous as the home of the Merchant Navy Cadet College and of Kenneth Grahame (*Wind in the Willows*), Pangbourne is now an outpost of Reading. There are a few shops although, apart from the butcher, I prefer those at Goring, and the same applies to the pubs, excepting the Swan. There are also the George Hotel and The Cross Keys at Pangbourne, and the Ferryboat Inn and the Greyhound at Whitchurch.

WHITCHURCH 1787

Fall 3'4" : 1.01m | Shallow | Sanitary station

Upstream There are no navigational difficulties. The pilings are on the left. The last 100 ft stretch has a walkway and gives access to the Sanitary Station. The pilings are dog-legged, so make a determined approach if the lock is emptying, or the stream thus produced may take your bow off them.

Downstream Be prepared before you reach the sharp left-hand bend in front of the weir. The pilings are short, 100 ft or so, which means that only four boats of average size can tie up. It is important to assess the situation before committing yourself to the lock cut. Once in, you cannot turn round and, if you lose steerage way, you will be washed against the weir. In the summer the weir posts are always covered with paint of different colours, and bits that have broken off boats. The DANGER notice is frequently bent. Contact with the weir in reasonable stream conditions is not particularly hazardous, but it is the very devil to get off again. So, always manoeuvre in the river above the bend, until you know it is OK to proceed. The odd idiot may push past but, if you have done your sums right, your revenge may be sweet and swift! Large boats coming out may squeeze you towards the weir. Do not let them, there is plenty of water to the right going up.

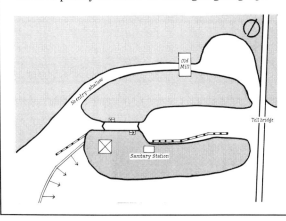

Keep well to the right as you leave Whitchurch Lock. Those coming down will be trying to avoid the weir, and there is precious little room for the first 100 yards. As the river

The pilings run alongside the weir above Whitchurch Lock.

turns right, you will see the Swan Hotel on the left, at the end of the weir. There is a landing-stage, but I do not advise it if there is a stream running or unless you have plenty of power available. It is simply not worth the risk.

The railway is back, at high level, behind the mainly Edwardian villa properties built almost into the cliff up the left bank. On the right you will see the first of many 1940 'pill-boxes' we shall pass. These were built as part of a plan to stop a German invasion at the Thames. The idea was that lightly armed men could, with the help of a concrete fort, hold the enemy long enough for reinforcements to arrive. In this case, the box was positioned to command the railway. The plan almost certainly would not have worked, but it was all that was then available. Now, the line of defences provide an inter-

This is a good place to moor, especially if you have children. My British Bird book almost got chucked in the river here, a few years ago. It had failed to identify three water-birds in half an hour. On the last occasion, in furious frustration, I asked a woman standing on the bank if she had any idea what we were both looking at. 'Yes', she said, 'Chinese geese!' It was then that I discovered Childe-Beale. It is well worth an hour or two after tea to walk round their gardens. You will find all manner of fascinating wild-life, including many endangered species of exotic birds, and lots of ducks and geese from foreign lands. These are perfectly free to come and go and you will find them dotted about from Goring to Whitchurch.

Hart's Lock was one of the more famous of the old flash-locks. Taunt's map of 1900 shows one large island, where the two are at present, and three more across the stream. Thacker has a photograph of pilings, which were being drawn when he passed in 1910. He says the lock was 'against the little islands under the woods.' From a study of the topography of the site, I think the *weirs* were on the right, with the lock in the narrow channel between the present islands and the left bank. This channel has the appearance of a man-made cut, the bank being curved in a way that does not seem natural. Also, the tow-path is on this side, although it is possible that this was not always so. It would be logical to have the lock against the tow-path.

The lock was still there in 1720 but history does not relate when it ceased to function. Certainly it would not have survived the building

esting glimpse of future archaeology, and perhaps a task for the children: spot the pill-boxes. There may well be several that I have missed. (I did not miss the one by the railway next to the mooring below Whitchurch Bridge. I simply thought it too far away to bother with!)

62　　The lovely trees on the right soon give way to the paddocks of another stud farm, Coombe Park. On the left, as the river again turns away from the railway, there are shallow moorings stretching from a point opposite the boat-house. There is another pill-box on the right.

63　　Hart's Lock Wood is now crowding in on the right. This has been compared to Cliveden, but that is a bit strong. It is nevertheless a place of great charm. Two islands mark the site of Hart's Lock, and the left bank has a wooden facing, allowing good mooring, as you run up to them. The Childe-Beale Trust is on this bank, with the moorings continuing up beside the islands. exercise care however; there is little water.

Hart's Lock. Taunt's photograph of 1880 shows clearly the lock-cut on the right.

of the pound locks at Goring and Whitchurch, in 1787. There is a massive concrete structure on the lower island, possibly the remains of a pill-box. I think the lock would have been about there. I searched in vain for any sure proof. All I found were some large stones on the river-bed against the right bank, in line with the structure on the island. These could have been the remains of the abutment for the old weir, if only because I did not find any others, and because they were in the right place, but I felt no glow of triumph!

This is the lowest of eight Thames flash-locks that have at one time or another been called Hart's. Generations of that family seem to have been fascinated by the river. However, a Hart was not the first keeper, for the place was known as Lockstigle, 'style by the lock', in 1181.

Shortly above the lock islands is another island. You have to keep to the right of this, for it is very shallow between it and the left bank. Above the island there are two or three moorings, after which mooring is prohibited on the left, and there is only one more between here and Goring.

The river swings left and west for about a mile and you will see the village of Basildon across the fields, looking medieval and deeply rural from this aspect, crouched around its little, square towered church.

64 Basildon or Gatehampton railway bridge is now in sight, and 200 yards before it is a ferry cottage, with a Thames Conservancy mark on it. The ferry was established in 1810, where the tow-path crosses to the right bank, and those who find its passing of some inconvenience may be mollified by the knowledge that it was reserved for the carriage of those involved in navigating during most of its existence.

The bridge itself, of brick and stone, is the least remarkable of Brunel's bridges over the river. I suspect him of leaving it to someone else, or having an off day. You have to turn quite sharply to shoot it. There are two main arches. Take the arch on your right, up and down. There is a pill-box immediately above it, and then a mooring, to the sandbagged and sheathed wall on the right.

The river now turns north again and passes three islands. There is no channel to the left of these and no mooring on them. Note the pill-box on the top one, the first of several 'suicide'

boxes. Your only way out would be to swim across the river, presumably under fire. I found shoal water on the right at this point, for 50 yards. There were two marker buoys 15 yards out from the bank.

There has been some bank rebuilding and reinforcing on the right up the last half mile to Goring. There is a shallowish mooring to the second of these places but the best moorings are in the last 200 yards up to Goring Bridge.

I suppose Goring and Streatley would figure on anyone's shortlist of archetypal Thames-side picture-postcard places. They are normally spoken of together, like Buda and Pest, Goring being much larger and relatively more spoilt by modern development, which is mercifully hidden from river users since the old village has not changed much in the last 100 years or so.

The two are joined by a long, flat, rustic looking bridge, which is actually two bridges, joined at the island in the middle. The effect is a pleasing one, since the bridges are attractive and yet make no attempt to intrude into or command the scene. Streatley Bridge, with the Swan Hotel at its foot, was a toll bridge until well into this century. There has been a major crossing here for three thousand years or so, for this is where the Ridgeway crosses the Thames, that great trade route of pre-history. The Ridgeway was improved by the Romans, who called it Ickleton Street. Streatley takes its name from this: 'clearing by the Roman road'. Streatley village now rests as quietly as it can beside the A329, its chief feature nowadays being the Bull at Streatley whose predecessor was quite possibly well patronised by the Beaker folk, a thousand years before Roman legionaries paused in their march. In the back garden is a great yew tree, with a legend inscribed on a tablet at its foot: 'In AD 1440 a nun and a monk here slain for misconduct and buried under the yew tree at the Bull at Streatley'. Doubtless to the glory of God and in the name of the Lamb, His son. It is a nice thought that nobody now knows or cares about the slayers of these two, while the yew tree still stands as a memorial to the sinners for us to muse over five and a half centuries after their brutal death.

The other place not to be missed at Streatley is Wells Store, which is almost opposite the pub. There may be a better cheese shop in England, but I doubt it.

Goring, on the other hand, has an internationally famous bakery. It also has all the other shops one is likely to need, including a delicatessen/coffee shop by the bridge, where you can obtain breakfast if you wish, as well as basic groceries. There are two pubs, The Miller of Mansfield, and the John Barleycorn. The latter would figure in anybody's list of favourite Thames pubs.

On the way from the mooring to the village, you pass Goring Mill, which is no longer working, although the mill-race is still there and the wheel is in place. If you are interested in antiquities, look left at the far end of Streatley Bridge and you will have the best view you will ordinarily get of a paddle and rymer weir, such as has been in use for eight centuries or so. Only a short section remains at Goring weir but it is worthy of study.

Goring is named after Gara and his tribe. The strategic and commercial importance of controlling the Ridgeway crossing must have been enormous. Gara had the power to stop trade dead or to do very well for himself. I have no doubt he achieved the second by threatening the first.

The reach from Goring Lock to Cleeve Lock is the shortest on the river, at just over half a mile. It is the very lip of the gorge up which we have been travelling since Maidenhead. For this reason, the reach is one of those best appreciated when moving downstream, towards the great woods behind Streatley. It was in these woods that the BBC did a famous recording of

Goring Lock and bridge seen from the village mooring.

GORING 1787

Fall 5′10″ : 1.77 m | Deep

Upstream The approach is complicated by the town mooring, on the right, with cruisers coming and going regularly. So it is a good idea to be ready early and approach warily. The weir-stream is from the left, but is not usually a major factor. However, you should be sure you can come alongside the lay-by (on the left of the lock), before passing under Goring Bridge, or you will be short of room between lock and bridge piles. In practice, almost everybody stops at Goring, it is that sort of place. In which case, one simply casts off and runs into the lock when it opens.

Downstream The lock is centre-left, and is such a short distance below Cleeve that it is best to keep your crew in readiness. There is no great difficulty, except that the pilings are very short. They lie to left and right, and there is no margin for error at all to the right (about 60 ft), while the left is only 20 ft longer. So, if you are not precise, you will be spread across the cut just as the gates open to let out a lockful. On the other hand, there is plenty of room to stooge in the wide river above the lock, if you decide on discretion rather than valour.

Note There is a rather good mooring down the old mill-stream, to the left of the lock, on the island and immediately beyond the pilings. This is subject to the lock-keeper's permission.

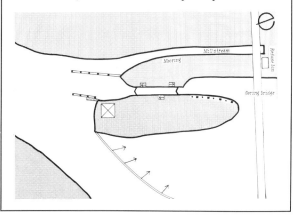

the song of a nightingale. That was in the thirties. I hope there are nightingales to sing there still.

66 There are three or four notable boat-houses up the right of this section and a modern development built round its own marina, on the left. There is just one mooring place, on the left, 200 yards below Cleeve Lock. Cleeve is 'cliff', of course, cf. Cliveden. There is a definite cliff on the right, so it is an apt name.

CLEEVE 1787

Fall 2'3" : 0.90m / Shallow

Upstream The lock is so close above Goring that you should remain in readiness. Although the weir is alongside the lock and close, the main stream actually runs behind the islands that line the right bank. Therefore the stream runs straight and creates no problems. There is a lay-by to the left and pilings to the right, which is the easier side for entering the lock.

Downstream The weir DANGER notice is visible for about half a mile, so this lock will not surprise you. It lies to the right. There are lay-bys to the right and left, and a short length of piling to the left as well. The right bank is easier. The only problem is the somewhat exposed position. A strong south-west wind would blow you off the right-hand lay-by and 'stick' you to the left. In such conditions, it is always best to oppose the wind and come ashore on the right, or to circle above the lock, where there is plenty of room.

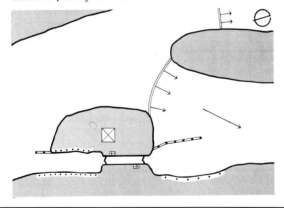

At Cleeve Lock is a notice saying: 'You are welcome to moor to the left bank for the next mile. Please do not leave litter. The farmer.' You leave the lock to face the longest reach on the locked river. It is 6½ miles to the next lock, a sure sign that we have reached the plateau.

the countryside changes perceptibly. It is still lovely, but now there is a greater feeling of space.

Riverside pubs are not many, now that most of them are turned into expensive hotels. So it is a pity in a way that the traveller now passes two of the best known, within a mile of each other. If you add the excellent hosteleries just left behind, these two miles are the best served on the river. The inveterate drinker must be hard put to progress at all for a day at least! Ye Olde Leatherne Bottel is on the right and incidentally has a hose for the use of patrons.

The field to the left, to which you are invited to moor, has shallowish moorings from just above the lock. They get deeper after the single piling post. They are still shallow on this bank until some way past the Leatherne Bottel, so exercise care. This is a particularly pleasant, quiet place to moor, especially if you have a dinghy in which to scull across river for a pint or two. At the top end of these fields I counted 52 coots, all together on the grass. A bobbin of coots?

Past the second fence, just before the right kink in the river slightly above 67, there are 50 yards of good moorings on the left. Opposite these are some shallow ones. There are a number of possibles up the right bank for the next half mile, but all shallow. There are no more on the left until after the second of the pubs. At 67 lies the County boundary. It is now Oxfordshire on both sides of the river.

The Beetle and Wedge Hotel is on the left. It is possible to moor eight large cruisers end on to the landing-stage here. It causes a good deal of merriment and camaraderie, and getting out in the morning is an interesting problem, but it is all well worth it. The hotel is at Moulsford, 'Mul's ford', and its existence and the road that comes down to the opposite bank, would indicate that the ford was at this spot. (Incidentally, 'mul' in Old English meant 'mule', cf. Oxford.)

There were two cruisers moored on the opposite bank, alongside and afloat. This is also a pleasant spot, which gives access to the charming village of South Stoke, its few houses, church and pub.

There is a mooring on the right, opposite Sheridan Line boatyard, and another some 250 yards below the railway bridge. This bridge is

the third and last of Brunel's Thames crossings and is worthy of him. It sweeps across at an angle, but the arches are twisted to allow the piers to be set straight in the stream. The resulting complications in the brickwork are one of the wonders of the Thames. Take time to look as you pass under. The bridge causes the least possible obstruction to the river and its users, as well, presumably, as saving itself a good deal of wear and tear. A pill-box stands guard at its foot.

Immediately above the bridge is a cluster of islands, which provide two or three super moorings, in addition to one on the right bank, except for the thunder of the railway. There was a flash-lock here, Moulsford Lock. Thacker found pilings here in 1910, near the top of the two upstream islands, and between them. I found no piles, but slight evidence of a stone abutment at the point Thacker mentions, but before I knew of his evidence. The piles were drawn officially in 1787, and the present channel opened up at the same time. As was usual in those days, for piles were the very devil to grub up with the instruments then available, the opening up was done with more efficiency

Moulsford Railway Bridge is one of the wonders of the Thames.

than the drawing, and there were several complaints over the next century of trouble with sunken piles at the site.

The present channel would seem to have been the relief stream, since the tow-rope had to pass over the island, according to a note of 1816, indicating that the lock was in mid-stream. The left hand stream could well have been dug for Checkenden Mill, last heard of in 1585. There is plenty of depth here but not a lot of space, so explore carefully.

There is a shallow mooring round the next bend, followed by a whole series in a delightful setting but frustratingly shallow, below the pill-box which squats on the right, threatening the slip-way opposite. The tow-path switches banks at this point, the site of Little Stoke Ferry and an ancient ford.

The next moorings are on the left, starting with a shallow one at 69. Another pill-box on the right at the left-hander has a mate on the opposite bank, which is followed by a better mooring, the last one for almost two miles.

MAP 3

Moulsford

A417

Beetle and
Wedge Hotel

.87

68
Sheridan Line D £ ⚓
H m

South Stoke Tu.

OXFORDSHIRE

BERKSHIRE

The Ridgeway Path

67

Goring S.C.
Ye Olde Leatherne
Bottel Inn MH

Wroxhills
Wood

Cleeve Lock
H WC

Park
Wood

Lough Down
.138

Lardon Chase N.T.

66

Swan
Hotel

The Miller
of Mansfield

Goring W.

B4526

Bull at
Streatley

Streatley

Goring Br.

Goring Lock

John
Barleycorn

Great Chalk
Wood

Common
Wood

B4009

65

Grim's Ditch

Gatehampton Fm

64

Bennet's
Wood

Lower
Basildon

Crown Inn

Hart's Lock
Wood

Site of
Hart's Lock

Cold
Harbour

B471

Whitchurch
Hill

Goring

Wildlife Trust
(Child-Beale)

N.T. Basildon
Basildon
House
Park

Coombe
Park

63

Bottom Woo

Hardwick

Whitchurch

Park
Wood

The Greyhound

Whitchurch
Lock

62

Swan Hotel

The Ferryboat 61
Whitchurch Toll Br.

N.T.
Pangbourne
Meadow

George Hotel

M 60

Mapledurham

Pangbourne Th.

Pangbourne
College

R. Pang

Purley

Purley Gar
Marin

Purley Hall

Ro

Tidmarsh

A340

Sulham Wood

Ti

Sulham

E

Ferry Eyot

Poplar Eyot

Harpsden
Wood

Hardbuck Eyot

Hennerton Backwater

Wargrave
Marsh

48 **M**

M Henley S.C.

Val Wyatt Marine

m ⚓ ⛴ 🔧 H ⚓ PD ⚓ £

Lower Shiplake

Swancraft Ltd.

49

🔧 ⚙ 🎵 H 🪣

St George & Dragon
Hotel **M**

Shiplake
Row

Shiplake Lock ≪

🪣 🍴 🔧 WC

John Bushnell Ltd
Wargrave Holiday Cruisers

Shiplake

m £ 🔧 🔧

Aquadine Ltd
(Nautical Souvenirs)

Wargrave w.

Phillimore's
Is.

50

Borough
Marsh

The Lynch **M**

M

Hallsmead Eyot **M**

M

Buck Eyot

St Patrick's Stream

A4

White Hart

M 51

St Patrick's Br.

Twyford

R. Loddon

A321

Flowing Spring

A4155

Sonning Eye

Shoulder of
Mutton

52

Sonning Br.

Mill Theatre & Restaurant

White Hart Hotel

Charvil

Reading
S.C.

Upper Bull
Thames
Motor Y.C.

Sonning Tu.

Sonning
Lock 🪣 WC

M

Thames & Kennet Marina **M** Horne
Park

D **M** ⚓ ⛴ £ 🔧 🪣 WC 🛶

🪣 Showers

53

A4074

F

OXFORDSHIRE   BERKSHIRE   Dunsden
Green

pledurham
Park

Wood

B481

Cane End

The Crown

Chazey
Wood

Caversham
Park

Shoulder of Mutton

Play
Hatch A4155

Caversham
Heights

Caversham w.

Lower Large

Bridge Boats Ltd. 🔧🔧🛶🎵 D m ○ — 🪣 🔧

St Mary's Is. 56

Elsan Disposal

See Map 3

Poplar Is.
Appletree
Eyot

St Mary's Is. **M**

Caversham
Boat Services

m ○ 🔧 WC 🎵

57

Reading R.C.

D & T Scenics

R.U.B.C.

🔧 🔧 🪣 H D 🔧

Better Boating Co.

Reading Marine Services Ltd. ⚙ Caversham Br.

M

Fry's
Island

54

The Bell Inn

⚓ ○ 🔧 H PD

£ 🔧 — 🔧 🔧

Salter Bros. Ltd.

🔧 ⚙ ○ 🛶 D

Reading Br.

Caversham Marina

🔧 ⚓ ⛴ 🎵 🔧 H D m 🔧 £

T.W.A. Area Navigation Office ≪

Caversham
Lock

55

Reading Marine Co.

Blake's Lock
Museum

D i 🔧 🔧 WC 🎵

£ — **M** 🛶

R. Kennet

Reading w.

High Br.

A329(M)

Palmer
Park

Prospect
Park

A33
To Kennet & Avon Canal

A329

69   The Ridgeway is still close to the river on the right. We pass North Stoke, which you cannot get at and barely see from the river. If you lived there, not many people would know it. This is a fine, broad reach, and if you were there in the depth of winter you might well come across eight dedicated young men and their cox, for this is where Oxford come for serious early training for the boat race.

70   Mongewell Park is on the right, guarded by a pill-box, and Carmel College, the Jewish public school, has a pleasant, riverside setting. As the river swings left-handed, Grim's Ditch is on the right. Grim is the devil, the ditch is thought to be pre-historic. It was either a tribal boundary, or inter-tribal/anti-Roman defensive line.

The river now bends right and there is a pill-box against the Ridgeway. On the left is a cottage on stilts, with a wall plaque 'Thames Conservancy, 1913'. At this point stood Wallingford lock, known as Chalmore Hole, and one of two pound locks which have been abandoned. The other is at Oxford. This one was built in 1838 and removed in 1883, much to Jerome K Jerome's embarrassment, related in

Three Men in a Boat. The lock was only used at times of low water, to assist barge passage through the shallows at Wallingford. By 1883 there was no barge traffic, and the navigation had been improved to the point where the lock was never used at all. The lock was on the site of a ferry, where the tow-path crossed again, and the ferry was reintroduced after the lock had gone, hence the date on the cottage.

Shortly above the cottage, Maidboats yard is on the left, where you can obtain all the standard services, the usual comment applying about Friday and Saturday not being the best days. On my way down, in a cross-wind and rain, I called here. The available space turned out to be 6 in longer than my boat. I went about below the yard, and crept in, making a perfect landfall, not touching anything except the shore, leaving 3 in at either end and stepping off with both ropes in hand to tie up. It was beautiful to witness in the conditions and the chap in the boat in front, having kindly jumped

Wallingford Lock – shades of Jerome K. Jerome. Henry Taunt 1865.

out to help, was fulsome in his praise. 'I couldn't begin to do that, and there are five of us,' he said. Naturally, I was quite unable to carry the thing off with due humility. I set off again, still feeling marvellous. Four miles later I made a complete hash of tying up at Cleeve Lock; I got stuck across the lock on entry and when I tied up below while I made some measurements, I failed to secure the boat properly and nearly lost her. Truly, the River is a great leveller!

Opposite Maidboats is a notice: 'Private, mooring fee charged.' It is deep enough at the down-stream end of this mooring but shallow towards the top.

71 A hundred yards above that the 'official' Wallingford moorings start. These are absolutely disgraceful. Nothing bigger than a punt can come alongside, and the bank is mostly so high that I go ashore from a plank off my roof. This shambles continues to the bridge. Above this, on the right, is a wall which has been allowed to deteriorate and which has a notice forbidding mooring. Two hundred yards above that, there are three or four places on the left, which are deep enough but against a high bank.

I mentioned that L T C Rolt complained about Marlow in 1951 and how heartening it was to call there now. He wrote of Wallingford: '. . . the old town of Wallingford offers no hospitality to the water traveller. The old Public Wharf just above the bridge offers the only reasonable mooring for large craft. . . .' Well, you cannot even use that now. The fault lies with South Oxfordshire District Council at Crowmarsh Gifford, if you would like to take the matter up. They own the public open space above the bridge and have an arrangement with the owner of the land below the bridge. 'It is agreed', I am informed, that moorings should not be provided.

The fault is not with Wallingford. The Town Council would love to offer moorings but own no land on the river. The Chamber of Commerce have been trying for 20 years to influence the South Oxfordshire lot (and their predecessors), but meet only a series of arguments of the type that local authorities that are determined to do nothing are so good at. I wrote to the senior Wallingford councillor on South Oxfordshire Council, to find out if he thought there was any hope for it, but he did not think

it necessary to reply.

If you *can* fight your way ashore, Wallingford is a delightful little town, with excellent shops, welcoming pubs and a long history. It is named after Wealh and his tribe, but the old town shows a cruciform design that is typically Roman, in which case they probably displaced the Britons who were living there. The ford was of crucial importance to the Saxons, who held it successfully until 1006, when the Danes finally sacked the town.

William the Conqueror passed through here, it is said, on his way to London. I think we may assume this was a deliberate strategy, rather than the result of being misdirected, which says much for the importance of the town then. He ordered a castle to be built, and there are rumours of an early twelfth-century bridge.

The castle was eventually destroyed by Cromwell's men, having been held for King Charles with great determination. You will see it on the left, about 200 yards above the bridge. Nothing much now remains but the mounds and ditches give a good indication of a powerfully large edifice.

For some reason, the town fell behind Abingdon in importance in the fifteenth century. One reason is the building of the bridge at Abingdon, which diverted the traffic. The town was also frightfully scourged by the Black Death around this time, and the presence of the disease, to say nothing of the decimation of the population, may well have been another cause. Certainly, Wallingford has never recovered, which is just as well for us, since this makes it the pleasant, unspoilt place it is.

Sixty thousand people a year pass under Wallingford bridge, according to the Chamber of Commerce, most of them as quickly as possible, making for the moorings and shops in Goring and Abingdon! It is one of the more difficult bridges to navigate, if there is a stream running. The piers are large and displace a great deal of water. In such conditions, do not attempt to turn above the bridge unless you are well above it. Proceed steadily and be sure your boat is straight to the bridge and central to the arch, particularly going down. Use the centre arch. Note the pill-box on the right, by the bridge, and the second one 100 yards above it.

Two hundred yards above the bridge, as you pass the castle mound, there used to be a flash-lock called Pollington's Weir, after the miller who built it. His mill-stream can still be seen as a depression in the ground between the river and the castle. The piles were drawn in 1791. When I was there, a Thames Water barge was moored and divers were at work, so I asked the foreman if he knew the whereabouts of the weir. He had not heard of it, but my query cleared up a mystery for him. They were dredging at the site of an old ford and he could not understand why they kept digging up old piling stumps! Was this the Wealhingas ford? The castle was excellently placed to defend it if that was the case, for it is less than half a bow-shot from the walls. A ford would be an obvious place to build a flash-lock, because you then maintain maximum water level at the minimum natural depth. I have two extremely disreputable pieces of timber in a bucket of water in my boat, which I believe are the last remains of Pollington's Weir!

Running down to Wallingford presents the best prospect of the town. The spire of St Peter's church rises above the castle mound, and there are a few attractive houses as well, to finish a pleasant picture. The countryside is now markedly different from that at Goring and not particularly interesting, so perhaps it does not matter that there are no moorings below Benson.

72   There is a pill-box guarding the small village of Preston Crowmarsh, after which a disused mill-stream enters from the right and then: 'Hands to mooring stations!' and Benson Lock ends the longest pound on the river.

As you leave the lock, there is an official Thames Water mooring on the left and two pill-boxes close together, which seem somehow to have got on the wrong side of the river. Perhaps the idea was to confuse the enemy by making him think he had crossed the river without knowing it!

73   The river now swings left and sets off on a ten-mile passage that is more westerly than northerly for a change. As it does so, it passes Benson Cruiser Station, on the right. Here the facilities are good, and include a laundrette (the only one I found), a general shop, a cafe which is open seven days a week, and overnight mooring. From here it is a few minutes walk into Benson village, which is heavily RAF, but good in parts.

BENSON   1788

Fall 6'2" : 1.87m | Deep

Upstream The lock is on the left, and the lay-by to the right of it, on a mole. Start preparing as you pass the old mill-stream, on the right. The lock is just round the next right-hander. The weir-stream will push you left as you approach the lay-by, but with foreknowledge, good steerage-way and determined steering, it is not difficult.

Downstream Start preparing at Benson Cruiser Station. The lock is on the right round a sharp right-hand bend, and has a very short lay-by, so look for congestion. You can pull in on the left, but there are no bollards there. There is plenty of room to manoeuvre above the lock cut, should you have to.

If you are working the lock yourself, and there are two boats, take care that they are not alongside each other, or that there is a gap of at least a foot between them if they are. There is a ledge running along the bottom of the lock on each side, which effectively narrows it when empty. Should there be too tight a fit between boats, they will jam absolutely. Last time it happened, re-filling the lock did not help either, the boats remained stuck at the bottom!

Note There is a mooring at the upper end of the lock island, in the weir stream, which the lock-keeper will let you use, if convenient.

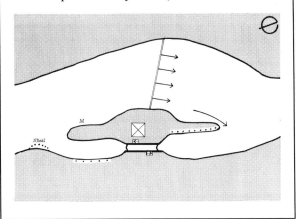

Benson used to be Bensington, but was commonly known by its present name at the turn of the century. The 'farm of Baenesa and his people' is mentioned in the Anglo-Saxon Chronicle in 911, Baenesa being a Dane. Here was a great battle between Mercia and Wessex, when Offa tried to smash the Saxon power and win final victory. Win he did, in the sense that he held his ground, but his victory was indecisive and his losses too great for him to advance further. Indeed, it is said that this battle marked the beginning of the decline of Mercia.

There are no moorings on either bank between Benson Cruiser Station and Shillingford Bridge. The scenery is improving again, although one could do without the vulgar 5 ft walling at the bottom of someone's garden. There is a pill-box, on the right, almost opposite this and then the river turns into a straight half-mile stretch, with trees on either side and Shillingford Bridge at the top.

There is a caravan site hanging to the cliff on the left below the bridge, but they have clearly tried quite hard to make it inoffensive.

Take the centre arch of the bridge, with care, although it is not a difficult bridge. Once you are above it, look back if you can. In the right light conditions, the view framed in the bridge arch, with two distant poplars forming a focal point, is one of the finest on the river. Shil-

lingford Bridge was built around 1827, and is of classically simple and therefore most pleasing design.

Above the bridge, the Shillingford Bridge Hotel owns the left bank up to the next bend. There is private mooring for 200 yards or so and then a notice invites you to moor and pay at the hotel. Do not be put off by the somewhat grand appearance of this hotel. They make boaters feel most welcome here.

For the next mile there are some excellent moorings to be had, starting from the footbridge beyond the hotel moorings. As the river swings sharply right (Did you see the pill-box?), there is a shoal on the left, and you then meet a feature that is common on the upper river but occurs for the first time here, a genuine Thames meander. On this occasion the river swings sharply right, in 50 yards hairpins left and in 50 yards turns right again.

After the left-hander there are several good moorings on the left, up to the next bend in fact. It is one of my favourite moorings. The field is a water-meadow, usually full of cows,

Shillingford's beautifully proportioned Bridge.

which runs back 200 yards to a hedge before rising steeply into woods. It is quiet here, and I met a white goose on both occasions that I moored here in 1985. He was a friendly fellow, broke bread with me, stayed for a chat and finally for the night.

On the point of the hairpin are two Thames Conservancy metal markers, driven into the ground. I think the ford ran across at this point. there is a road down to the other bank. They do not want anyone landing there now, the good people of Shillingford, the ford of Sciella and his tribe.

Opposite this hairpin is my *bête noir* among Thames houses. It is a monument to architectural idiocy on a stupendous scale. Built about 1925, I should think, it incorporates Norman, Elizabethan, Georgian, Scottish baronial, Flanders and Brothers Grimm, all in one splendid splodge. The garden is terraced in sharp angles and harsh lines, with walls and steps to various levels, all on a flat, riverside site in the depths of the country! On the other hand, the boat-house is lovely.

Architectural styles mix at Shillingford.

Waking early and going on deck when the day was young, I was rewarded by a flight of seven herons, followed by two great skeins of Canada geese, honking merrily to each other as they wheeled up river and away. My white friend waddled over for some breakfast.

Round the next right-hander there are two moorings on the right; another 50 yards up on the left; one against the next field on the right; in 100 yards, one on each side (that on the left being a beauty); another by the large road sign, which is the problem, A423. Beyond the pill-box there is nothing on the right for a mile. On the left there is another snug place at the apex of the next right-hander.

The tow-path crosses at the point, slightly below 75, where the two moorings are opposite each other, the site of another lost ferry. Round the next bend, the ground beyond the left bank starts to rise steeply and soon becomes thickly wooded. Dorchester Abbey church is now in sight across the fields, with its squat, square tower.

About 150 yards before the confluence with the River Thame, there is a mooring on the left, to an obvious, grassy bank. Above that you are not permitted to moor on either bank. If you are in a small cruiser, drawing a foot or less, and can get under the bridge, there are two or three nice little moorings just inside the Thame. Otherwise, you will have to moor along the right above the Thame bridge. Here there are moorings of varying depth for about 100 yards. Approach the bank carefully.

If you are feeling energetic, and can moor early, there is a lot to be said for mooring here. A quiet ramble up the Thame to Dorchester is well worthwhile. The Abbey has ancient foundations indeed, for Bede writes of it in *c* 730, and tells how Birinus baptized Cynegils, King of Wessex, and thus established Christianity in that kingdom. At the Dissolution, one Richard Bewforest bought the church for £140 and presented it to the parish. It is a magnificent building.

Dorchester itself is much older. The Romans found the British settlement of Dorcicon, a name too old for interpretation. This town was established on the river bank, protected by a system of banks and ditches, known as Dyke Hills, which are still clearly evident. The Romans built their own town next to it. The whole area is rich in ancient artifacts, some of which are in the Ashmolean at Oxford. Two pill-boxes are built into the Dyke Hills, so that we might have used 2000-year-old British defences to hold up the Germans, if things had worked out differently.

Dorchester used to be crushed by traffic, but has now been by-passed and is a quiet, retired sort of place, full of pretty cottages and attractive houses, to say nothing of its pubs.

On the other hand, you might walk up to the lock, cross over the footbridge to Little Wittenham, another charming little village, and ascend to the Wittenham Clumps, which tower above, on the Sinodun Hills. I recommend doing this in a summer hailstorm, as the twins and I did once a few years back. It was impossibly primeval and evocative as we marched up the hill in the teeth of the weather, with a steadiness and resolution that would have earned the approval of the sternest centurion. One could almost hear the shouts and clash of battle as we breasted the hill.

The clump of trees that give this hill its name has been here since 'before the memory of man'. Certainly the Romans would have known it. The trees have been replaced in the last few years, having threatened to die out. From the top of the hill you can see forever. There is an adjoining hill, where you can explore the massive iron-age hill fortress, the first town in this part of the country, from which it appears the inhabitants later moved to Dorcicon. You can walk on past this fortification, down the hill to the left and back through the woods to where you started, all of which will take an hour.

We came straight down that day, in the wonderful light that follows a summer storm, and with a fresh, warm wind to dry us out completely by the time we reached the boat again. We paused at the first footbridge to play Poohsticks, which can be purchased there, in aid of the RNLI.

Under this bridge was the flash-lock that preceded the present lock. There was a Thames Water gang working at the lock, whose leader told me he had found timber across the bottom and old pilings, when working under the bridge a few years ago. Actually, I expect this was the weir, with the lock in a cut dug under the second footbridge, which cut has now been extended for the present lock.

My reasons for suggesting this are that the resulting configuration is typical of the more advanced flash-locks, and that I do not see why the pound builders would have broken through into the weir-stream to form the present channel between the upper and lower islands, which is an awkward navigational problem that could have been avoided. Thus, I do not think they did break through, because the channel was there already.

While you are moored at Thame mouth, you can see for yourself how ridiculous is the assertion of certain romantic souls, that it was the confluence of Thame and Isis that formed Tamesis, or Thames. If the whole water of Thame were to be cut off tomorrow, I doubt if the lock-keeper at Benson would notice any appreciable change in his levels.

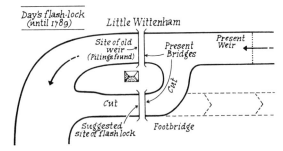

Below the lock, there is a wicked outflow from the weir, which may cause you to moor accidentally against the upstream pilings, or the boats already there! Keep out to the right to overcome this, but beware of activity at the Sanitary Station, or from upstream boats that may baulk your exit at a critical moment.

Above Day's Lock the river starts a remarkable horseshoe bend, sweeping from NNE to SSE in $3\frac{1}{2}$ miles, while it gains about one mile. Quite why it does not come straight across from Long Whittenham, is not apparent, since the land is very flat. Not that it matters, for the countryside is pleasant enough. It is dominated by two features, the Sinodun Hills, with the Wittenham Clumps on the crest, and the cooling towers of the Didcot Power Station, placed with that unerring feel for the landscape one always associates with the CEGB. The Sinodun Hills, like Dorchester, received their name too long ago for us to establish why they were so called.

DAY'S 1789

Fall 5'2" : 1.58m / Deep / Sanitary station

Upstream Start preparing as soon as you have passed the Thame confluence. The river bends at right angles and the lock and its traffic is then close ahead. The Sanitary Station is on the island, to the left. The pilings are on the right. There is no shore access from these so, if you have to work the lock yourself, the only thing to do is to scramble onto the footbridge wall on the right. Although the main weir-stream runs behind the old lock island, there is a sharp stream across from the left, from the moment you pass under the bridge. This can be rather disconcerting.

After leaving the lock, do not allow downstream traffic to push you too far to the right. It is muddy and very shallow up the right hand bank, and the cut is not wide. Downstream boats will not see you until late.

Downsteam You will see the DANGER notice in reasonable time. Keep off the weir and, if you have to circle, do so well above the cut. The lock is on the left, round a sharp, blind, right-hander. The weir will pull you as you try to enter the cut, and upcoming boats will not see you until late. Do not let them push you into the weir-stream, but remember, they have very little room to their right. Once in the cut, there is a good lay-by on the right, and no problem.

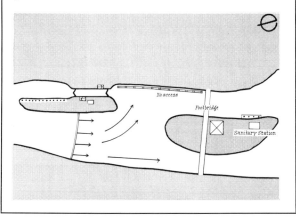

Mooring is difficult in this reach. Immediately above the lock, the water is very shallow on the right. There is a shallow mooring 50

77

yards further up and a deep one 50 yards beyond that, but against a knobbly bank. There is one more, by some willow trees, 50 yards before a fence comes to the bank. I found nothing practical on the left, until several shallow ones above and below mile 79.

78   The country on the right, chequered with large gravel workings and a haven for Canada geese, soon gives way to houses. These are mostly some way off up enormously long gardens, and vary between rather fine and horrid. The river is running past the hamlet of Burcot, Bryda's cottage, or possibly Brydingscot, now of no interest to the boater, except in passing.

It was not always thus. Had you been travelling to Oxford at any time in the hundred years up to 1630, you would probably have stopped here and taken to wagon or horse. There were blockages at Oxford, Iffley and Abingdon, and serious shallows at the top of Culham Reach. The result was a thriving barge port at Burcot wharf, bringing large profits for Oxford merchants, for all the wool and other goods from the Cotswolds and Wales had to pass through their hands.

In 1605, King James I set up the Oxford–Burcot Commission, charged with overcoming the problem. There followed twenty years of resolutions and worthy meetings, including another Act of Parliament. Then a detailed survey was made, followed by another five years of silence. (How excellently has bureaucracy worked to wreck the best laid plans over the centuries!) Finally, in 1631, King Charles I lost patience and issued a royal rebuke, combined with the threat that he would have the work done himself if the Commission did not. Within five years, the Commissioners had built three of the new-fangled 'pond' locks, at Swift Ditch, Sandford and Iffley, based on an idea imported from Italy; dredged the stream and opened the river to Lechlade. So Burcot wharf disappeared into history. Where exactly it was I cannot discover, although the 'hotel' building which now belongs to the Gas Board, at about 79, seems most likely because it is closest to the road. I have found evidence of old pilings half a mile below this, but they could relate to something else, or the wharf may have stretched for half a mile.

79   The river now starts to turn back towards the Sinodun Hills. On the right the bank rises steeply and the houses are high above. There are 'No Mooring' notices at the bottom of several gardens. I particularly liked the spinney, with this legend nailed to a tree: '*Danger Adder Sanctuary*'!

Clifton Hampden Bridge is one of the newer ones, built in 1865. There is a passage in *The Thames Illustrated* which appeals to me. 'The structure has not yet lost its newness, but, when time has gently toned it, it will rank among the finest bridges on the river.' This was written in 1899. The Victorians were often wrong, but this writer was absolutely right. This graceful brick bridge is one of the pictures of the Thames most often seen. It is most photogenic and comes at a point on the river which needs a strong statement of the type it makes so well.

Clifton Hampden is a curious name, since Clifton means 'farm or homestead on a hill' and Hampden 'village on a hill'. Perhaps a chap called Hampden, who came from a village on a hill, became lord of Clifton? Margaret Gelling does not think so. At all events, there certainly is a cliff, with the unusual and pretty little church sitting on the edge of it. There is a village store, which shuts firmly at all the times boaters can be expected to wish to use it, but which stocks most things you might need, if you can catch it off guard or hang around long enough. Further up the road is the Plough, an old village pub as yet unruined by improvement. On the far side of the bridge is the Barley Mow, which is probably the quaintest pub on the river. It certainly has the lowest beams! Here J K Jerome is said to have dashed off a few chapters of *Three Men in a Boat*.

Take any of the three middle arches of the bridge. It presents no difficulty. The only mooring is on the right bank above. The first 100 yards is very shallow. Then there is 100 yards which is OK, after which nothing to Clifton Lock.

The lock is not far above the bridge. If you are   80 feeling adventurous, the weir-stream is navigable for the half mile up to the Plough Inn at Long Wittenham, which has a mooring for visitors. If you lunch there on a Sunday, you should visit the Pendon model railway and museum, which is open in the afternoon and which is well worth the trip. They think nothing of spending five years making a model

CLIFTON 1822

Fall 3′5″ : 1.03 m / Shallow

Upstream The lock is on the right. You will see the weir-stream splitting from the lock cut first. The piling is on the left of the cut, and is short. There is room to spare for circling however, and no navigational difficulty.

Downstream Start preparing as you pass the footbridge. There is a lay-by on the left and piling on the right. Use the lay-by. The piling is against a small overflow weir, which is just strong enough to hold you on and create difficulties where none should be.

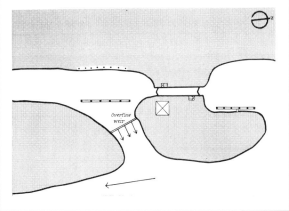

Left. *Clifton Hampden Bridge and Church.*

Clifton Lock.

of a single house, with detail down to a robin the size of a pin-head, sitting on a garden fork! It is about 150 yards from the Plough.

At the start of the weir-stream, on the right just past the overflow weir, are two moorings to a pleasant meadow. There were several other interesting possibilities, but I could not come alongside any of them. On the first mooring stood a heron. I came to within ten feet of him and he made no attempt to move. I have never been anything like so close to one before. I was so amazed I mentioned it to the lock-keeper. 'Oh, that's George', he said. Apparently George has been around for years, and is something of a character, given to fishing in the lock before it opens.

Little and Long Wittenham are aptly named: 'Witta's place by the bend in the river'. We are now at the end of the most remarkable bend on our journey.

There is a brick-clad pill-box on the lock-island, the only one that has had a useful life. It is the lock-keeper's garden shed. Opposite this, on the left of the stream, is a tank-trap, one of only two I found. On both occasions I was unable to account for why it was placed where it was, of all places!

Clifton and Culham are relatively new locks, the first locks on the sites being 1822 and 1809 respectively. Both have remarkably long cuts, the opportunity being taken when the lock was placed to shorten the stream, by cutting off a bend and thus speeding up the commercial passage time. So, at Clifton, the cut runs for over half a mile, and shortens the river by that distance. It is quite pleasant, and of course makes the lock simple to use, there being no weir to worry about near the lock.

The weir is on the left as you leave the cut, and there are three or four good moorings on that side, immediately above it, followed by several middling deep ones in the next field.

There is a pill-box on the left at the top of the cut, and another further down the weir-stream. Just above this stream there is a distinct pool shape in the main stream. I wonder if this was once the site of a flash-lock. Thacker is silent on the subject, but prints two lists by John Bishop, in 1580 and 1585, both of which refer to a 'weare' at Long Wittenham belonging to widow Sawyer, and another variously described as Thomas Trullock's lock 'dwelling

at Appleforde' and 'in Sutton parish'. Either of these stations could fit the bill.

The countryside is now noticeably flat. There are distant hills but they make no impression on the eye. All around are broad acres of arable and pasture land. The only houses are in the hamlet of Appleford, which lies around its squat church, 200 yards or so across a low meadow on the left bank. On a summer's day, with the cows up to their hocks in the river, the scene is straight out of Constable's England, provided you view it from the angle that misses the electricity pylons. There is nothing to visit the village for, but it is a gentle spot, and it has one mooring, almost abreast the church, with reeds at one end and a tree at the top. It is just 40 ft long, so nudge in gently.

Shortly above the village is the first of a series of fairly unattractive railway bridges, and the reach above brings you closest to the power station, with its water intake and dirty yellow outfall. So it is not my favourite stretch, although the first view of the Sinodun Hills greets the downstream voyager about 200 yards below Culham Lock.

The railway bridge and the road bridge by the lock each has its guardian pill-box. The weir-stream is not inviting and I did not attempt it. It is crossed by a charming stone bridge, and was the navigation stream until 1809.

Above Culham Lock, where you can obtain ices and soft drinks, and immediately before the foot-bridge that crosses the cut, there is a lay-by on the left, where you can moor. This is the only mooring in a lock cut on the river. From here, a short walk across the fields brings you to Sutton Pools, the great weirs and pools making a splendid sight. The weir-stream is lined with superior, 'much sought after' properties, and the path leads into Sutton Courteney village. It is a most agreeable walk, and not over a mile in all.

At Sutton Courteney, there once stood a great mill, infamous among the barge fraternity as a place of difficulty and cost, the millers being especially bloody-minded and grasping, even by the standards of their peers. A pound lock was built here, about 1638, at the time similar works were being undertaken by the Oxford–Burcot Commission. One set of doors was actually under the mill, and the lintel supporting the building was so low that barges frequently

FIRST PAGE. *The weir running strongly at Marsh Lock. (AA Picture Library)*

OPPOSITE. *Adventure under sail in a quiet corner.*

ABOVE. *Running down to Henley.*

RIGHT. *Regatta launch on her mooring at Henley. (AA Picture Library)*

Cows in conference at Shillingford.

The River below Goring.

CULHAM 1809

Fall 7'11" : 2.41m | Deep
This unobstrusive lock is the second deepest on the river above Teddington.

Upstream Start preparing when you see Culham road bridge. The lock is on the right. There is no difficulty with the stream. The lay-by is on the right, and is in two parts. Beyond the narrow bridge, it is quite short and bellied. Therefore, approach the bridge dead slow.

Downstream The lay-by is to the left, while there is a short length of piling to the right, without shore access. You will see the lock in plenty of time. Wind is the only cause of trouble here. A strong south-westerly wind will blow you off the piling and against the lay-by. Getting off this will then be difficult. The best bet is to try hard to get on to the piling. Failing this, the best way to proceed from the left is to have your bow crew 'tow' you in; ignominious but practical and expedient.

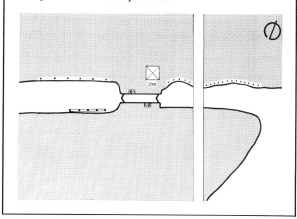

down, there is no sign of the cut until you are almost upon it, although the Thames Water Danger sign standing in the middle of the river, marks the spot. The new sign reads 'DANGER KEEP AWAY', an unusually emphatic instruction with which I heartily agree. The Sutton weirs are no place to be unless you live there and know what you are doing.

There is no mooring allowed in Culham Reach, which tends to be rather bleak in any case. You are approaching Abingdon Sailing Club, and can expect to come across racing dinghies for the next mile. On my way down, the scene was greatly brightened by a kingfisher, surely the loveliest sight on any river journey!

As the river turns left at the top of the reach, the Swift Ditch runs in on the right under an enchanting old bridge (1416), which no longer carries the traffic, but has been left as a thing of beauty. The Swift Ditch has a chapter to itself. Suffice to say here that it is unnavigable now but was the main navigation channel, on and off, for 600 years. Swift means short cut, rather than quick running.

The entrance to the Swift Ditch and the bridge of 1416.

had to unload before passing under. The lower gates were at the far end of the mill-pool, making the lock huge and the amount of water required to fill it, and the time this took, enormous. Add the highest single toll on the river and it is clear that there must have been considerable ill-feeling and so forth. The cutting for Culham Lock was the best news the bargemen had had since the removal of the Folly flash-lock, of which more anon.

From the mooring, an even shorter walk brings you to Culham village and the Red Lion.

At the end of Culham cut, turn sharp right into the wide stretch of Culham Reach. Coming

84 Andersey Island is on the right, and there are several moorings to be had against its low banks, especially at the downstream end. The island is named after the church of St Andrew, which once stood upon it. It is a peaceful place.

The outskirts of Abingdon are now on the left, and you can moor to that bank, close to the road, for about 200 yards. Red Line Cruisers offer all facilities.

The town moorings at Abingdon are excellent and extensive. They stretch from 200 yards below the bridge, right up to the lock. There are good moorings to the park on the left bank as well, although these are shallow for a narrowboat. All are subject to a mooring fee.

Having travelled this far, you will know at once that Abingdon must be 'the farm or homestead of Aebba's people'. Well no, actually, this is the exception! It was known as Aebbandune (Aebba's Hill) in 699, the name apparently brought by some monks in honour of their founder, an uncertain, misty holy man, alleged to have come from Ireland and settled at Boar's Hill, near Oxford (hence the hill). Earlier records suggest a Roman British village, and then the Saxon settlement of Senekesham.

The great Abbey that grew up here was notably vigorous and of huge benefit to the populace. It is said that, at the Dissolution, nobody could be found to speak against the Abbot, a rare thing indeed. The town throve under monastic impetus, firstly with the digging of the Swift Ditch, and especially after the building of the bridges in the town and at the Ditch, in 1416. At the height of the canal era, the Wilts and Berks canal was built, to link the Thames and Kennet and Avon navigations. It has now gone, but a few feet of wall are still visible, about 100 yards below the confluence of the Ock and Thames. There is a bridge with Wilts and Berks written on it, which crosses the Ock at its mouth, and can be confusing. It is simply that the bridge was built by the Canal Company.

The town centre has now been largely ruined by bad town planning. There are some good pubs starting with the Nag's Head, on the bridge itself. The King's Head and Bell is interesting, in the old town. Go up to the Town Hall and double back, left. The Town Hall, with the Museum above it, and the old streets running back to the river, are all worth exploring. The

The charming town of Abingdon comes slowly into view.

Old Gaol is now a sports centre, where a hot shower can be had, a luxury much appreciated after the somewhat cramped ablutionary arrangements of most cruisers. A few yards beyond the gaol is a corner shop, 'open all hours', and then a newsagent. The banks are in the centre, and if you bear left there and walk down to the old cinema building, you may find a fishmonger's van. He sells good fish. Otherwise, you are stuck with the shopping precinct.

Abingdon Boat Centre, by the bridge, has the usual service facilities, and a good chandlery.

Abingdon Lock lies a short half mile above the bridge. You can buy ices and sweets at the lock, and moor above it on the right, an official Thames Water mooring place. I do wish Thames Water would dredge their official moorings properly. All too often they are shallow and awkward, which rather defeats the object. This one is typical.

The countryside is now open farmland, and

Abingdon backwaters.

ABINGDON 1790
Fall 6'2": 1.89m | Deep | Sanitary station

Upstream Start preparing once you have cleared Abingdon Bridge. The lock is on the right. So are the pilings, which are the shortest on the river. So, if there are two boats there, go dead slow, or touch on the right bank, short of the lock. There is an interesting backwash here. Secure your stern quickly, or you will turn right round and face downstream again, as I did once.

Downstream You will see the DANGER sign in good time, but the lock is round a sharp left-hand bend. The pilings are on the left, and curve left. At the end by the lock, they are cut off level with the horizontal walkway, so that a crewman trying to hold a boat has nothing to hold on to. This is where Alison fell in. The combination of the weir-stream pulling you off the pilings, and these turning away from you as you try to lie on to them, calls for some precisely controlled approach work. Fortunately, there are four triangular pilings opposite, to catch you if you fail. These are called dolphins, and are provided for the use of steamers.

The Sanitary Station is at the upstream end of the pilings, which have a decking attaching them to the shore at this point. I understand this is to become a bankside lay-by in the near future.

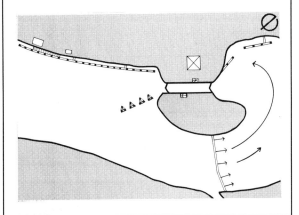

Abingdon Lock, well-hidden among the trees.

right, the overflow weir for the old Swift Ditch Lock. There are some shallow moorings on the right round the right-hand bend before the weir, but the best ones are on the island formed by the weir-stream and the old lock channel, which is marked by another weir two hundred yards above the first. There is also an excellent mooring 100 yards above this weir. It is only 40 ft long and very snug, but deep. All these will give you access to the Swift Ditch and the old pound lock.

There is another mooring on the right, 100 yards further up, and one roughly 200 yards below the railway bridge. On the left, there is one 200 yards above the first of these, and then from 200 yards above the bridge, there are a few dotted all the way up to Lock Wood Island, a distance of about half a mile. The railway bridge is another iron lump, with two 'arches'. Use the arch on your side of the river, up or down.

pleasant enough, although the modern tendency to plant oil-seed rape everywhere is not altogether scenery enhancing, especially as the smell is unpleasant and strong.

In about half a mile, there is a weir on the

87 Lock Wood Island is a very good place for pirates, in the spring and autumn. In midsummer there are man-eating nettles to be overcome, when the mooring by the 'Channel' notice is not viable. You can still anchor offshore though, and land from the dinghy. The channel runs to the left of the island, and is somewhat narrow, with a blind bend at the top. The island was probably formed by the cut made for the flash-lock that was here until about 1798. I deduce this from the sharp, unnatural way the lock channel turns off the main river. The flash-lock stood at the lower end of the lock channel, where the bridge shown in Taunt's photograph used to stand. The pilings of this bridge are still clearly visible. Of four additional pilings that I found, one was a bridge support. The other three were placed such that they might have been used for tying up to when using the lock. There is a massive piece of masonry just below the surface in the centre of the channel. This can also be seen in the photograph. I think this used to stand at the same height as the walls, which are still there.

Its shape suggests there was a relief weir in the left channel. These remains are of the last lock here, which had single doors, like those at one end of a modern lock. So it is not a flash-lock in the normal, paddle and rymer tradition, although it had the same effect. The lock in this form only lasted about five years before it broke, not to be replaced, but there had been a lock here for 300 years before that. The whole makes the most complete flash-lock now available to us on the river.

The channel to the right is just navigable. If you decide to have a go at it, always approach upstream, never exceed a speed of $\frac{1}{2}$ knot, and hug the right-hand wall. You will clearly see the underwater obstructions to your left. Once through, the water is deep but the trees low.

During the last half of the last century, the romantic, rustic bridge, the excitement of the island, and the availability of teas at the old lock cottage, made this a popular place for days out

Rustic bridge at Lock Wood Islands, site of the most complete flash-lock. Henry Taunt.

from Oxford. It is said that this was Alice Liddel's favourite outing with the Rev Dodgson, and her sisters. The magic of the place makes it the twins' favourite mooring, 100 years later, although both bridge and cottage have now gone.

The early evening brings out the bats, which can sometimes be 'caught' in the light of a torch, the only way of seeing these exquisite little creatures. The night is punctuated by the chilling calls of owls in the woods. In the morning you may see a pair of kestrels hunting in Nuneham Park. There always used to be kingfishers here, but I saw none in '85 or '86.

The river, having taken eight miles to move $1\frac{1}{2}$ miles from Clifton Hampden, now turns due north once more, and for the last time. Nuneham House is on top of the hill on the right. Nuneham Courtenay was called New Ham in 1086, Curtenay being added in 1242, when the Courtenays came to live here. Interestingly enough, when the Harcourts, from Stanton Harcourt, took over, they decided the village spoiled their view, and moved it bodily, to its present position. So Nuneham Courtenay is in fact quite new. It is also an example of enlightened landowning, being immeasurably superior when built to the usual filthy, insanitory hovels to which the lower orders were normally consigned at the time.

No sign of the village is available to us, only the great park of Nuneham House, which is now owned by Oxford University. The first thing of note we see is the water conduit from Carfax in Oxford, removed here when it got in the way of Oxford traffic, and now standing in a little dell, looking just like a gothic folly.

The Carfax Conduit, removed from Oxford to Nuneham Park.

The great house is next. It was started in 1710, and the impression from the river is Palladian. Beyond it is the chapel of the Harcourts, which used to be the village church, before the village was moved. It is an amazing edifice, the brainchild of a much travelled Harcourt and looking more like a temple to Diana than the church of All Saints.

There are two moorings on the left, shortly before Nuneham, and then nothing on either side below Sandford. Nuneham boat-house is on the right, now overgrown, apparently empty and disused, but a super place for a party, for which it surely must once have served.

This is Radley College river, and you should expect considerable activity from racing boats on summer afternoons. The boat-house is on the left, but there is no sign of the College itself. There was once a plan to build a bridge here, and the approach roads were built to the riverside before these plans were abandoned.

The run from here to Sandford is severely blighted by a positive rash of electricity pylons. The left bank is uninspiring, but the right is easy on the eye. Nevertheless, I am always pleased to see Sandford Lock in the distance. Perhaps the five mile pound from Abingdon is too long for a restless spirit.

Sandford Lock is huge by the standards of this part of the river. There used to be a great mill and weir on the right. The last vestiges of the mill vanished in 1984, together with a tall, ugly chimney, which was a landmark for miles around. Now there is a modern development where the mill used to stand, and the weir has gone too. This last makes life easier for the likes of us. Here was the second pound lock built by the Oxford–Burcot Commission. It opened in about 1633.

Above the lock, there is mooring on the left. You can also moor at the King's Arms on the right. There are then private moorings up the right bank, and a small marina, followed by a ship's graveyard, a most depressing sight. Among the boats slowly collapsing into the mud is an old College barge, and a torpedo-boat. It is amazing that somebody is not made to clear up this eyesore, but presumably there is nothing to be done unless the boats become a hazard to navigation.

In a short distance, the river turns sharply left and right, round Rose Island. There is a

SANDFORD   *c.* 1633

Fall 8′10″ : 2.69m | Deepest above Teddington

Upstream Recent developments have made this lock one of the simplest on the river to approach. The removal of the mill outfall weir that used to hurl one cheerfully against the lay-by on the left, is a great boon to navigators, although it has reduced the majesty of the river. There is about 100 yards of lay-by on the left, and a double-decker steamer piling to the right. For preference, moor on the left anyway.

Although small by the standards of Bell Weir or Romney, Sandford is a huge lock compared to anything above Mapledurham. The lock chamber is bellied, so that you have to turn towards the walls, after passing the gates. So enter slowly. All four steps run the right way, but this is not an easy lock, because the width is so great that failure to make a landfall will invariably leave a boat broadside across the chamber, or stuck in the middle, yards from the shore. There are some recessed pipes in the side, which you can grab, or pass a rope around.

Downstream There is no stream above the lock. There is a row of bollards on the bank to the right, which finish 100 yards before the lock. Approach slowly, so that you can turn inside the lock, which is wider than the gates.

Note If you need to work the lock yourself, you will find it a most exhausting experience, because of its size. It may help you to know that the open/close label on the upper gate is back to front. So turn to 'close' if you wish to open sluices or gates, and to 'open' if you wish to close either. This will at least save you five minutes of turning the wheel for nothing.

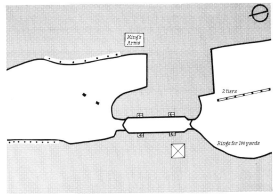

mooring round the left-hander, after which the railway line comes too close for comfort. Ahead lies another iron railway bridge. Take the centre arch, both ways.

Just above the bridge, the Hinksey Stream runs into the river. This is one of a network of rivulets that surround Oxford. It is linked to the Seacourt Stream, which leaves the Thames above King's Lock. There was once a plan to canalise these two, to shorten the stream past Oxford, but this was fortunately abandoned.

The left bank above the Stream is an official mooring site. It is the most uninviting on the whole river, gloomy and dank. I have never seen it with the sun on it. I prefer the mooring immediately above the by-pass bridge, although I do not recommend this either. To be frank, we are in yobbo country, and there are altogether too many off-duty football hooligans about for my liking.

Iffley Lock is now ahead, and the village is on the right. The origin of the name is apparently obscure. The village was Gifetelea in 1004, but whilst lea means clearing, nobody seems to know what Gifete was. Is it possible perhaps that it records the gift of a plot of land? The old English for 'gift' was 'gift', and while they used another 'e' in the plural, 'giftes', we are still short of an 'e'! Nevertheless, spelling was remarkably haphazard in those days, so perhaps I may be allowed my suggestion.

The first pound lock on the Thames was built at Iffley, by the Oxford–Burcot Commission. No exact date is available for its completion, but we may assume it was not there when King Charles issued his ultimatum on 18th August, 1631, whereas a contemporary account, published in 1632, mentions both Iffley and Sandford. The actual quotation is: 'a new turne pike doth stand amisse'. (Turn pike is frequently used for pound locks.) The tract was written in rhyming couplets, so that the author had to use a word that rhymed, rather than an exact description. I take 'stand amisse' to mean 'to one side', or 'unready', but in course of erection. So, 1633 may be the earliest that the lock can safely be assumed to have existed.

Note the boat-rollers on the left, with the delicate stone bridge over them. A predecessor of the present lock used to lie in the channel which now holds the rollers, except that it was placed about 50 yards further upstream. At the top of the lock lay-by, above the lock, a bronze bull's head is built into a niche in the wall. There used to be a ring in the bull's nose but it seems that somebody has gone off with it. It was presented by Lord Desborough in 1924. This was where the tail-boat in the Oxford bumping races used to start. The start is now a few yards higher.

IFFLEY *c.* 1633

Fall 2'9" : 0.81 m/ Shallow

Upstream The lock is visible in plenty of time. It is in the middle of the river. The piling is on the left. It has now been fitted with a pontoon to give shore access, which makes life easier. As you approach the lock you will see the original lock chamber on the right. It now has a small weir, known as Stoney Sluice, under the covered wooden bridge. The weir is no problem.

Downstream Prepare as you pass the Isis Tavern. The lock is on the right, with a sharp bend immediately before it. The lay-by is on the right, and curves away from you. However, there is no interference from the weir, except when a strong stream is running and Stoney Sluice is open, when you should take especial care. Otherwise there is no difficulty in coming alongside. The boat rollers at this lock are still operational. They are approached under the pretty stone bridge.

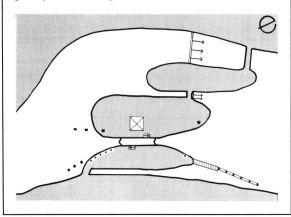

The Isis Tavern lies on the left, and it is possible to moor outside it, with care. There are some awkward submerged obstacles along the bank. Do not expect the pub to be open. It keeps strange hours for an hostelry that is only really approachable from the river. You *may* get in shortly after midday and at about 7.08 pm on a Saturday evening. It is an attractive spot for a drink though, with a low bank opposite, usually full of geese.

This is the reach on which the Oxford Colleges do their rowing. Whenever the University is 'up', you will find considerable activity from the practising crews, and when the students are away, the private club crews come into their own.

The idea of bumping races came about because the river is not really wide enough for two eights to row alongside each other. So they race in groups of 12 boats, in line, with two lengths separating each boat at the start. The idea is to bump the boat in front of you, although, in practice, the beaten crew will usually signal acceptance of defeat, to save excessive damage to valuable racing hulls. The races are held over four days, starting from the positions reached the year before. Each day, victorious boats move up above the boats they bumped. The leading boat in each division also rows at the rear of the division above, into which it moves by making a bump.

There are two regattas, one in February, called Torpids, and the other in June, the Summer Eights. The groups, or divisions, start in reverse order, so that the standard of rowing improves during the day, from 'appalling', through 'rabbit', to 'national club'. Summer Eights is one of the events of the year in Oxford. The University crews are available to stiffen their top boats, and the rabbits have had another term's practice, so that the rowing is better than in the Torpids.

The University packs its boat-houses. Families, friends, and a large section of the public at large, come to drink Pimms, meet each other and sometimes to watch the rowing. The climax is the final race of each day, Division I, to determine the Head of the River.

Of recent years there has been a considerable increase in the number and efficiency of women's crews at these events. They have their own Divisions, which are fought with as much determination and style as are the men's.

I digress. We were at Iffley Lock. From there we can make our more leisurely progress, past

A restored College Barge hides in a backwater near Iffley.

Salter's lower yard and under Donnington Bridge. Above the bridge, up a short creek to the right, somebody has breathed new life into an old College Barge, to magnificent effect.

In another hundred yards, is a stone on the left bank marking the boundary of the City of Oxford. Shortly above this is a footbridge, and some bollards on the bank, to which it is possible to moor.

From here there is no mooring until after Oxford University Boat Club, on the left, a large, late Victorian/Edwardian edifice, opposite the College boathouses. These are on an island, formed by two arms of the River Cherwell, which runs into the Thames here. It is this quiet stream (pronounced Charwell by the way), which has been the setting for a gentle afternoon's punting, or romantic, moonlit idyll, for generations of Oxford undergraduates.

There is good mooring, on the left, all the way up to the head of the reach. These moorings are within ten minutes' walk of the centre of the City, and are in an attractive position, looking across Christ Church Meadow at 'The House' itself, with Merton to the right of it.

The Oxford University Boat Club on the last day of the Summer Eights, 1987.

Hirers of punts are usually blissfully unaware of approaching dangers.

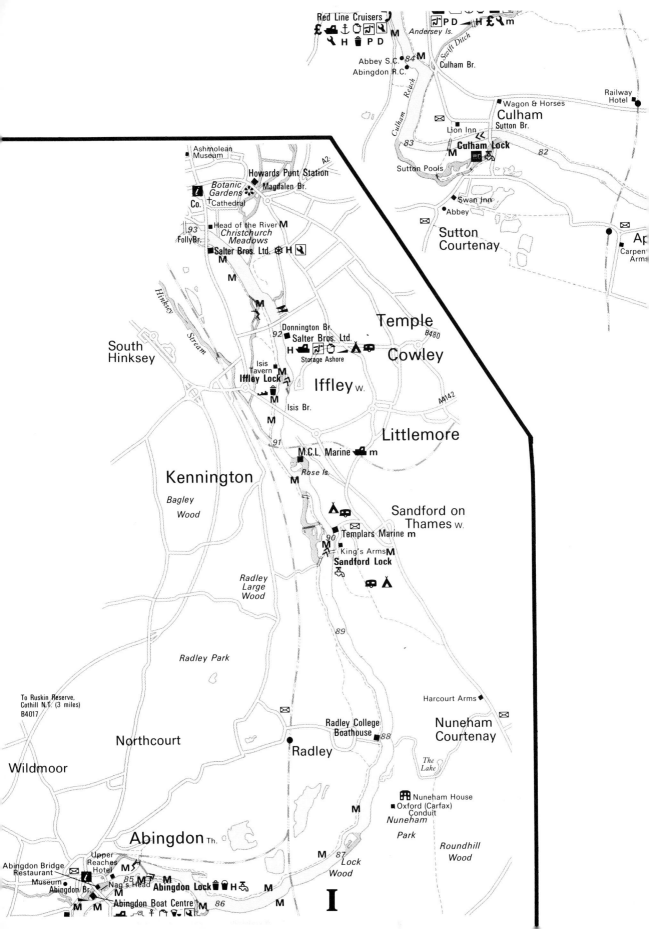

Red Line Cruisers
£ ⚓ ⌚ ⚒ ☎ ♫ P D → H £ m
🔧 H ⬛ P D

M
Andersey Is.
Swift Ditch

Abbey S.C. •84 M
Abingdon R.C.   Culham Br.

Wagon & Horses   Railway
Hotel

✉   Culham
Lion Inn   Sutton Br.

Culham Reach

83
Culham Lock   82

Sutton Pools

Swan Inn
• Abbey   ✉

Sutton
Courtenay

A
Carpen
Arms

Ashmolean
• Museum

Botanic   Howards Punt Station
🌸 ◆ Magdalen Br.
Gardens
Co. ⊕ †Cathedral

Head of the River M
.93   Christchurch
FollyBr.   Meadows
■ Salter Bros. Ltd. ⊕ H 🔧
M

M

A2

South
Hinksey

Hinksey Stream

M ✖

Donnington Br.
92 Salter Bros. Ltd.
H ⬛ 🖾 ⬛ ☎ → ⚠ 🚐
Storage Ashore

Temple

Cowley   B480

Isis
Tavern M ⚓
Iffley Lock   Iffley W.
⬛
M
Isis Br.
M

A4142

Littlemore

91
M.C.L. Marine ⚓ m
M
Rose Is.

Kennington

Bagley
Wood

⚠ 🚐

Sandford on
Thames W.

■ ✉
Templars Marine m
90
King's Arms M
✖
Sandford Lock
⚓
🚐 ⚠

Radley
Large
Wood

Radley Park

To Ruskin Reserve,
Cothill N.T. (3 miles)
B4017

89

Harcourt Arms •

✉

Northcourt

✉

Radley College
Boathouse
■ 88

Nuneham
Courtenay

Wildmoor

• Radley

The
Lake

🏠 Nuneham House
■ Oxford (Carfax)
Conduit
Nuneham
Park

M

Roundhill
Wood

Abingdon Th.

M

87
Lock
Wood

Abingdon Bridge
Restaurant
ℹ Museum
• Abingdon Br.

Upper
Reaches
Hotel
M ◆
85 M →
Nag's Head Abingdon Lock ⬛ H 🔧   M
M
86
M   M
Abingdon Boat Centre M

M ◆   M

I

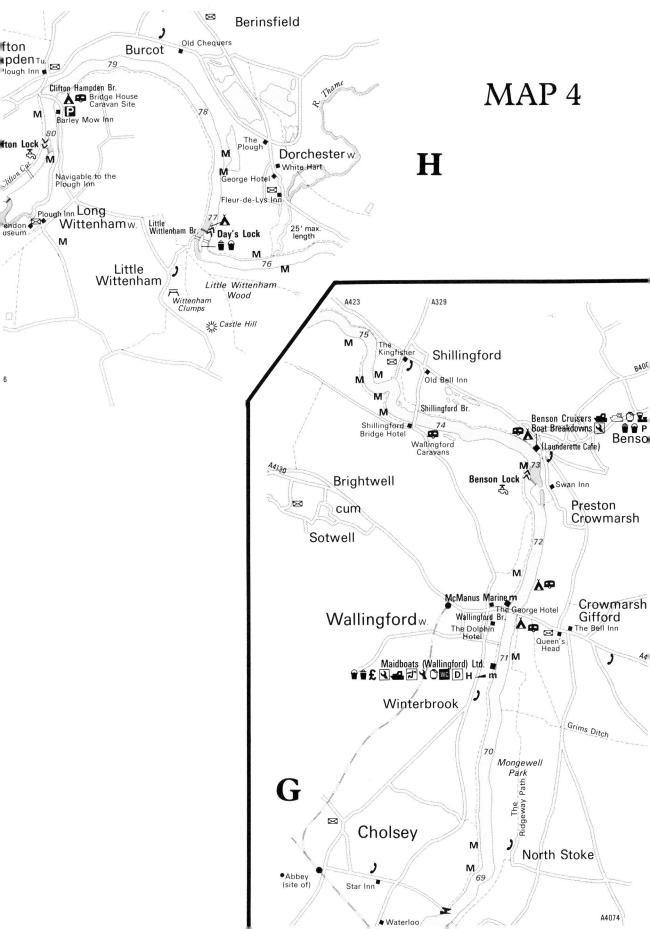

Part Four

OXFORD
TO
LECHLADE

QUITE why Oxford developed as a place of learning is not clear. It has ancient roots, but is in a particularly unpleasant situation, the area being mainly natural marsh between numerous water-courses. In this it is very like Cambridge of course. Perhaps brains work best when the body is damp and chilled to the marrow? Perhaps scholars might expect to be left alone in a place that nobody would be likely to covet? What is certain is that this beautiful little city is placed about as far as it is possible to get, in

these islands, from the sea. Or, to put it another way, it is almost exactly in the middle of England.

It is an extraordinary place architecturally, full of extraordinary people intellectually; the most English of towns, all those traits and peculiarities about us which our friends and enemies alike find amusing, charming, puzzling and infuriating, are here writ large. It is known as the home of lost causes: what Oxford thinks today is usually proved to be rubbish tomorrow. On the other hand, mostly ordinary people have come here for over a thousand years, to read and to talk and to listen. A very large number of these came here simply for the joy of knowledge. Great men and, more recently, great women, have issued from this place in a steady stream, like some rich vein of gold in the national heritage. To speak English correctly is to speak Oxford English; the *Oxford English Dictionary* is the standard work.

Because it is Oxford, there has been a great debate about the origin of the name. Theories abound, the more far fetched the better! How about the supposed words of St Frideswide,

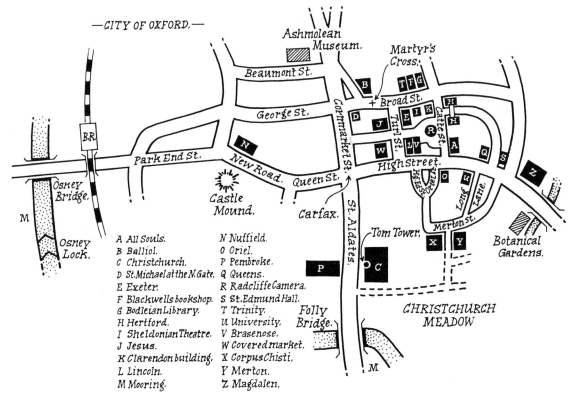

—CITY OF OXFORD.—

A All Souls.
B Balliol.
C Christchurch.
D St. Michael at the N. Gate.
E Exeter.
F Blackwells bookshop.
G Bodleian Library.
H Hertford.
I Sheldonian Theatre.
J Jesus.
K Clarendon building.
L Lincoln.
M Mooring.

N Nuffield.
O Oriel.
P Pembroke.
Q Queens.
R Radcliffe Camera.
S St. Edmund Hall.
T Trinity.
U University.
V Brasenose.
W Covered market.
X Corpus Chisti.
Y Merton.
Z Magdalen.

the patron saint, when leaving the city to be a hermit? 'Ox, go forth!' Recently, it seems that there is a consensus that Ox-ford may mean a shallow or ford over which oxen pass! There is also considerable discussion as to where this ford could have been, the favourite at present being North Hinksey. History does not relate why Hinksey (Hengist's Eyot) is not called Oxford in that case. It would have been the least useful place actually. The area between Hinksey and Oxford is still the boggiest approach to the city, and must have been sheer hell before land-drainage and roads. This approach would also have required the crossing of four streams of varying size, when only two crossings are necessary almost anywhere else.

For me, the ford was either of Cherwell or Thames, and of these Thames seems more likely, because it is a much larger obstacle to traffic. Of the various Thames sites, I favour Port Meadow, for reasons I shall discuss when we arrive there.

It may be useful to consider the thinking behind the naming of certain fords after animals, given the need for names to be precise and meaningful to the Anglo-Saxons who originally gave them. None of the books I have read discusses this matter, and I am well aware of the dangers of lack of scholarship. Nevertheless, it seems logical to suggest that the names were meant to be of fundamental use to travellers.

I have already suggested that Moulsford was not named after Mul, a Saxon, but from the Saxon word mul, a mule. Now we have Oxford. We shall come to swine-ford and sheep-ford.

We can take it that the Saxons had no schooling in or access to precise measurements. There were units of measurement, but they would have meant as much to the average Saxon as metric measurements do to present middle-aged Englishmen, or imperial measures to the younger generation. On the other hand, there would have been no Saxon who, asked to indicate the height of a mule, ox, sheep or pig, could not have done so immediately, by holding his hand the correct distance from the ground.

Thus, the names do not indicate, charmingly but unusefully, that mules, oxen etc. cross here. Rather, the message is: 'In normal conditions, the water at this ford is of a depth such that an ox could cross.' Merchants, travelling on the Ridgeway, could have saved several miles by

crossing the Thames at Moulsford with their pack-mules, instead of at Goring, whereas people on foot would have had to go the long way round because the water at 'mules' ford' would be up to their chests.

On this basis, the importance of Oxford is that heavy goods, drawn invariably on ox-carts in those days, because there were no heavy horses, could cross here.

It would not be proper, in this book, to devote a great space to a detailed description of Oxford. Since, however, it is likely that most boaters will stop here for shopping or a pub, I offer a short tour of the City, which should not occupy more than $1\frac{1}{2}$ hours, including the former activity.

You will observe, from the map, that there are two mooring places for access to the City, below Folly Bridge, and between Osney Lock and Osney Bridge. Both are excellent. They are roughly equidistant from Carfax, the centre of Oxford, and therefore from the shops.

Christ Church Meadow at Oxford, Merton Tower and a 'best-boat'.

The approach from Folly Bridge is the more interesting, since it passes Christ Church, the largest of the Oxford Colleges, 'the House of Christ', and therefore 'The House' to its members. Within its precincts is Oxford Cathedral, the smallest in England, and well worth a detour. Alice (in Wonderland) Liddell's father was Dean (Master) of Christ Church, where Charles Lutwidge Dodgson (Lewis Carroll) was a mathematics don (teacher).

Here also is Great Tom, the largest of the bells 'liberated' by Cardinal Wolsey from Oseney Abbey, at the dissolution. It is now housed in Tom Tower, at the St Aldates entrance to Christ Church, and is rung 101 times every night, commencing at 9.05, in commemoration of the number of students at the foundation of the College. If you are moored overnight below Folly Bridge, you will probably hear it.

The main shops are in and around Queen Street, Marks & Spencer, Sainsbury; and Cornmarket Street, Boots and Smiths. For food shopping you should visit the Covered Market, a short way down High Street, a veritable Aladdin's Cave of delights.

The cross-roads at the top of St Aldates is known as Carfax. It is the centre of the medieval town. This is where the water conduit stood, which is now at Nuneham Courtenay. Observe the Carfax Tower, with its singular clock. If you climb the tower, which is open to the public, you will have an excellent view of the whole City.

Walk down Cornmarket Street from Carfax, and you will come to the old church of St Michael at the North Gate. If you have come from Folly Bridge, you can appreciate precisely how small was the medieval town. You entered it roughly half way up St Aldates, and have now walked across to the far wall. The part-timbered house just before St Michael's is the last surviving medieval house in Oxford.

Turn right into Broad Street (The Broad), which was once open space outside the north wall. There is a slightly raised and cobbled cross in the middle of the road, which marks the spot where Archbishop Cranmer and Bishops Latimer and Ridley were burnt at the stake, for espousing the wrong religious sect. They were Protestant, when it was wiser to be Catholic, or

vice versa. It is said the fire scorched the door of Balliol, on the other side of the street.

Trinity is next to Balliol. Its beautiful gardens can be glimpsed through the wrought iron gates. Then comes Blackwells bookshop, where you can easily spend another hour, browsing, and the Bodleian Library, where you cannot, unless you are a member.

The Bodleian is entitled to a copy of every book that is printed, and keeps these and large numbers of priceless manuscripts from the past in literally miles of storage, much of it underground.

The Sheldonian Theatre is opposite, where graduates receive their degrees. It stands back behind a line of serious looking busts. It is one of Oxford's minor mysteries who these represent: Greek gods, Roman senators, great actors or statesmen, or simply the caricatured heads of the committee that put them there? Apparently nobody bothered to record the facts at the time, and now nobody remembers.

The Clarendon Building, next to the theatre, is interesting in that it is the Headquarters of Oxford University, and meeting place of the Hebdomadal Council. The *OED* tells me that this word is adapted from the Latin, presumably by someone with a heavy cold. It means, weekly!

Hertford is the college at the head of Catte Street. Its two halves are joined by a Venetian 'Bridge of Sighs' over New College Lane. Further down the street, All Souls, on the left, is peculiar in that it has no undergraduates, only Fellows. It is dedicated to higher study, probably the cleverest place in England.

Across the square is the Radcliffe Camera, another part of the Bodleian, and beyond that Brasenose (BNC), a college named after a brass door knocker, now carefully preserved within.

Brasenose Lane passes between Exeter and Lincoln and, by crossing Turl Street, you gain access to the Covered Market, from its other side. Catte Street, Turl Street and the Market itself all give access to the High Street (The High), from where you have a number of options: turn right, walk up to Carfax, and from there back to your boat; take a slightly longer route back to Folly Bridge via King Edward Street; or walk down the High to Magdalen.

This last leads past Oriel and University Colleges on the right, and All Souls, Queen's, St

Edmund (Teddy) Hall and Magdalen on the left. It also passes Oddbins and Frank Cooper's Oxford Marmalade shop, which is worth visiting just for the smells!

Magdalen is one of the more visually attractive colleges, with its lovely tower, from which a choir heralds the dawn on May Day, in the presence of a huge crowd of tired, dishevelled, hung over or drunken and usually soaking wet undergraduates, and large numbers of locals and tourists to boot. Magdalen Bridge crosses the Cherwell at the base of the tower, and opposite are some fine botanical gardens. Among the hot houses is one of special interest to children. It contains all the trees and bushes from which come all the things they eat and drink from foreign lands: orange, lemon, banana, coffee, tea, and so on.

A side road by the gardens takes you to Christ Church Meadow, and thus by various routes back to St Aldates and the river.

The other alternative from the High, down King Edward Street, takes you to Merton Street, Corpus Christi and Merton. Merton Street is cobbled, the last such in town, and therefore frequently taken over by film or television crew who want to shoot a 'period' scene. It only requires the removal of a few, tastful 'No Parking' signs, and the cars and bicycles, to transform the street to the eighteenth century. There are no television aerials, no overhead wires, just the soft, immemorial stone of the colleges, old style lamps, and the worn cobbles underfoot.

There is much more, half the colleges, for instance, numerous nooks and inviting lanes, the Parks, three museums, brass rubbing at St Mary's in the High, an ironmonger which was well established when Shakespeare was a lad. Something like the tour I suggest will give you the flavour of the place though. The colleges are usually open to the public. They are all lovely, so it does not matter which one you choose to visit. There are, of course, a great many pubs in the town, too many for a list to be any help. A few are interesting as places to see as well as to drink in: The Bear in Blue Boar Street, off St Aldates; The Turf, off Holywell Street, at the end of the Broad and the White Horse, in the Broad itself, are three such.

Salter Brothers yard, which nestles against Folly Bridge, is probably the most famous on

The house at Folly Bridge.

the river, due to the fleet of steamers that used to run as a regular passenger service from Hampton Court to Oxford. They still do shorter trips, and are available for special functions. Now they are diesel powered, although obviously old-fashioned. They are still majestic, when viewed from a small boat, and always graceful. When I first travelled on them, they sported a smoke stack, which often had to be lowered to pass under bridges, when passengers were covered in smuts. I well remember racing 'Oxford' up the Henley regatta course in a double camping skiff, my father at stroke, while I applied all my twelve-year-old strength at bow, and some enthusiast at Remenham shouted 'Come on Cambridge'! Alas, it was a rather one-sided contest. I think we were too much hampered by the camping canvas over the top of the boat!

Folly Bridge is so called because its predecessor had a folly, known as Friar Bacon's study, because he lived there, at one end of it. There is still a most unusual building at this place.

In earlier days the bridge, which was placed

at a bad angle across the stream, had a number of narrow, pointed arches, under which was built a flash-lock! It was the most infamous on the river, and crowds used to gather to listen to the language of the bargees, and look and cheer at the frequent wrecks and disasters that occurred there.

The present bridge was built in 1827, and is quite handsome. It is no problem navigationally, except that in common with the whole reach from Iffley, it is likely to be choked with skiffs and punts throughout the summer. There is a punt hire point immediately above it.

Up to the left of Salter's is a narrow channel, which was cut for the pound lock that stood here from 1821–1884. The brick chamber is still clearly visible at the lower end. I always use this channel when going downstream, as it saves an awkward turn down to Folly Bridge and the possibility of becoming tangled with upcoming traffic under the single useable arch of the bridge. Do take the channel slowly however, since it is only just wide enough, and you will very likely find your exit blocked by some ass in a punt, who is not looking.

Shortly above the bridge, you have to pass between two channel markers and then swing sharply right. If there is a stream running it tends to sweep past here and down the side channel, thus pushing you towards the left-hand marker. So, be prepared for this. The markers are on the site of the old weir which served the pound lock, and of which some of the piles are still in position, to right and left of you.

Oxford has had a richly deserved reputation for the worst treatment of the Thames by any town on its banks, since at least the eleventh century. The reach you are now entering was little better than an open sewer when I first passed up it in 1947. Fortunately, times now seem to be more enlightened. The last outrage was the architecturally bankrupt Council flats, built c1960, which you pass on your right, by the footbridge. Before this, there is a new development of riverside town-houses, which is imaginatively conceived, and should become better with age. At the same time, the Grand Pont houses to the left have been greatly smartened up in the last few years.

The great gasworks, that until recently besmirched the whole neighbourhood up the next half mile, has now been replaced, via a municipal rubbish tip, by instant Council vegetation. It is not attractive, but to appreciate it you should have seen it before.

On the right is another attractive development, with a disused railway bridge, which has been decorated by someone at the Council with imagination, to make it the happiest bridge on the river. Just above the bridge, on the right, a small stream runs diffidently into the river.

Until 1227, this stream was the main river. By that time, the wholesale neglect and misuse of the river in Oxford had caused it to become clogged and only navigable with difficulty. Since it was, even then, a main artery for trade, which the good fathers of Oxford were alone in not understanding, this produced a major difficulty. It was then that the Abbot of Oseney delivered a masterstroke. He applied to the King for a licence to dig a cut. It runs from here for about $1\frac{1}{2}$ miles, through Osney Lock, where the monks built a mill.

The King, Henry III, was so grateful that he wrote to the Abbot, thanking him for going to so much trouble. No doubt the Abbot laughed all the way to the coffers. The Abbey became one of the richest in the kingdom, while Oxford was cut off from its trading river 'at a stroke', and has never got it back.

There are two arches to the bridge. Take the left-hand one going up. The right arch takes you almost into the old river and the turbulence of its stream.

Take the left-hand arch at the next bridge too, the modern railway bridge, which is sited a little awkwardly. With both these bridges, look for down-coming traffic, to which you should give way. An arm of the Seacourt Stream runs in on the left, above the bridge. On the point of the confluence is an obelisk, in memory of Edgar George Wilson, who in 1889 saved two boys from drowning, but lost his own life in doing so. He was twenty-one years old.

Osney Lock is now 250 yards ahead.

One hundred and fifty yards above the lock, on the right, the entrance to Osney Marine Engineering Co's yard is blind, going upstream, and anything coming out will be in your way and will not have seen you.

On the left is a Thames Water mooring, running for 250 yards, and with bollards for most of that distance. There is also a riverside

The River glistens across Port Meadow, Oxford. (Chris Donaghue)
Oxford, city of spires. (Chris Donaghue)

ABOVE. *Radley senior eights in training at the Swift Ditch, Abingdon.*

LEFT. *Love by the riverside.*

OPPOSITE. *The Wittenham Clumps stand guard above Day's Lock. (S & O Mathews)*

LAST PAGE. *St Leonard's Church, Lechlade. (S & O Mathews)*

OSNEY 1790

Fall | 6'3" : 1.89m | Deep

Upstream Start preparing after passing the railway bridge. The lock is on the right, and is not visible until late. It is almost alongside the footbridge that crosses the weir-stream, which you *will* see. The piling is on the right. In a stream, there will be a marked push to the right as you approach the piling. In a stream or wind, it is difficult to get off the piling to line up with the lock gates.

Downstream Start preparing below Osney Bridge, and slow down as you pass the Waterman's Arms. The lock is not visible until the last moment, although you can infer it from the lock cottage and the flag-pole in front of the local Headquarters of Thames Water Navigation Service. The pilings are on the left, and curve away from you, so approach slowly but under power. There are two weirs off the lock cut, on the right. The first is no problem. The second, to the right of the lock entrance, will pull hard if there is any stream running. Do not attempt to stop on the right, and make sure of your tie-up to the pilings. There is no access to the lock from the piling, so that, in order to work the lock, it is necessary to stop on the right, before the first weir.

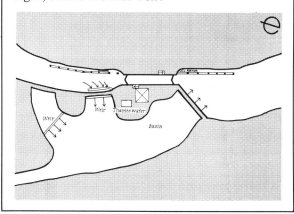

Osney Lock can only be seen late, and mind the weir!

Osney, Osa's Eyot, is pronounced Oseney, not Ozney. Indeed, it was spelt Oseney until fairly recently. The great Abbey stood all along the right bank, from below the lock to Osney Bridge. Only a fragment of an archway now exists, in the boatyard.

Opposite the mooring, is the old power-station, which used to cover Osney in a perpetual layer of coal dust, but is now part of the University Science Department, and only looks awful. It has a pretty, oriel window, a typically Victorian whimsy.

There is a weir immediately before the bridge, on the left. It is only a problem when there is a strong stream running, and then only if you stop. Osney Bridge replaces one that collapsed in 1885, causing four people to fall

94

Osney Bridge is *the lowest on the River!*

pub, The Waterman's Arms, a second pub, The Hollybush, and a village shop with bakery. With another little store across Osney Bridge, which opens on Sundays, in addition to long hours for the rest of the week, this is a better mooring than that below Folly Bridge, if you do not want to go into Oxford for shops etc.

in, one fatally. Despite a self-congratulatory plaque from Oxford City Council, recording the new bridge, it is one of the least attractive of Thames bridges, and the meanest. At 7ft 6in above medium river level, it is impassable to a great many cruisers. If you hire a boat and it says in the brochure that it will not pass Osney Bridge, believe it. Lots of people are unconvinced by such warnings, and it is a favourite summer entertainment of the locals to watch such people smash their boats up.

It is possible to moor on the right, above the bridge, but not ideal, and I should only advise it in emergency or for shopping, when the Osney mooring is full.

Three hundred yards above the bridge, the Oxford Canal link joins from the right. Anyone emerging from this blind entrance will have to turn in a wide sweep into the River. This arm is only accessible to boats of a maximum width of 6ft 10in overall, and having a current British Waterways Licence. The stream to the left is unnavigable. It runs to a bathing place.

There are scattered moorings to the tow-path on the right above the canal. Do exercise care though, there are some nasty things below the surface in many places. There is also a good deal of foot and bicycle traffic on the tow-path, so do not put your ropes across it.

At the top of the reach, just before the steeply arched foot-bridge at Medley, is Medley Weir Cottage, on the left, at the site of one of the last flash-locks, which was in use until 1930.

Above the bridge are two boatyards; Bossoms, on the left (an ancient Thames family that), and Medley Boat Station on the right. The latter offers most services, including chandlery, but avoid Saturdays, when they are busy with their hire fleet. There is even a dry-dock here. Bossoms are boat builders, and do not offer services. Incidentally, Medley Boat Station lies on the old river, since we have now reached the top of the Oseney Cut of 1227.

Above Bossoms is Medley Sailing Club, so expect sailing activities on this reach, particularly at weekends.

Now the river widens dramatically. It will never be as wide again, to the end of the journey. On the right is Port Meadow, an ancient common, and present home of horses, cows and flocks of geese and plovers. There was a ford here, almost exactly at mile 95 in fact, well into this century. Both Taunt and Thacker record it. I would guess it was dredged away in 1930, when Medley Weir was removed. I think it was the most likely site of the ford that gave Oxenford its name.

Port Meadow was originally Portman's Eyot, burgher's island, suggesting either common land or land held for the common good by the Council of Elders. I think it reasonable to suggest that it could have been a market place, for sale and barter of stock, wool, cheese, etc. The juxtaposition of ford and meadow was surely not coincidence. The importance of the first led to the establishment of the second.

The great objection to this site is its distance from the town itself. Would not a ford at, say Grand Pont, or in the region of the Castle mill have been more likely? There is great force in that argument, but we have to put ourselves in the position of the Saxons who built the town. They recognised the importance of the ford, both for trade, and strategically. On the other hand, the site chosen for the town uses the defensive possibilities of the Thames/Cherwell confluence to the full, whereas to have built the town a mile to the north would have wasted these. Oxford did not simply happen over a period of time, it was built by the Saxons to a rigid, cruciform plan, like a Roman military camp. So, while the nucleus of the town may have already existed, (there are the remains of an ancient settlement on Port Meadow itself, for instance) the decision as to where to build was clearly taken by someone in authority, who knew what was required to make the town safe, as well as prosperous.

The other piece of implied evidence for this being THE ford, lies across the river, in the village of Binsey, 'Byni's Island'. Binsey Church has a miraculous well in its yard, of great efficacy in the treatment of eye trouble, stomach pain and infertility in women. It appears that St Frideswide, a vague ethereal figure, of whom almost nothing is known, had a male admirer, called Algar, who one day had the temerity to touch her. He was instantly struck blind! Frideswide, distraught, prayed for the intercession of St Margaret (of Antioch?). Lo! A well appeared, of which the waters instantly cured the wretched Algar. For whatever reason, whether connected with this event, or preceding it, Frideswide dwelt by the well, as a hermit, and many came to be cured. Fortunately, the well continued to work after she had died, and its popularity was such that many hostelries were built at Binsey, to accommodate those who came seeking its aid.

Given that the water table is only 3 ft below almost anywhere around Oxford, and that clean water and a knowledge of herbal medicine will cure most things, and Frideswide's choice of site for her 'surgery' seems eminently sensible, if the oxen-ford was nearby. The traffic at the ford would rapidly spread news of her prowess far and wide, resulting in greatly increased business for all concerned around Oxford. No wonder the Church sainted her, and the burghers of Oxford adopted her as the town's patron. She put Oxford on the map, figuratively at least.

It is impossible now to imagine the sleepy hamlet of Binsey as a busy transit camp, full of inns and teeming with people and animals, but so it was, by all accounts. Port Meadow, on the other hand, still has great personality. It is easy to think of it thronging with the farmers and merchants and their herds and produce.

Although this reach has much to appeal to the eye, with the broad river having that great common on one side and a line of mature poplars on the other, it is unfortunately rather shallow up both banks, the whole way to Godstow Lock. The only mooring, a handsome one, is to the landing stage at the Perch. Otherwise, only boats of the shallowest draught can expect to come alongside.

Such a boat did land in 1862, on July 4, for it was on that day that Lewis Carroll first started to relate *Alice in Wonderland* to Alice, her sisters and his friend Duckworth, when they rowed up from Oxford, on one of their expeditions. Alice always remembered it as a lovely day, while the Met. Office insists it was overcast, with occasional showers! Well, the Thames is a magical sort of place, where the weather is usually how you wish it to be, but I cannot imagine the following remark, which is what the weather men would have us suppose is something like Dodgson must have made to Mrs Liddell: 'I see it is overcast, with occasional showers, so I propose taking your children, in their summer clothes, in an open boat, out into the country, where we shall lie about on the wet grass and tell stories.'

GODSTOW 1790

Fall 5'2" : 1.57 m | Deep

Upstream You will see the lock quite early. It is on the left. The weir-stream is not a problem, but you may find some reluctance to lie up to the pilings, which are on the right. The angle of approach to the lock from the pilings is a bit awkward. You have to get off and round quickly. For these reasons it is probably easier to tie up to the lay-by on the left.

Downstream The Trout weir, which is under the bridge, is the one normally open, and in average conditions the weir at the head of the lock cut is not a problem. The lay-by is on the right, and so is the prevailing wind. You may well have trouble getting onto the lay-by. Make sure your bow is in and then drive your stern in firmly, for there is no room to manoeuvre for a second try. On the other hand, you should never have trouble coming off the bank to enter the lock!

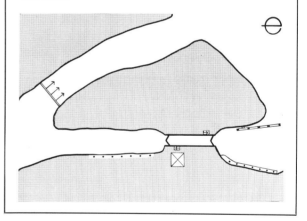

The weir-stream flows in from the right, just below Godstow Lock, but does not, of itself, cause difficulty. St Edward's School boathouses are up the channel, and you may therefore meet racing shells, in the summer term, all along this reach. They will turn into the weir-stream, so if you have to wait for the lock when they are about, keep up to the left more than you usually would.

Above the lock, mooring is only possible to the end of the cut. Beyond this, it looks all right, but is not. There is a relief weir on the right at the end of the cut, but this not not normally a problem. On the left, just below Godstow

96

Bridge, is the ruin of Godstow Nunnery. Here 'Fair Rosamunde', mistress of Henry II, retired and died. Some said her death was at the hand of Queen Eleanor of Aquitaine. Since Henry was anxious to discredit his wife at the time, I should not be at all surprised if it was he who started the rumour!

Godstow, 'the place of God', survived the ravages of Henry VIII, only to suffer destruction at the hands of Parliamentarian Artillerymen in 1645, during a skirmish for Godstow Bridge. The battle was fought for control of the continuation of the present bridge, over the weir-stream. The Roundheads, who held sway on the left bank, sought to test Royalist defences around the King's Headquarters, at Oxford. The Royalists held the bridge, which must be one of the most easily defensible on the river.

The bridge has two arches. Take the one on your right, up or down. The structure crosses at an awkward angle, and is a tight fit, so keep close to the right hand bank until the last moment, and do not hurry.

Above Godstow Bridge, there are three or four shallowish moorings, on the left, from which to gain access to the Trout, or if you feel like a one mile walk, the White Hart at Wytham, in the opposite direction. Wytham is pronounced White-um. The moorings on the right are private.

About 200 yards above the moorings, the Oxford by-pass bridge crosses, and puts a sudden finis to Oxford and all that has gone before. The river is now noticeably narrower, and the countryside has an emptiness that slowly deepens from now on. Nor is it the soft, comforting country of Middle Thames. There is an alien feel about it, almost hostile at times. As if to emphasise this change, and stamp its new identity on you, the river immediately performs a most intricate meander. If there are other boats ahead of you, you will literally not know if they are coming or going.

Between here and King's Lock there are three moorings, for four boats, all on the right, and all immediately after right-hand bends. Of these, the first is the best, a grassy bank fringed with bushes and trees. Unfortunately, everybody else knows of it, so it is usually occupied.

97   The great clump of Wytham Hill and its woods, which has been a companion on the left for the last couple of miles, is now receding,

though not for long, while King's Lock cottage seems for some time to be so near and yet so far. At last the river stops mucking about, and straightens up for the lock, which marks another change. It is the first of the manually worked locks, with their distinctive, spoked wheels for operating the sluices, and the massive balance beams for opening the doors. All the locks from now on are like this, making them much easier to work yourself, if you have to, and adding a new dimension to the enjoyment of the young and the active. For the lock-keeper will usually let you help, provided that you ask him, and he is not too busy. King's is almost the youngest of the pound locks (see

---

KING'S 1928

Fall 2'6" : 0.77 m | Shallow

Upstream. Because of the meander, you will think you have arrived here for some time before you do. Then you will find the weir, on the right, can be rather pushy. The moorings are on the left, and you could well arrive a bit suddenly, so hold off and take it gently.

Downstream. There is no problem with the weir. Wind is the only likely difficulty, for the mooring area is exposed. In a south-westerly, you will find it difficult to get on to the pilings on the right, and virtually impossible to come off the lay-by on the left. If the lock is not open, I find it better in these conditions to stooge in the main river above the lock cut, where there is no lack of space. On a calm day, there is no problem, but choose the pilings for preference because the angle of approach to the lock is better.

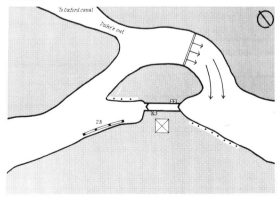

'Passing of the Flash-locks'), and has a stone on the right of the entrance, commemorating its opening, in 1928. I have discovered no explanation of the name. The most likely reason for it is that an early lock was run by a man called King.

Immediately above the lock, the Duke's Cut runs out of the weir-stream. This is the other entrance to the Oxford Canal, and is only of use to properly licensed, narrow-beam boats. The Duke was the Duke of Marlborough, who owned the land. There are two or three moorings to the lock island, for a fee and with the lock-keeper's permission, and two, grassy moorings opposite, at the top of the weir-stream. If you moor here, you will be at the most northerly point on the river.

The route now swings south-west, and runs straight for about half a mile. Two hundred yards before the first left hand bend, there is a mooring on the right; another, on the left, just after this bend, where an old fence runs down to the bank, and another round the next right-hander, on the right. This last is opposite the Wytham Stream, which forms a parallel watercourse, via the Seacourt and Hinksey Streams, to link up with the Thames at mile 91, by the railway bridge. There was once a plan to enlarge this network and use it as the main channel, thus shattering the peace of Wytham for ever. This plan was abandoned on the grounds that it did not actually offer any advantage.

The basin from which Wytham Stream leaves the river is known as Hagley Pool. I think there may have been a flash-lock, or fish weir here at some point. There used to be an island in the bend below Wytham Stream, which would have been a likely site, using Wytham Stream as a relief overflow. This is only a hypothesis, although Thacker mentions Clay Weir 'between Eynsham and King's in 1796', without suggesting a site.

The next reach is wide and straight, and rather exposed to the south-westerly winds that tend to blow down it. Wytham Great Wood now begins to return on the left. There is an excellent looking mooring under some trees, with 'No Mooring' written on it. Immediately beyond it is a good one, which does not appear to be prohibited. A little further on the next likely place is not practicable, being muddily shallow.

Cassington Church can now be seen, nestling in its village across the right hand fields. Round the next right hand bend, there are two or three moorings before the River Evenlode flows in. It is unnavigable, but this is a charming spot, with the pretty stream fringed by trees, and the Wytham wood now striding along the left bank of the main river. There is a shallowish mooring, for a boat of 25 ft or so, immediately above the confluence, and if your boat fits it, I envy you. Otherwise, there is only one more between here and Eynsham Lock.

Shortly above the Evenlode is an old canal, the Cassington Cut, which used to run to Cassington Mill, about a mile away. It was in this reach, a couple of years ago, that a bird-watching friend of mine announced that he heard a nightingale singing in Wytham Wood. I cannot hear myself think above the thump of the Lister, but if he says so, I believe him. The mooring is on the right, 100 yards above the cut, against open fields, so you might moor there and be serenaded. If you have never heard one, a nightingale sounds a bit like a blackbird, but the notes have greater clarity and greater musical range, with splendid coloratura passages if it really gets going. In fact it is safe to say that if you heard it, you would know.

As Eynsham Lock comes in sight, there is another old canal on the right, the Eynsham Canal. This ran up to the village, about $1\frac{1}{2}$ miles, but is now quite unnavigable. There are the remains of a flash-lock about 100 yards up from the river. The tackle has all gone, but the beam and sill are still in place. You have to walk up to the Talbot and back down the stream, if you want to look at it, there is no way ashore from the river.

Eynsham Lock seems to me to be the youngest pound lock on the river, by a couple of months, (See: 'Passing of the Flash-locks') although it was opened on the same day as King's.

About 100 yards above the lock is Swinford Bridge, the second and last of the remaining toll bridges. The mellow stone bridge, of 1777, is said to have been commissioned by George III, after a nightmare crossing in the then ferry. Unfortunately, the toll, of two pence, was fixed by Act of Parliament, and is now inadequate to provide for the sadly needed work of maintenance and restoration. The various political

EYNSHAM 1928

Fall 2'9" : 0.84m | Shallow |
Sanitary station

Upstream. The weir pushes hard onto the lay-by, which is on the left. This has a profound effect on activity below the lock. The Sanitary Station is at the beginning of the lay-by, so it is necessary to give boats there a wider than usual berth, or risk joining them inadvertantly. If possible, avoid using the service area when travelling downstream, unless there are no other boats tied up to the lay-by. This is because you will have to turn round having passed these, and this can be a very interesting experience. Note also that there is a reverse stream, close to the lock on the right, to catch a boat with insufficient way on and wrap it round the post which has presumably been put there to stop such unfortunates from running hard aground.

Downstream. Be ready once you have passed Swinford Bridge. It is not difficult. The weir is to the left and the pilings to the right. The only slight problem is the angle off the pilings to the lock entrance.

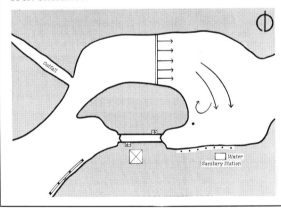

factions will not help, for various political reasons, including not buying it when it is for sale. One day it will fall, killing a few people, no doubt. Then there will be wringing of hands, and public enquiries, and VAST rebuilding costs. It is a microcosm of petty, bureaucratic futility. Meanwhile, we can enjoy it.

Eynsham, pronounced Ensham, is probably 'Aegen's place by the bend in the river', and was mentioned in the Anglo-Saxon Chronicles for 571. It is a fine old village, but about a mile from the river, so probably too far away for most boaters. The Talbot is about ¼ mile from the river, and there is a farm shop 150 yards from the bridge, to the left. It stocks basics and is the last shop of any description before Lechlade.

Swinford means 'swine ford', and is, I believe, another of those fords the name of which specifies the mean depth, for the benefit of unlettered people. Thus, it is not a place to which swine from all over the country came to cross, but a place where a standard sort of pig *could* cross, if it happened to wish to. My generation might have called it 'Two Foot Ford', now the term would be '600 mm Ford', which I am happy to note lacks any charm at all.

Moorings start about 50 yards above the bridge, on the left, and carry on, at varying depth, round the sharp left-hander, for 150 yards in all. It is a good, reliable place to stop. The moorings on the right are private, incidentally. There are apparently no signs of fortifications on the nearby Beacon Hill, which commands the ford. I would have thought it an obvious choice for an iron-age hill fort.

There is another mooring 100 yards or so above the last ones, opposite a curious backwater, which leaves the river only to return to it, 50 yards higher. This is the remains of an old meander. There is a standard progression in the development of meanders, which happens when the river is running through flat country. This progression is best illustrated:

The process starts with a simple bend, having two pressure points when the stream is running fast. The scouring at these points causes the next stage.

The action of scouring actually increases the interruption to the stream and thus the forces bearing on the pressure points, of which there are now three. This leads inevitably to the last stage.

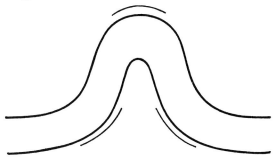

From here it is only a matter of time before the river breaks through the neck, leaving the loop to return gradually to nature. This pair of inlets is the only perfect example on the river at the moment, although there are a number of places where it has happened earlier, and may happen at any time.

So the river is not as winding as it once was, but it still manages a good meander up the next half mile or so. There are moorings on the upstream sides of the next two left-hand bends. I found no moorings on the right between Swinford Bridge and Pinkhill Lock.

Oxford Cruisers Ltd offer the normal services. They are the highest hire-cruiser yard on the river.

One more bend takes us to Pinkhill Lock. Pinkhill is probably a corruption of the delightful 'Pinkle', which Taunt calls it, alias 'Pinca lea', Pinca's place.

Round the next bend above the lock is a Thames Water mooring site, under the lee of Farmoor Reservoir. I saw a water rail here in 1985. The large mass of open water on the reservoir has attractions for other birds. I understand there is a colony of cormorants, who cannot believe their good fortune at having found apparently limitless supplies of succulent trout. There is also a colony of cross anglers, who cannot believe the number and size of the trout they see lifted out by the cormorants! There are also 'foreign' ducks, which you will see from here to Bablock Hythe. I think they are Tufted Duck. They have cross-bred with the local Mallards to produce some unnameable offspring.

The river turns away from the reservoir, briefly, before returning and sweeping round a right-hand bend. You will see a backwater on

PINKHILL 1791

Fall 3'6" : 1.05 m | Shallow

Upstream Start preparing once you have passed Oxford Cruisers' yard. There is a sharp left hand bend into the lock, so you will not see anyone coming out until very late. So approach slowly. The pilings are on the right, as is the weir-stream. You can do no wrong if you keep up to the right.

Downstream This is a simple lock. You can see it in good time. There is plenty of room to circle above it, if you do not wish to tie up. The pilings are on the right and are reasonably sheltered. There is no interference here from the weir.

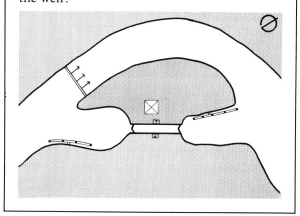

the right, unnavigable, and a rather untidy, bush covered lump of land. This is all that remains of another meander, which looked like this around 1900:

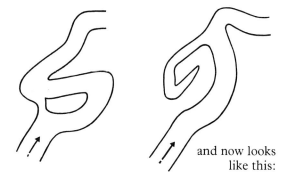

and now looks like this:

Note that the left-hander round which we have just passed is building up to be the next neck to be lopped off.

At the apex of the next left-hand bend, there is a fence and some bits of masonry, on the left. You can moor just below the masonry, which is the abutment of Skinner's Bridge, a foot-bridge that used to cross here. The bridge was on the site of Skinner's Weir, a flash-lock that was removed in 1880, which is recent enough for a modern writer to have first hand knowledge. Henry Taunt knew this weir, and this is what he wrote of it:

The old weir, with its couple of quaint that-ched cottages, was one of those picturesque places that artists love. It had been in the possession of the Skinners, from father to son for a long number of years. It was a little inn, and the last landlord, Joe Skinner, was one of the best hearted, quaintest fellows that ever lived. He was original in the highest

Skinner's Weir 1863. The flash-lock was removed in 1880. Henry Taunt.

degree, and it was a rich treat to spend an evening with him and listen to his talk of havoc wrought among the wild ducks, with his stalking horse and tremendous duck gun, or his curious remarks on someone who had been there, and, not understanding him, had rubbed old Joe the wrong way of the wool, getting perhaps a rough setting down. This is all swept away by the march of improvement: the old cottages, the tumbledown weir, and old Joe are all gone, and the place entirely lone and deserted.

It still is, although the reservoir is close evi-dence of modern man. If you moor here, you will easily follow the old course of the lock cut, as it runs dry through the field for about 150 yards, before meeting the river again, where a wall stops the river from continuing to use it. It runs downstream past where you are moored for about 50 yards, again clearly visible. I should judge the most likely spot for the lock

to have been more or less where the culvert carrying the footpath now is, although there is some evidence of a basin above this, in which case the lock would have been further back. I found no evidence of the 'couple of quaint thatched cottages', perhaps you will. I did find some damson trees though, full of delicious fruit.

Round the next bend I came across a large flock of Canada geese, together with what I suspect were domestic geese but which looked like Greylags, as well as some hybrids, suggesting both breeds. They were doing what we used to call, in the RAF, 'circuits and bumps', which in the restricted water space was quite exciting, and full of loud conversation. Geese remind me of nothing so much as a junior school football team, all dashing about shouting instructions to each other!

There is a mooring on the upstream left side of the next left-hander, after which there is only one more in the next hour and a half of cruising.

The reservoir now starts to slip astern. The country is very flat but with plenty of tree cover. The poplars in the distance are at Bablock Hythe. Round the next right-hand bend there commences half a mile of caravan park. The best time to see this is in mid-winter, when it is usually under a foot or so of water. Otherwise all you can do is hurry past.   103

Bablock Hythe, 'the landing place at Babba's stream', has a long history. There was a ford here, and then a ferry, and an Inn since 'before the memory of man'. There was a chain ferry there in my life-time. The chain crossed the river about two feet above the water. If you did not know about it, or were not looking, it brought you up, all standing, when it struck the camping canvas fore-stay. The dreadful pub is now closed. Maybe it will rise again from the ashes of its recent past, to delight the traveller once more.   104

The ferry at Bablock Hythe, 1880. Henry Taunt.

There is now thick woodland on the left and a high bank on the right until, at mile 104½, you will see a section of wall on the right. Two hundred yards above that is another section. It is quite high, but the water is deep, and it is a perfectly practical and rather interesting mooring. The upper wall closes off the lock cut of the flash-lock known as the Ark Weir, known also as Hart's, Ark Island Weir and Noah's Ark. It closed about 1860. Here again, you can follow the lock cut round the field, until it reaches a pond, right down by the first section of wall, which is where it used to run out. The pond is the remains of the weir scour or basin, and the old lock walls are just above this, although you will have to scrabble about in the bushes to find them. They are on both sides of the channel, but the side further from the river is more obvious. Why 'The Ark'? Gelling says it means a small building by a stream. Thacker says it is a frequently used name for a desolate house. He also remarks a house or inn of that name, 1½ miles further up. This is nearer Ridge's than the Ark weir though, so is likely to be mere coincidence, unless the landlord of the Inn was also the lock-keeper here at one time.

105 The electricity pylons are rather intrusive up the next reach, which is otherwise wild, with deep woodland on the left, which actually gets into the river in places. Here I saw a kingfisher, who darted ahead of me for perhaps two hundred yards. They are always such a thrilling sight. Also, two double camping skiffs came down, in good order technically, the coxes gaily acknowledging my salute.

Northmoor is one of the loneliest stations on the river. Its cottage is the only sign of habitation. This serves to give you notice that you are approaching the lock. You can see it 200 yards before you arrive, which is 170 yards before you see the lock itself!

Northmoor Lock has one of the only three remaining paddle and rymer weirs, which perpetuate a system that has been in use for a thousand years or so. This is what a flash-lock looked like. The lock-keeper removed a few paddles and rymers, swung back the beam, if you were lucky, and whoosh, through you went! I am jolly glad we no longer have to. The idea of hauling up against the stream does not appeal much either, although one would at least be on dry land.

Northmoor was never in fact a flash-lock, indeed it is the second youngest lock on the new site on the River after Shifford, having been built in 1896. Nor is the weir's continued existence purely an anomaly. Apart from an admirable desire on the part of Thames Water to preserve such features as they reasonably can, the paddle and rymer weirs are still there because they are extremely efficient and inexpensive to maintain.

NORTHMOOR 1896

Fall 4'1" : 1.24 m | Shallow

This lock has stanchions for tying up to, rather than bollards.

Upstream This is a very sudden lock, somehow, both ways. Going up, there is very little warning. Look for the cottage over the field ahead, and prepare as soon as you see it. The pilings are on the right. The weir-stream meets the river at a sharp angle and tends to rush out at one. The push to the right is quite strong, so keep up to the left as you approach the pilings, or you will undershoot.

Downstream You will see the lock in good time. Most of the tie-up, on the left, is exposed to the weir-stream. The weir seems oppressively close. It is difficult to get alongside in a strong stream, especially in an offshore wind, but you must, because circling is not an alternative. When I came down in August '85, the notice MOOR ON THIS BANK had been snapped in half. That is the right attitude. Make sure you get your boat in, even if you have to hit the bank with it.

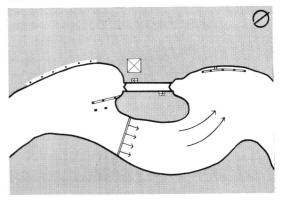

The paddle and rymer weir at Northmoor, one of the few remaining.

There is no mooring up the next reach until Hart's Weir Footbridge. The countryside is unspectacular but pleasant enough. You can moor on the right bank, directly you pass the bridge. Hart's Weir was one of eight locks known as Hart's, starting with the one at Pangbourne. Taunt calls it Ridge's, and since it closed in 1880, he would have known it well. Thacker found Ridge's, Langley's, Old Hart's, Cock's, Rudge's and Butler's under this site. Quite why the name of Hart has become re-attached to it during this century, after it had closed, is not clear.

The lock cut and cottage were on the left. If you are interested in exploring the site, cross the footbridge and walk down the path until you come to a small, concrete bridge. The cut lies to the right of this, and you can still follow it for about 200 yards, when it opens onto the river. At the far end of the bridge there is an old stone wall, curving towards you; the upstream shoulder of the lock wall. It is still two ft high. To the left is an old privet hedge and two gate posts. Clearly somebody lived here much more recently than the closing of the lock. If you push through the hedge, there is a quantity of stone walling and loose stone on the right, the remains of the cottage. The line of the lock wall can be traced along the front of the building. The channel was perhaps 35 feet, and search in the grass at this distance will quickly reveal the other wall.

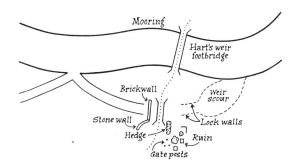

Ridge's flash-lock, home of Betty Rudge, Lady Ashbrook. Henry Taunt.

A real-life Pygmalion took place here. Lord Ashbrook, then an undergraduate, met Betty Rudge, the lock-keeper's daughter, while out fishing, and they fell in love. He arranged for her education, and they were married in 1766. This almost unbelievable experiment in social realignment appears to have been conspicuously successful. Betty married a theologian of Jesus after the death, in 1784, of her lord, and died in 1808, much loved and respected, leaving many descendants, including a future Duchess of Marlborough. I hope she looked after her father. As for Lord Ashbrook, one wonders if his mother was alive when he decided on his bride. If so, there must surely have been a positively Wildeian exchange: 'Mama, I am going to marry the sweetest girl.' 'Indeed! And who is this paragon, pray?' 'Her name is Betty, she is a lock-keeper's daughter.' 'A LOCK-keeper?' 'Yes mama, Rudge's Lock.' 'The lock, Sir, is immaterial!'

Shortly above the bridge, the good-looking mooring on the left is not in fact practical, it is too shallow. Then there is a tank-trap!

There is a pleasant mooring 200 yards below 107, just above two ancient willows, and another on the left apex of the bend at 107. On the right a little above the pill-box, two boats can moor against the concrete piling. Then, just as Newbridge comes in sight, there are two moorings to the meadow bank, between some bushes. Beyond these is another pill-box, hidden in a hedge across the field. It is interesting that the pill-boxes have come back, there having been none since Culham, 25 miles away by river, but only seven for a flying swan. Perhaps the idea was to encourage the enemy to enter the cul-de-sac formed by the loop of river, and hope he got bogged down with narrow communications and limited room, so that he could be shelled and bombed into a shambles? The river has now turned due west, in which direction it remains for the rest of the journey.

The Rose Revived at Newbridge has a short

landing-stage, but you can moor all along their frontage of 150 yards as well. The bank is rather high, but it is worth the effort. It was well worth it one April night a few years ago, when I went up from Oxford with the twins. There was a strong stream running, which delayed our progress, and we passed Northmoor at 6.30, just as it was getting dark. I did not know the mooring points in those days, and three or four attempts to tie up proved fruitless. So we pressed on, in wind and rain and darkness. It was 7.45 before we finally came to Newbridge and marched, dripping in our oilskins, into the warmth and welcome of the Inn.

Newbridge has six arches. Use the largest going up and the one to the right of it coming down. There is not a lot of room for error, and the River Windrush, which runs in from the right immediately above the bridge, will try to push you across, in any stream. So set yourself up with care and proceed steadily, with reserve power. I once watched, on a gale lashed morning, as a Thames Water tug went through, with a huge barge in tow, without a scratch. Half an hour later it took me three minutes of hard struggle to swing my boat off the mooring.

There has been a good deal of discussion over the years as to whether Newbridge is so called because it is the oldest on the river. From all the evidence I can find, it is the oldest structure over the navigation channel. Radcot Bridge, *c*1225, is older, Newbridge being called that because it was built twenty five years later. However, Radcot Bridge is now over a side stream. They are both lovely old structures. The patina on the sandstone at Newbridge, gently weathered over 700 years, is very easy on the eye, as is the simple excellence of its design.

I have been somewhat exercised by a remark by Mr and Mrs Hall in *The Book of the Thames*, *c*1859. 'They note that, at New Bridge, there is a small inn on the Berkshire side and busy mill on the Oxfordshire bank. They add: 'A short distance below, the Windrush contributes its waters to the Thames.'

The May Bush is still on the Berkshire side, now ridiculously called Oxfordshire, as a result of the local government stupidities of the early 'seventies. On the Oxfordshire bank is the Rose Revived, alias the Rose and Crown, alias the Rose. In 1462, this was said to have been an alehouse 'beyond the memory of man.' It has also been a wharf, a toll house and a hermitage, but never a mill. There was a Newbridge Mill, but it was situated some way up the Windrush, which, at the time the Halls passed, ran into the Thames about 200 yards *higher* than it does now. It was moved to its present course because it was disturbing the flow of the main river by pushing an island of silt, round both sides of which it flowed, into the stream.

How did the Halls miss the Rose, confuse it with the mill, and mistake the confluence of the Thames/Windrush?

The Maybush is difficult to approach from the river. Indeed they have a notice advising you not to try. I got within a foot of the bank, and walked ashore on my gangplank. There is no mooring allowed further up, so it is either a question of trying as I did, or sneaking across from the other bank!

There is a pill-box a short distance up on the right. Beyond it, on the left, I found shoal water up to 10 ft out from the bank. Watch out for this coming down river. It appears to be a collapsed wall or sandbagging, approximately 150 yards above the bridge.

There are no moorings on the left between Newbridge and Shifford Lock, and the next on the right is above Shifford village.

At about 108½, just above a crossing power

The Thames' gentlest inhabitants graze the waterside meadows.

line, and before the sharp right-hander, a ten yard section of stone wall on the right marks the site of Limbre's Weir, alias Daniell's, Langley's and, almost of course, Hart's. It closed in 1872. I found evidence of a dry channel, but no masonry, nor a weir scour.

The river is becoming narrower all the time. There is an island on the reach above the bend. Keep left of it going up, there is hardly water for a dinghy to the right. The high banks, the winding river and the trees and bushes that line one's view make it very difficult to see approaching craft. Be extra careful not to cut corners. There are places where you will have little more than a boat's length warning of another.

109   I saw several flat bottomed boats piled high with reeds in this reach. Apart from the outboard motors, that is a sight that must have been unchanged for centuries, millenia perhaps.

Shifford, on the right, comprises a church, a farm, and about one other building. It used to be a notable town, so vital to Alfred that he held a parliament there. As discussed under Runnymede, earlier, I do not think that meant anything more than a wooden camp, with an open space large enough for everyone to bring his men-at-arms along to see fair play. There were hereabouts two major fords, Sheep ford itself, which we may take on our previous hypothesis concerning fords named after animals, to indicate about 1ft 6in at mean water level, and Duxford, little more than a mile away. At low water a duck could cross this ford now, but it is actually named after Duduc. Clearly Wessex, must hold these two at all costs, for they guarded Wantage, barely ten miles to the south.

What became of Shifford then? I suspect it was left high and dry, literally, by the building of Radcot and New bridges, each side of it, and gently withered.

I spent some time looking for Shifford Old Weir, until I decided I must be in the wrong place. So I asked myself where I would build a flash-lock. Since the stream known as Great Brook flows in a little above Shifford village, it seemed to me the best place would be above the confluence, to avoid the additional pressure of the stream at times of high water, and to prevent backing up and flooding by effectively damming

this stream. So I started to creep up the right bank looking for evidence. After about ten yards, the boat came to a sudden stop. When I went forward to find out why, I found masonry on the bank and under the water, which is what I had hit, together with evidence of old wooden pilings as well. So I am fairly confident this is where the weir was. It ceased to function in about 1800.

The country is now wild and open, with no

SHIFFORD 1898

Fall 7'4" : 2.23 m | Deep

This lock employs stanchions for tying up, not bollards.

Upstream The lock is just past the weir-stream, which enters from the left. Since the weir is nearly two miles away, there should not be too much push from it. The pilings are on the right. This is the fourth deepest lock above Teddington. Naturally the steps run back to front, so careful judgment of the approach is called for.

Downstream The cut is half a mile long, so that there is no problem with the weir. There is an overspill weir to the right of the lock, but it is unlikely that this will make itself felt. The lay-by is to the left. The first section of this has suffered from the collapse of the bank and is unusable and liable to cause damage. Keep off the bank until close to the lock.

Note There are a couple of pleasant moorings in the overspill weir-stream, which the lock-keeper will allow you to use in normal circumstances, for a fee.

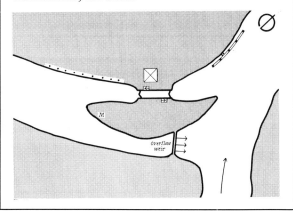

other sign of habitation than Shifford farm. The great march of progress is marked by the inevitable power lines, but after the Great Brook the river turns away from these. There is a field on the right with the fence close to the bank, with two moorings at the beginning of it.

These moorings are the only possibles on this whole section, and we are now approaching the River's most isolated lock, Shifford. Shifford is the newest lock on a new site to be built, 1898. This is not to confuse dates with King's and Eynsham, which are much younger pound locks, but simply replace flash-locks on the same sites. The cut for the lock by-passed Duxford, saving a mile on the navigation channel.

From the moorings at the lock you may walk across the island to Duxford, which is guarded by a pill-box, and cross the ford, with the aid of wellies, in quiet conditions. There is nothing to see but countryside and about six houses, but this whole area is full of peace. If I was only allowed one bit of river, I should choose the reach from Shifford to Tenfoot, precisely because it is the loneliest, quietest place on the river.

The old navigation channel is still practicable most of the way to Duxford, from below the lock. There is plenty of water usually but little width. Only try it if your boat is not over 25 ft, and turn well before the ford, which is cluttered with debris of all sorts.

I made a voyage in the dinghy, from the top of the weir-stream. There was a strong stream, and I progressed rather like Eeyore, turning round slowly as I slid along. It is a wild, unspoiled stream, and I watched it idly, half asleep. It was some time before it was borne in on me that there definitely was an approaching rushing noise. Too late I realised there was a drop at the ford, there was no stopping and no friendly bank. I was swept over into the maelstrom below, all of a foot below, I am happy to say, to the derisive cheers of three small boys, who were there to throw stones apparently. Shaken and damp, but feeling suitably heroic, I took greater care over the second half of the voyage, and returned to Shifford lock unscathed. There was a flash-lock a little below the ford until 1869, but I have found no sign.

Shifford was, for 35 years, my highest mark on the Thames. I had not been higher since the ill-fated expedition of 1946, on which the whole crew (me) except the captain went down with cholera (Shiffo' tummy actually), and lay close to death in Shifford lock cut for three days. At least while there, growing friendly with the lock-keeper, I was allowed to help him with his weir, which was a paddle and rymer weir at that time. The thunder of the weir and the great pressure on the paddle, suddenly released as the water ran behind it, are still vivid in my memory.

The country into which one emerges from the somewhat dark and dank environs of the cut is yet another facet of the Thames scene. Here the banks are low, green and inviting, and the river meanders unobtrusively between them, leaving the boater to wonder which side of the stream those distant cows are grazing. There are several moorings on the right, the last one just past the pill-box, after which there is nothing until after Rushey. On the left there is one mooring opposite the pill-box, and another half way between it and the second pill-box. It is difficult to imagine that anything much can have changed in this landscape for centuries, unless there are fewer signs of human habitation than once there were. In rain and gale it has little to recommend it, unless you are snugly and warmly moored. In sunshine, or in the dappled light of a sky scattered with summer clouds, it is enchanting.

Shortly after the second pill-box, the footbridge called Tenfoot crosses the river. There was a weir here until 1869, and Taunt's map of

Tenfoot Weir in 1864. Note how full of rushes and water-lilies the river was in the days when Henry Taunt took the photo.

1897 shows three dwellings on the left. I found no sign of the weir from the river, and the houses are certainly not above ground. There is speculation about the name. The present bridge was 11ft 3in in 1985, when I passed, as I discovered by stopping against a piling and dropping a perpendicular, a piece of string, which I later measured. The name predates the bridge anyway, so I think it must have indicated the width of the flash. The objection to that is that it is awfully narrow for the passage of barges. But this would surely be why it was so named. It may in fact give us a clear indication of the width of an upper Thames barge. Certainly, a boat of, say, 70 ft, 10 ft wide, would present quite an interesting navigating problem in these narrow reaches, let alone anything bigger. Thacker decided it must be flash width too, and quotes one Jessop, in 1791, as referring to 'the 10 foot weir.'

The river now runs between higher and uninviting banks, while the scenery closes in and the course of the stream becomes rather more extravagantly convoluted. This is one of those reaches where there is nothing much to do but get to the far end of it as quickly as possible. There are stands of poplars on the left, like soldiers on parade, in rigid lines: waiting only to be big enough to be cut down.

At around 112½, there used to be a weir called Thames. It was removed about 1821. the Thames Water chart shows its site as the sharp left-hand bend, just above the pill-box. An outflow here used to connect with the Great Brook, which we met below Shifford, so a likely position for the weir would be immediately below this. Thacker was assured it was the place, by some haymakers, in 1910, although he found no signs of it. I find no signs either, and am not happy that it is a sensible place, bearing in mind the siting of the other flash-locks that can be studied. The practice, as you may observe, was either to erect a simple weir across a straight stretch of river, or to make a cut across the inside of a bend, such that the main force of the current was taken away from the flash-weir. I know of no example of making a cut on the outside of a bend, and this bend is so sharp that a cut on the inside would have to

The low, green country above Shifford Lock in 1987; it could be 1887.

be so far back that the river would flow straight through it, the opposite of what one would want. If it was a simple type, putting it on the apex of such a bend would have caused endless uproar amongst one's customers. Two bends and 250 yards lower, a drain issues from the right bank, and some old stone wall runs for thirty yards above this, and a short distance below it. A lock at this point *would* satisfy the above criteria, and the stone wall is much too extensive for a drain support, so I offer this as an alternative site.

113   The next item of interest is a mile further on, Tadpole Bridge, a single span, uncomprising structure, next to which is the Trout pub. About 100 yards below the bridge, now forming the start of the pub's mooring, is the wall of Tadpole, Rudge's or Kent's weir, which was removed in 1869. Until 1986, the landlord forbade mooring at this pub, and would come out and shout at you if you tried to be a customer. The new management are delighted to see boaters and are pleased for you to moor and the pub is once more a delight to look forward to.

114   Above the bridge the banks are the highest on the Thames, partly as a result of dredging and partly for flood protection. The only company is a pill-box. Another place to press on. Note, there are no moorings, except at the Trout, between the meadows above Shifford and the meadows above Rushey, one hour's cruising apart.

Rushey Lock comes as something of a relief. And what a relief! The gardens are immaculately kept, and the older lock house graces them well. This is another lock with a paddle and rymer weir, with the largest weir scour basin on the river. Make an excuse to dawdle around if you can without being a nuisance. Rushey derived from 'rush island by the weir'. I saw an Arctic Tern here twice in 1984.

115   The reach above the lock fully compensates for the reach below it. You can moor in several places on the right, from 115 to a point just past the pill-box, which is one of several from which there would have been no survivors, withdrawal being impossible. On the left, there is a mooring round the first left-hander above the lock, another underneath 115, next to four old willows, which will be anxious to join you aboard! Also, on the apex of the next left-

RUSHEY   1790

Fall 6'0" : 1.8m2 | Deep |
Sanitary station and pump-out

This lock is the middle of five using stanchions instead of bollards.

Upstream You will see the lock some time before you arrive. The weir is on the left, so keep to that side if there is any stream running. The pilings are on the right, past the weir-stream.

Downstream The lock appears rather suddenly, but the approach is straight and uncomplicated. The weir-stream is to the right, quite early, so does not interfere with the mooring. There is a piling on the right and a lay-by on the left. There is no advantage in using either and both are simple. The Sanitary Station and pump-out are on the left.

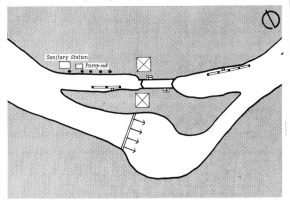

hander. This reach is very like the one above Shifford.

At about $115\frac{1}{2}$ was Old Nan's Weir, until about 1861. There is a well defined cut, now simply a depression in the field on the right. From the river the only sign is a large stone, close to the river bank and nearly buried, but too much of a coincidence to be random. I also found an unusual number of stones on the bottom, roughly in line with this stone. The name conjures an interesting picture of the lady. It was by no means unusual for a woman to work a weir, usually after the death of her husband.

There are moorings on the right; just before the next pill-box, and on both sides of the next right-hand hairpin, at 116, under some trees. On the left there is a fair position to an attractive, tree lined bank, a little above the pill-box, another exactly at the 6 of 116. Lastly, two left-handers further up (three bends down from the bridge, if you are coming down), there are three good moorings.

Old Man's footbridge stands stark, improbably, a short distance below Radcot Lock. The site of Harper's weir until 1868, the bridge was probably built on or into the old weir walls. I found nothing else, except bits of masonry scattered on the river bed.

Radcot Lock has the last of the three remaining paddle and rymer weirs. It replaces Clarke's flash-lock, which also disappeared in 1868. It is worth noting that Clarke's and Harper's weirs, only a quarter of a mile apart, must have been the closest two locks in the history of the river.

The weir is deeper in the middle than at each side, hence the two different lengths of rymer. There are three different lengths of paddle. The longest ones have the pole in the centre, and are for the bottom of the deepest part of the weir. The medium ones have the pole on one side, and the short ones have the pole on the other side. With all three placed in position, one above the other, the weir is fully shut and the poles level at the top. The rymers are fitted into holes prepared in the sill on the river bed, finding which in a strong stream is the trickiest part of the business, so the lock-keeper informs me. The rymers are spaced so that the paddles rest against and between two of them. The paddles are held securely by the pressure of the water. *Tout simple!*

7 Above the lock is the first sign of softening of the countryside again. The river winds past another plantation, and a reasonably civilised camp-site, to Radcot bridge and the Swan Inn. The old navigation channel runs in on the left as you turn to face the bridge, and you can moor from just above this almost to the bridge. Radcot: 'reed cottage or red cottage'.

The present navigation bridge was built in 1787, for what reason it is difficult to judge, since it appears no larger than the old Radcot Bridge, which it replaced. The navigation channel makes an absurdly abrupt departure from the river, and a sharp turn through the bridge, which is the most difficult on the whole stream. Here, as Thacker remarked, the reputation of a lifetime can be destroyed in seconds. Apart from its narrowness, the shape of the

RADCOT   1892

Fall 4′10″ : 1.48m | Deep

There are short, wooden stanchions in this lock, rather than bollards.

Upstream Start preparing at Old Man's Footbridge. The weir runs in from the right, and tends to push you away from the pilings against a fairly uninviting left bank. Keep good way on and hold up to the right as you approach.

Downstream Good, open approach. The weir is on the left, but is not a factor. Moorings to left and right. Use those on the left for preference. There is a hose on the left, before the lock lay-by.

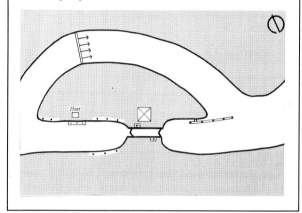

Paddles and rymers of various lengths at Radcot. When in place the top of the weir is level.

bridge and its approach leads to it being a funnel for wind. Take care coming down additionally, because you will not see anyone coming up until it is too late to do anything about it.

The old bridge, well protected by two pillboxes, has a nasty little kink just above it, which would have made the approach difficult. Surely it would have been easier to remove this than to make the new cut? Indeed, it was quite likely formed by the disturbance caused to the stream by the presence of the new cut. There was an old mill, Monk's mill, in the stream below, which might have caused difficulties with the channel, but this was removed about 1760, before the new cut was made. It can only have been that the arch of the old bridge was too tight for the barges. Someone has rounded the centre arch at some time, causing settlement at the keystone. Perhaps that was at the back of the decision to abandon the bridge for navigation. It is a truly lovely old structure. If you can, take your dinghy round to it and examine the work closely. If not, you can always walk over it or climb down beside it. There used to be a cross on that boss on the down stream side.

118   The river now runs absolutely straight for about half a mile, under some power lines, which presently come to march alongside. The straight ends with a sharp right-hander, known as Hell's Turn. There are no moorings above the bridge, just a pill-box and one house, which intrudes into one's solitude for quite a long time, until it turns out to be Grafton lock cottage.

Grafton Lock was opened in 1896. Taunt says it was placed just below the weir pool of East Hart's Weir. At some time at the beginning of the century, someone planted some conkers on the lock island. The horse chestnuts that stand there now are a magnificent sight, to which the lovely gardens, which are such a credit to the lock-keeper, are a worthy foil. Grafton is 'homestead in a grove', which the lock certainly is.

There is a pill-box on the right, above the lock. Shortly afterwards is Eaton Hastings church, and a large house whose gardens run down to the river bank, almost the first to do so since Oxford! There are two or three other houses but the village is now a mile away, the old village having been deserted, possibly due

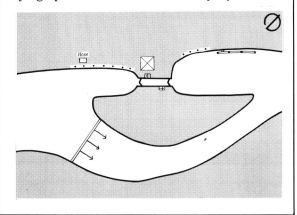

GRAFTON 1896

Fall 3'8" : 1.11 m | Shallow

This lock has wooden stanchions for tying up to, not bollards.

Upstream The lock cottage will be seen in good time. The weir runs in from the left, but is below the moorings. These are on the right, and comprise a short length of piling, followed by 150ft of lay-by.

Downstream Easily visible. 150ft of lay-by on the left. The weir stream is not a factor when tying up. There is a hose on the lay-by.

to plague, but possibly also as a result of the industrial experiments at Buscot House. Eaton Hastings is 'farm by the river, held by the Hastings family'.

There follows another pill-box and there are two moorings beyond it and two more round the next bend, which is a sharp right-hander.

From here you can see Kelmscott Manor across the fields. Two more bends bring you to a concrete wall on the right, allowing mooring for three or four boats and access to the village of Kelmscott, 'Caenhelm's cottage', and the Plough Inn. There is usually a bit of a traffic-jam on a summer weekend, but there are four moorings just above the Thames Water towpath bridge, which are the closest to the village, followed by another three or four round the field, up to the pill-box. Lastly there is one hard above Eaton Bridge, which is about five minutes' walk from the Plough.

Kelmscott House, once the second home of

William Morris, the socialist, poet, artist and designer, is now a museum of his work and art. It is open on the first Wednesday in the month, in the afternoon. The village is small and picturesque, if somewhat self-conscious, with some attractive houses and farm buildings. There are no shops, just the pub.

Opposite Kelmscott one can see Buscot House clear in the distance, on a hill, the first hill, it seems, since Beacon Hill and Wytham Wood, 20 miles away.

We shall come to Buscot shortly. In the meantime, let us pause at Eaton Bridge, the site of Eaton Hastings flash-lock, the last to operate on the Thames (See: 'Passing of the Flash-locks'). Here there used to be a pub, the Anchor, but this was burnt down a few years ago, and razed. Only its footings remain. Beyond where it stood is a side-stream, in which was once a mill-wheel. You can still see the axle mounts and the grooves in the chamber wall worn by its action.

The weir, known to Taunt and Thacker as Hart's, is described by Taunt with great clarity:

Hart's Weir has the greatest fall (nearly 4ft sometimes in low water) of any among the weirs of the upper Thames, so perhaps a word or two upon passing through would not be out of place. In winter there is a swift stream through, but very little fall, the weir-paddles being all out; and the only thing to guard against in shooting is the bridge that carries the rymers. I recollect one winter in passing this very weir, when lying on my back in the boat to get through, scraping a fair amount of skin off my nose and face, through contact with the bridge while going under. In summer there is no fear of that, as the bridge is a long way above the water; but what must be looked out for is, the nearly direct fall of a foot or so in ascending or descending, and this perhaps in a spot only just wide enough to get a boat through. Weirs are built in a very different way from locks, and, to a person not used to them, are very puzzling. They take up the whole breadth of the stream, so that in opening them fully, you let the whole of the penned-back water above pass through; they are generally composed of three different parts, viz., the bridge, the rymers, and the paddles. The bridge is longer

than the span of the stream it has to cover, and works round on a pin; the part on the shore side being weighted to balance the other, and notches cut to let the rymers in and keep each one in place. On the sill, at the bottom of the river, exactly underneath the bridge, are corresponding sockets to hold their end, and then the paddles fill up the spaces between each; the weight of the water above keeping all tight. Generally, for small boats, only a few of the paddles and rymers are moved, so that there is always a fall, and the best way to get up is to fasten your tow-line to the head of the boat, and gently haul her, one person being on the bridge of the weir to guide her through. As a rule, when the weir is all out, you will not get through by any other way. Going down is different, and much easier, though somewhat dangerous (most of the weir-pools being very deep); but, having ascertained everything is ready, pull gently on, and keep your boat's head straight to the centre of the opening, just before reaching which the oars must be shifted, yet kept ready to be used again the moment you are past, as the stream rushing through causes a strong back-current. It is always better, if you have not been through before, to get help from the neighbouring cottage, refreshing yourself, if needed; and a

Eaton Bridge, Kelmscott, site of the last Thames flash-lock.

small quantity of the Englishmen's buck-sheesh (beer) will always find you a willing assistant. Sometimes it is wiser, and saves time, to drag the boat over (if you can), rather than pass through; but this must be a matter for consideration at the time.

Until the voyage that forms the basis for this study of the river, Eaton Bridge was the highest I had managed to come. From here on, I was breaking new ground, or rather water, since I had been to Buscot, St John's and Lechlade several times before but not by boat.

So it was pleasant to have an escort up the surprisingly long, straight and wide reach above the bridge. It was a Sandpiper, admittedly only a Common Sandpiper, but I was delighted with it. It led, in a series of short flights, all the way to Buscot.

There are no moorings between Eaton Hastings Bridge and Buscot Lock. There are two pill-boxes; the first having a hedge behind it, so that one can feel with relief that the garrison might have escaped in need: the second is sitting on such a thin neck of land that it seems in imminent danger of crossing the river, as no doubt it will, one day.

The country up this reach is noticeably more rolling. The river, after its straight, makes a sharp right-hand bend, following this with another to the left. Farmer's Weir, an undistinguished flash-lock which seems to have disappeared about 1770, used to lie halfway between Eaton and Buscot Locks. There is a largish clump of trees and tangled growth, on the left, about half a mile above Eaton, with a weir scour shape in the river, which seems a likely spot. The hairpin round the pill-box is followed by a violent left-hander, and so on. This is a highly skittish bit of river.

Between the two pill-boxes you will see a pair of cottages on the left and the remains of an inlet. This was a short canal that ran up to the cottages, which were known as Buscot Wharf.

Buscot, 'Burgweard's cottage', was the subject of an interesting experiment during the nineteenth century. Robert Campbell Curtis, who had made money in Australia, took Buscot House and proceeded to improve the lot of the local people by introducing industry to the village. He pioneered advanced farming methods, dug a reservoir near his house, and

pumped water up to it by means of steam turbines. He rebuilt Buscot village as a 'model', which is why church and village are now half a mile apart. He built a kiln for the manufacture of bricks, which were shipped out from Buscot Wharf. Lastly, he built a factory where the present Thames Water building is, above the lock, for the production of brandy from beetroot. This he solemnly exported to France! Alas, this last idea was not too successful and was of short duration. Now, all that really remains of all this energy is the sleepy hamlet

BUSCOT 1790

Fall 5'7" : 1.69 m / Deep

Upstream Start preparing as you swing left by the weir-stream bridge. The pilings are on the right, give no shore access, and are exposed to the old weir-stream, which issues from the left. Watch for the push from this. 200ft further up, there is a 40ft lay-by on the right, next to the lock.

Downstream The lock is clearly visible in good time. There are pilings on the right, without shore access, but easier than the lay-by on the left in a tail wind. This is a surprisingly difficult lock. There is a pull from both the old weir, on the right and the new, on the left. If you are approaching the left-hand bank, keep plenty of way on, or the main weir-stream will take you into the bank too early. Stand off too far and the old stream will stop you from getting to it at all. This is why the piling is easier. Nevertheless, in a strong stream, it will be difficult to get off this to enter the lock!

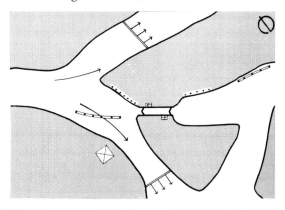

121

he built, and the reservoir, but what a man he must have been.

Do not pass under the bridge that suddenly presents itself, it is the new Buscot weir-stream. Instead, turn sharply left and then sharply right, and there is Buscot Lock. The weir-pool surrounds and several buildings at Buscot are now owned by the National Trust, who keep the place up very well. Beside the smart, new lock cottage is another, which is the oldest lock cottage on the river. It is now in private hands but is a funny, quaint little place, full of interest. Beyond it is the small building which, I am assured, used to hold the steam turbine for the Buscot House reservoir. You can still see the mark and axle supports of a mill-wheel, next to it.

Above the lock, there are two moorings, on each side of the first right-hander, opposite the inlet. The mooring upstream of the bend is better. There is another suicidal pill-box on the island opposite.

The spire of St Laurence, Lechlade, is now clearly visible above some distant trees. Buscot church and its old vicarage, with riverside garden, are on the left. They make a lovely, soft picture, nestling among the trees, although I was told that the churchyard is so wet that to be interred there is the next best thing to being buried at sea! There are now willows all along the left bank. The river makes an amazing loop to the right, past a rather bedraggled pill-box, and then loops crazily back to the left, after which it settles down, with three merely sharp bends. The last of these has a large basin, known as Bloomer's hole, whose origin is obscure.

Shortly above this basin take the left hand channel to St John's Lock, past the River Cole, whose fairly recent channel is on the left. (It used to flow in above the lock.) Up the weir-stream, to the right, is the confluence with the River Leach, and the mooring at the Trout Inn.

Lechlade takes its name from the River Leach, and from lade, meaning: to load, to take on a load. Thus, 'the wharf by the Leach'. Some authorities say it was named after the field by the wharf, which was called 'the Lade', but I think they confuse cause and effect.

Activity was stimulated by the monks of St John's Priory, early in the thirteenth century. They built a bridge, said by some to be third only to Radcot and Newbridge in antiquity. Thacker says 1229, which makes it only four

---

ST JOHN'S 1790

Fall 2′10″ : 0.85 m | Shallow | Sanitary station and pump-out

Upstream Start preparing as you enter the cut. There are pilings on the right, before the bridge, without access to the shore. Beyond the bridge is a basin, with lay-by on the left. An overspill weir discharges into this basin, which may be awkward in bad stream conditions.

The Sanitary Station and pump-out are also on the left in the basin. There is no hose, only a tap.

Downstream The lock is visible for some distance. In strong winds from the south-west, the pilings by the lock are extremely difficult to get on to. In these circumstances, the relief pilings, which are on the right, fifty yards before the lock, are the ones to use. The weir-stream leaves on the left, and is not a problem.

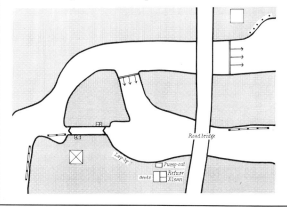

---

years younger than Radcot, and older than Newbridge. It seems to have been on the site of an ancient ford. They then obtained the right to hold a fair, in 1234, after which the place became a thriving port. Thacker has an excerpt from the seventeenth century Baskervile MS, from which I quote:

> ... in the Meadow below ye bridge on Glocester shier side ... Oxford boats & others resort to sell Ale, Beef & Carrots, & to carry goods. ... at a Mill below this Meadow, Leach flu runs into Tems. ... I have seen 6 or 8 boats togeither at their Wharfe. ... besides corn. ... from Severn and Avon ... in Carts & Wagons by land great weights. ... of

MAP 5

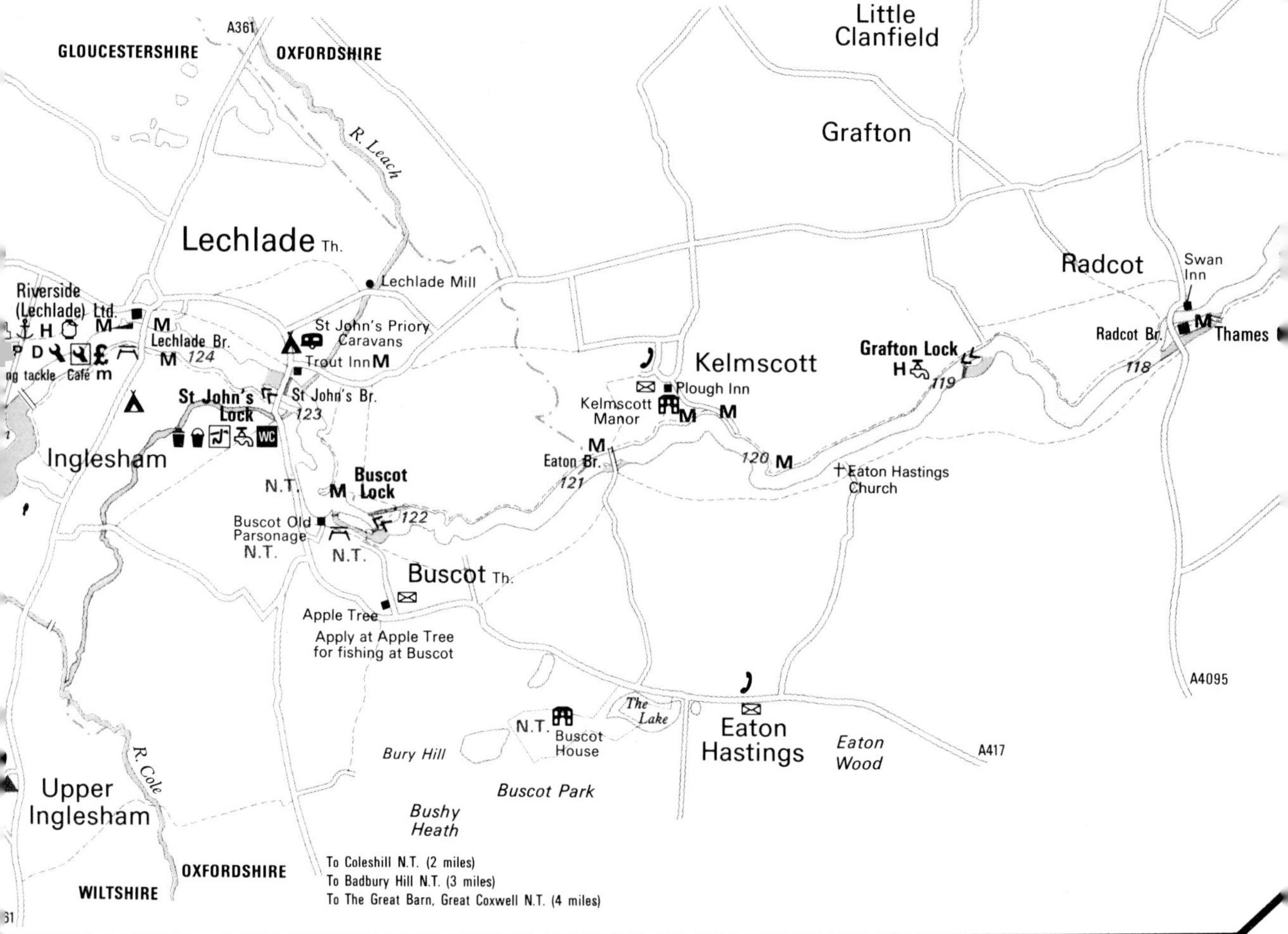

GLOUCESTERSHIRE   OXFORDSHIRE

A361

R. Leach

Clanfield

Little
Clanfield

Grafton

Lechlade Th.

• Lechlade Mill

Radcot

Swan
Inn

Riverside
(Lechlade) Ltd.
M
Lechlade Br.
M *124*

St John's Priory
Caravans
Trout Inn **M**

Grafton Lock
H *119*

Radcot Br.
M Thames
118

P D
ng tackle Café **m**

St John's
Lock

St John's Br.
123

♪
Kelmscott

Plough Inn
M M   **M**

Inglesham

WC

N.T.

M
**Buscot
Lock**

Kelmscott
Manor

Eaton Br.
121

120 **M**

✝ Eaton Hastings
Church

Buscot Old
Parsonage
N.T.

122

Buscot Th.

N.T.

A4095

Apple Tree

Apply at Apple Tree
for fishing at Buscot

R. Cole

**Upper
Inglesham**

N.T.
Buscot
House

*The
Lake*

♪

**Eaton
Hastings**

*Eaton
Wood*

A417

Bury Hill

Buscot Park

*Bushy
Heath*

OXFORDSHIRE

WILTSHIRE

To Coleshill N.T. (2 miles)
To Badbury Hill N.T. (3 miles)
To The Great Barn, Great Coxwell N.T. (4 miles)

61

K

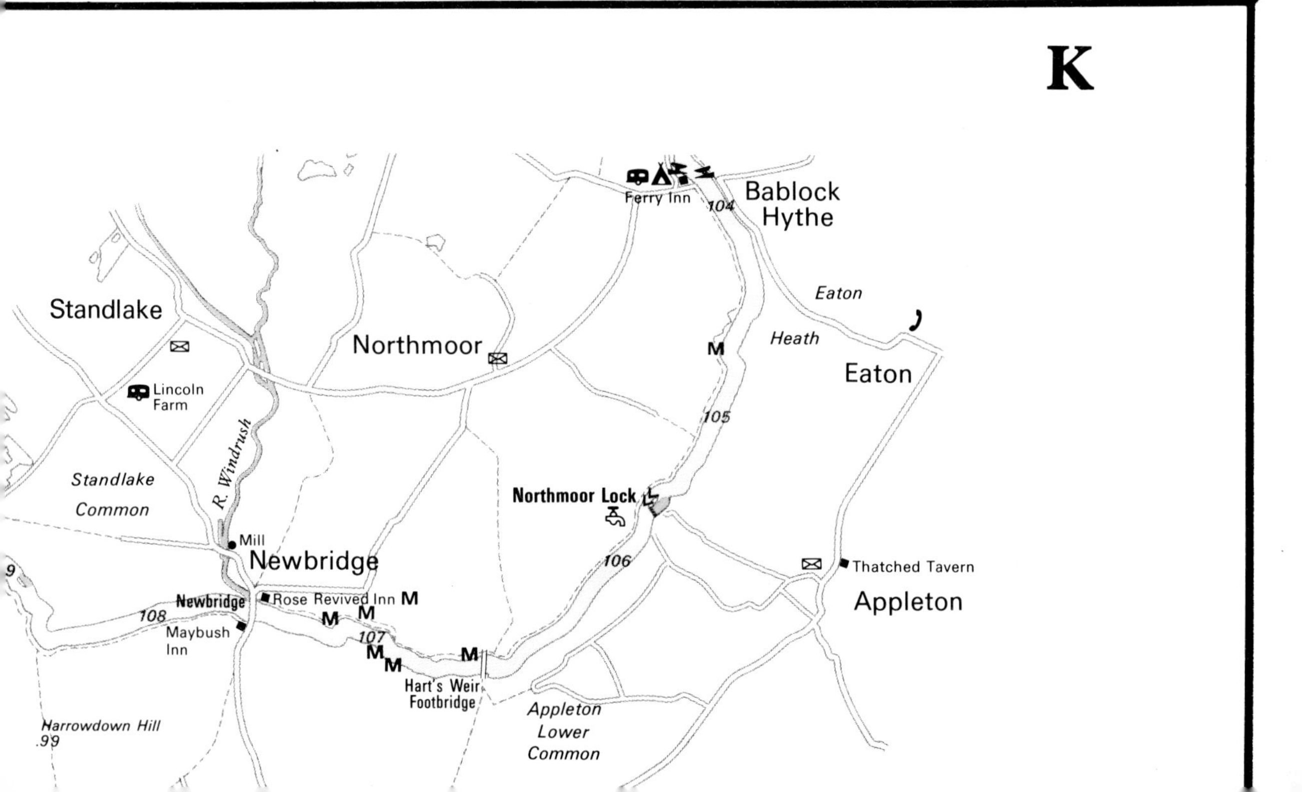

Ferry Inn
104

**Bablock
Hythe**

Standlake

Northmoor

*Eaton
Heath*

M

♪

Eaton

Lincoln
Farm

105

*Standlake
Common*

R. Windrush

Northmoor Lock

Mill

Newbridge

106

■ Thatched Tavern

Appleton

Newbridge
108

Rose Revived Inn **M**
M   **M**

Maybush
Inn

107
M
M M

Hart's Weir
Footbridge

*Appleton
Lower
Common*

Narrowdown Hill
.99

9

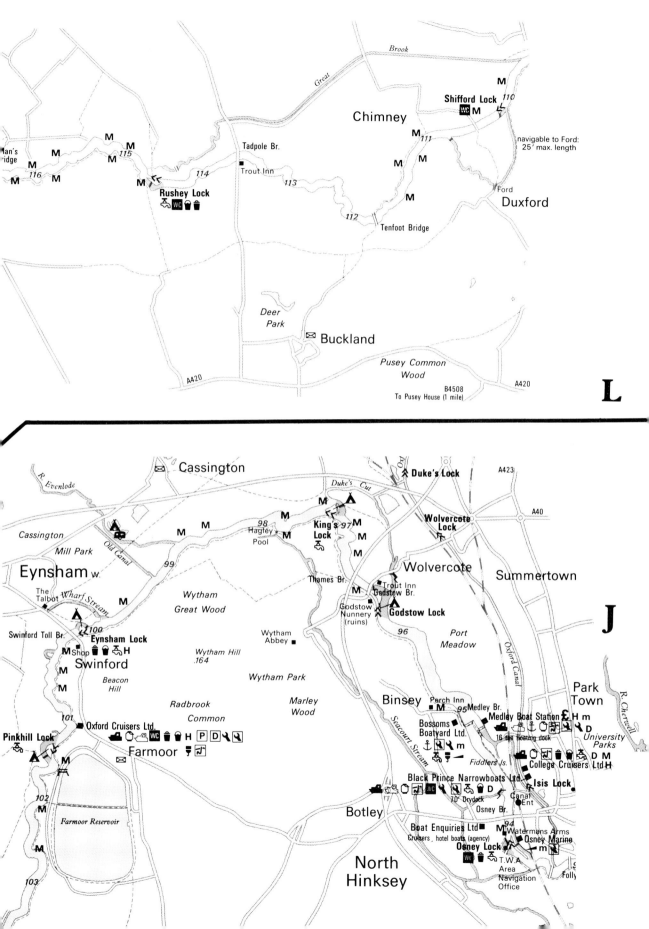

L

J

Chimney

Shifford Lock 110
navigable to Ford:
25' max. length

115
114
113
Tadpole Br.
Trout Inn
111
112
Tenfoot Bridge
Ford
Duxford

116
Rushey Lock

Deer Park
Buckland
Pusey Common Wood
A420
B4508
To Pusey House (1 mile)
A420

R. Evenlode
Cassington
Duke's Cut
Duke's Lock
A423
Oxy
A40
A423

Cassington
Mill Park
Old Canal
98
Hagley Pool
King's Lock 97
Wolvercote Lock
Summertown

Eynsham w.
99
Thames Br.
Wolvercote
Trout Inn
Godstow Br.

The Talbot
Wharf Stream
Wytham Great Wood
Godstow Nunnery (ruins)
Godstow Lock
Port Meadow
96
Oxford Canal
Park Town
R. Cherwell

Swinford Toll Br.
100
Eynsham Lock
Wytham Abbey
Wytham Hill .164

Shop H
Swinford
Beacon Hill
Wytham Park
Binsey
Perch Inn 95
Medley Br.
Medley Boat Station H m

Radbrook Common
Marley Wood
Bossoms Boatyard Ltd.
16 ton floating dock
University Parks

101
Oxford Cruisers Ltd.
WC H P D
Farmoor
Fiddlers Js.
College Cruisers Ltd H
D M

Pinkhill Lock
Seacourt Stream
Black Prince Narrowboats Ltd.
70' Drydock
Isis Lock
Canal Ent.

102
Farmoor Reservoir
Botley
Osney Br.
Boat Enquiries Ltd.
Cruisers, hotel boats (agency)
94
Watermans Arms
Osney Marine
m

103
North Hinksey
Osney Lock
Wf
T.W.A. Area Navigation Office
Folly

Cheshire Cheese. ... & other goods comes from London-ward. ... hether & are sent as aforesaid by land to Severn and thence in Boats to Bristol and elswere, & in ships to Ireland.

At some point, I infer after 1750, activity moved up river about a mile, to the present town and wharves by Half-penny Bridge. I suggest that Bloomer's Hole was formed by a flash-lock erected below the wharves, to give deep water at them and provide a flash for down-going barges. (cf The Swift Ditch). In this respect, I find the lack of any evidence of a lock at the present site before the middle of the eighteenth century of significance.

124 From St John's Lock, a tower has appeared beneath the spire of St Laurence's Church. The somewhat breathless excitement of the last two miles gives way to a gentle meander between low meadow banks. There is one more pill-box but no moorings between the lock and the town mooring, which is on the left, before the bridge, and runs for about 150 yards.

You can moor, for a fee, opposite this, at the New Inn, or there is mooring 150 yards above the bridge, for a fee to Riverside Lechlade Ltd, who offer fuel, water, chandlery and a cafe.

Lechlade Bridge is known as Half-penny Bridge, because that was its toll when built in the late eighteenth century. The old toll-house still stands at the town end.

Lechlade is a most attractive little town, with all the necessary shops and banks. At its height it was prosperous indeed from the barge trade, which probably accounts for the presence of three more pubs, the Red Lion, the Swan and the Crown, as well as the New Inn already mentioned, and the Riverside, which is a modern and recent addition. Now, it is comfortable, standing a little diffidently back from the river, presumably to avoid flooding, a circumstance which adds to the pleasure of its prospect from the Thames.

Above the bridge, there is about half a mile of navigable water, past the Riverside Marina, until Inglesham Footbridge. Turn below this, there are numerous shallows above it. The Thames continues to the left. The River Coln joins from the right. Ahead was the start of the Thames and Severn Canal, and there is a pleasant house, the old canal round-house and a short inlet of about 10 feet, with a bank across it, which is all that is left at the Thames end. The canal was built about 1790, and was remarkably beautiful but never profitable, mainly due to the failure of the Thames Commissioners to keep their water navigable, and the excessive tolls charged by the mill-owning lock-keepers. The railway finally killed it, as it did the trading Thames itself, but it was still navigable well into this century. Perhaps one day it will flow again.

Since we cannot go on, it is only left to drop back down to the mooring at Lechlade, for that best part of any Thames day, peaceful contemplation of the day's events, and planning for the morrow.

Journey's end. The head of navigation.

WATERMANSHIP

THE WRECK

Wrecked on an uninhabited island

THE ART OF AVOIDING SHIPWRECK

ONE OF THE curiosities about boating is the assumption that newcomers will somehow automatically know what to do and what the various boating terms used mean, without being told. Rivermen have either been boating all their lives, in which case such things are actually second nature to them, or they had to learn the hard way and do not see why others should have it easier.

The results of this assumption can be seen by anyone spending a few minutes at a lock, or in watching the passing scene from the river bank. This chapter is an attempt to set the matter a bit straighter, to improve the level of watermanship and thus the peace, comfort and safety of river users as a whole.

The main problem in this subject is simply communication. A Riverman in full flow might as well be speaking a foreign language as far as a novice is concerned. You and your crew may elect to speak land English or water English, or a combination of both. That is unimportant. What does matter is that everybody understands everybody else, especially in emergency.

Although you may be an expert, you will often have crew members who are not, which is why the information included here assumes complete ignorance of the subject. There will happily always be moments of pure bliss. I took

a friend through her first lock where the keeper, holding out his hand for the stern rope, was startled to have it shaken fervently! On the other hand, the case of a hirer complaining to a lock-keeper that pulling the 'Stop' button switched off the engine but did not stop the boat, may become less frequent.

The information is in alphabetical order for speedy reference, although this does have the effect of fragmenting the narrative.

TAKE CARE ON THE RIVER

As a general principle, impress on your crew that the Thames like all rivers is potentially dangerous and must be treated with respect at all times. This remark applies especially to those who have been on the Broads or the canals, or both, and who regard the River as a rather narrow Broad or unusually wide canal. It is neither.

The Thames is usually deeper than a man can stand and the edges normally shelve steeply. After heavy rain, especially in the spring and autumn, it can be swift running and awesomely powerful, particularly in the vicinity of weirs. So, always err on the side of safety and caution.

When moving on deck, from one end to the other, crew should always hold the rail with one hand.

RIVER TERMS

Abaft Behind.

Abeam The area that lies to each side of a boat.

About To GO ABOUT, in the case of a motor-cruiser, means to turn round.

Aft The rear part of a boat. It varies with each boat. In a rear cockpit cruiser it would include the cockpit, while in a centre cockpit boat it

NAUTICAL WORDS

would be the rear cabin, which might be called the AFTER cabin, and whatever deck space lay to the rear of that.

After deck The space from which a narrow-boat is controlled. Otherwise, any deck space that is at the stern of the boat.

Ahead 1 The scene in front of the boat. Used to draw attention to what lies in the direction of travel: 'Do you see that buoy ahead?'
2 GO AHEAD; SLOW AHEAD; FULL AHEAD. Instructions to the person working the GEAR LEVER, meaning: 'Cause the propeller to turn to drive the boat forward.' (See STOPPING)
3 GOING AHEAD. Proceeding in a forward direction.
4 'AHEAD!' Used as a warning to another boat crew that they are in danger of running into something, probably you. Shout 'ahead skiff' or 'look ahead eight', as appropriate.

Ahoy A warning shout, used to attract the attention of another crew. Use it in conjunction with the boat's name, colour or type

Ait See EYOT

Amidships The centre section of a boat. It has no definite limits, lying between FORWARD and AFT. It is usually reduced to 'MIDSHIPS.

Anchor You will have (or should have, and get one if you have not), at least one anchor aboard. There is no reason why you should not use this for anchoring in the stream, except that you have to allow for the boat to swing right round on the end of it, and if this blocks, or could block, the stream, then clearly it is not practical. There are places, but not many. The main purpose of having an anchor is as a last line of defence when the engine has failed or the drive has sheared and you are about to disappear over a weir. In other words, you will only ever want it once in a lifetime but, when you do, it will matter awfully. So discover where it is and ensure that it is secured to the boat. You would be amazed how many people have solemnly paid out the anchor *and* all its rope, because they did not make that check.

There are at least two sorts of anchor. One looks just like an anchor, but the other has ears locked under a collar when not in use. Before dropping it in the water, you have to release the collar. Check what you have got and make sure you know how to use it in a blind panic. When using the anchor, particularly in any sort of stream, do not make the mistake of using too little rope. Remember, it will be at least six ft to the bottom of the river. Then, the anchor has to lie on its side and be trawled along until it digs in or snags on something. As far as possible, you will want to pull it straight along the river bed, as any upward angle will tend to stop it digging in. So 24 ft of rope or chain would be necessary in normal circumstances. When you have paid out what you need, secure the rope to a deck bollard.

Astern 1 The scene behind the boat. Used to draw attention to what is happening to the rear. 'Have you noticed that eight approaching fast astern?'
2 GO ASTERN; SLOW ASTERN; FULL ASTERN. Typical instructions to the person working the gear lever, meaning: 'Cause the propeller to turn so as to drive the boat backwards.' (See STOPPING)
3 GOING ASTERN. Proceeding backwards.

Beam Width. The extreme width of the boat, from gunwale to gunwale at its widest point.

Below Not on deck. To 'go below' is to enter the cabin or saloon space.

Bilges The area between the bottom of the boat and the lowest deck. Here collects any water that falls into the boat, or comes in, through the fabric. There will be a bilge-pump aboard, and this should be used to pump the bilges dry daily, or as often as experience dictates. (My narrow boat needs pumping about twice a year, but daily is more usual.)

Boat-hook An excellent instrument, about 12 ft long, having a metal point with a hook about 2 in short of this, a bit like a Beefeater's pike! It can be used for pushing one end of the boat off the bank, against a wind; to pull the boat against a bank, either by hooking the hook round something, or by driving it into the ground; and for fishing things out of the river, like a towel or the dog. (It is just the thing to hook round a dog collar.)

CAUTION: Do NOT use the point for pushing yourself away from another boat, particularly a wooden one. It can do a lot of damage. Either reverse the boat-hook or, better still, slide the point over his hand rail, so that the back of the hook does the pushing.

Bollard a 'T' shaped device, screwed to the deck of a boat and also to be found at most locks and many mooring places, to which mooring ropes are attached.
Securing to a bollard: see KNOTS.
(See also 'Locks and Locking'.)

Bow Pronounced 'bough' (as cow), from which it derives. The front end of the boat. Also, BOWS, being the whole bow-shaped part.

Bridges Bridges require thought and care, where they have piers built into the river. These piers form an obstruction to the smooth flow of the current, and the increased stream which results from this is further complicated by the displaced water rushing into the arched spaces, creating turmoil and eddies. To add to this, bridge builders in the old days tended to take the line across the river which suited them, without regard for the problems of river traffic. They probably still do, but it is now mercifully cheaper to throw a span clean across the river, so that it does not matter.

As a general principle, approach piered bridges with good steerage way but with power in hand. Always aim for the middle of the arch you choose to take and always take the centre arch unless this will cause difficulty with an oncoming boat, or unless the navigation notes suggest otherwise. Never cut a corner in your approach. Open up the arch until you can see both walls, right through the bridge. In a strong stream, be ready for the current to pull you towards one side or the other, so that you can steer or accelerate your way out of trouble. Unless there is another problem, never slow down in these circumstances.

Always give way to craft running down river, which necessarily have less control than craft pushing against the stream. Make a clear choice of arch. I once watched fascinated as the cruiser

ahead of me drove straight into a pier at Newbridge!

It may be that you are running down stream and wish to tie up above a bridge. If there is a stream running, or if you have any doubts, it is much better to shoot the bridge, turn below it, and come back up. Otherwise, of you miscalculate, you may end up broadside across the bridge. There was a certain destroyer did that in London, you may remember, and I saw a motor-cruiser do it at Wallingford. Once you do, you will never get off unaided and risk being turned over in a strong stream.

Unless the helmsman is good at it, having the fend-offs down at bridges is good policy.

In the past year or two, there has been an increasing tendency for the hooligan element to jump off bridges when craft are passing. Usually the idea is to frighten you and to splash you. Occasionally, they aim to land aboard, or climb aboard. You can prevent this last by lifting your fend-offs. With large spans, like Donnington Bridge, you can spot them preparing. They stand on your side, until they can see your line, then run across and wait for you to appear. Once they run, change course radically and you will appear 20 ft away from where you are expected. With small spans, like Godstow or Wallingford, you have to run the gauntlet.

The size of the problem may be judged from the fact that I have been attacked at all three of the bridges mentioned, during the last two years, as well as being interfered with by swimmers above Abingdon Bridge, who closed from opposite sides. Swimmers cannot hurt you if your fend-offs are lifted.

The police do now seem to take the matter seriously, although they were quite diffident to start with. My incident at Godstow took place while a Panda car with two policemen in it was actually standing on the bridge! Neither got out while the bridge remained in my sight. Eventually someone will be killed, and then the practice will no doubt cease. Legally, a boater whose propellor damages a swimmer may be liable to the full rigours of the law.

Buoys Floating, anchored markers, typically found marking a course for sailing dinghies, occasionally acting as tie-up points for private launches, but usually and most importantly, as hazard and channel warnings.

These are used to mark obstructions such as wrecks or sandbars, and you should steer clear of them. As a convention, red represents port and green starboard. Therefore, you leave red buoys to port and green ones to starboard. There is a complication. That instruction applies if you are heading up river. If you are heading down river it is fairly important to do the opposite. I once hired a boat and came across my first buoy, green, about 250 yards down from the boatyard. I left it to starboard and spent an interesting 20 minutes getting off the sand-bar. In all the excitement of setting off, I had forgotten to reverse my brain!

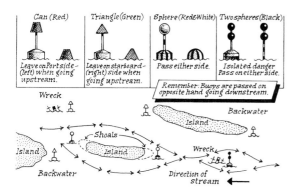

Cabin Bedroom.

Cast off Release the mooring ropes. Start off. (See MOORING).

Cat-walk The boarding attached to the tops of lock gates, allowing passage across a lock. Also, the planks that enable one to reach the bank from a lock piling.

Cockpit The area from which a boat is controlled, if it is a centre or rear cockpit cruiser. It usually doubles as a sun-deck, since it can be uncovered if the weather is reasonable.

Deck The floor. Especially in a cruiser, the walkway and standing space outside.

Displacement The volume of water which a boat moves aside when it is floated. This volume of water has to be moved continually as the boat moves, causing the wave formation which accompanies a boat and is called its WASH.

Draught (Pronounced DRAFT) The depth of water displaced by a boat.

Eight A racing boat, so called because it has eight oarsmen. There are also 'fours' and 'pairs'. (See SHELL).

Eyot (Pronounced EIGHT) Also AIT. A small island.

Freeboard The shortest distance between waterline and gunwale constitutes the freeboard.

Flags Only the red ensign is allowed on the stern of your boat unless you are particularly entitled to fly another. The fine for ignoring this is £500, and you will not get through a lock unnoticed. Any pennant, such as your local club flag, the RNLI pennant, or the skull and crossbones, if you are a pirate, will have to be flown from a flag mast on the cabin top. Foreign nationals are allowed to fly their national ensign astern (and should fly the red ensign also as a courtesy if they do).

Fend-offs Fend-offs are plastic, rubber or rope, sausage or ball shaped objects which, when hung over the side, ward off the worst effects of your own or others' miscalculations. They prevent damage to your boat when it is moored against the bank or moving through a lock and secondarily, they prevent damage caused by other people hitting you when you are moored. It follows that fend-offs have no function when the boat is cruising, and rivermen will raise them in these conditions and stow them neatly along the gunwales. You may be too idle to do that, and certainly you will not attract the attention of many people by leaving them down. There is one thing you *can* do to improve the appearance of your boat and that is to make sure they are all level and particularly that they do not drag in the water. That really does look scruffy. This exercise has the added advantage that you will notice all the fend-offs that are about to come undone and be lost.

It is well to note that hands and feet do not make good fend-offs, although the inexperienced use them all the time. Crew should not dangle legs over the side to push away a wall. It is so natural to do this that it takes will-power not to. Although the water is carrying the weight of a boat, allowing an object weighing several tons to be moved quite easily, it is quite

Neatly levelled fend-offs compliment this hire-boat as it leaves Shiplake lock.

a different matter to stop it moving by means of soft tissue and bone.

For the same sort of reason, it is good watermanship for crew to sit down in fend-off situations, like mooring and locking. It is remarkable what a shock it is to stop suddenly even from 1 or 2 knots, and it is easy for an off-balance crewman to go straight over the front on these occasions. So, when he has sorted out his rope and put the correct sections in each hand, he should sit on, or lean against, the cabin.

Fire-liquid gas Your cooking, and often your heating, will be done with liquid petroleum gas. This has one nasty peculiarity. It is heavier than air. So, if it escapes, it drops to the bilges, in which it collects and can blow you out of the water. So, make sure the supply is operating correctly, always light a match *before* turning on the gas, and never leave a gas appliance unattended. If you do, and find it has gone out and the gas is still on, get off the boat and find

help. Do not in any circumstances light a match or start the engine, until you have done so.

The boat will be equipped with fire-extinguishers. Find out where they are and how they work.

Forward The front end of the boat, from amidships to the bows. This is usually corrupted to FORR'ARD.

Galley Kitchen.

Gear lever/throttle Most Thames motor-cruisers are equipped with a lever which is pushed forward to make the boat move in that direction, and pulled back to make it reverse. In the centre of its travel it is in neutral. There will also be a knob or lever which will engage or disengage the drive shaft and propeller.

Once the drive shaft is engaged, the speed of the propellor is regulated by the lever. With the lever pushed right forward, the propellor will turn 'full ahead'; when it is pulled back, 'full astern'.

The engine may also be used for charging the batteries, when the boat is moored for an appreciable time, and sometimes for running the central heating. In these cases the drive must be disengaged.

Gunwale (Pronounced GUNN'L). Originally the gun wall on ships of war, this is the point where the sides of the boat meet the deck. There is usually a ridge at this point, to which the fixings for fend-offs are attached, and which helps to keep the crew from slipping overboard.

Hand signals There are no laid down hand signals, you can make them up as you go along. I have always found them very helpful. They are the only signals I would dare to make to a lock-keeper, for instance. With the hand, you can tell him you are not going to use his lock, but are turning round. You can ask him which side of the lock he wants you to use, or tell him which side you propose to use. It is always a good idea to wave someone past who you know wants to overtake. At the very least, you will tell him that you know he is there and will not turn suddenly across his path.

Hard over See STEERING.

Helm The steering wheel or tiller.

Horn The horn on a boat is not like that in a car. That is, you do not use it to let that idiot over there know what you think of him. Nor do you use it to require space for passage. It is not an offensive weapon, in other words. You use it to tell others what *you* are doing. There is a standard code:—

1 short blast: I am turning to starboard.
2 short blasts: I am turning to port.
3 short blasts: My engines are going astern.
4 short blasts: I am unable to manoeuvre.
4 short blasts, pause, 1 short blast:
   I am turning round to starboard.
4 short blasts: pause, 2 short blasts:
   I am turning round to port.

You will already have spotted the reason why you will hardly ever hear a horn used on the river! Effective is it not?

In emergency, a LONG BLAST will at least make everyone look at you, and this is now also an approved signal.

As to the standard code, even if you learn it by heart, how many people will understand what you mean? Furthermore, the only reason you would wish to tell someone you were turning to port is if you were thereby going to cross in front of him, and that would be bad watermanship anyway.

Never hoot to obtain the services of a lock-keeper....

Keel The lowest point of the boat, below the waterline. Actually, the longitudinal member from which all the rest of the boat is built up.

Knot (See SPEED). A knot is a nautical mile, one minute of a great circle of the earth, 2026 yards.

Knots There are lots of seamanlike knots, and they are difficult to remember. Unless you are unlucky, you will only need two, and possibly a reef knot, which you should know already. The two are the clove hitch and the round turn and two half hitches.

1 *The Clove Hitch* This is an excellent and simple knot for use when the mooring post is short enough for you to drop the knot over the top, such as those you have with you on the boat. It has a tendency to work loose slowly, when applied to a smooth post, so I do not use it over-night.

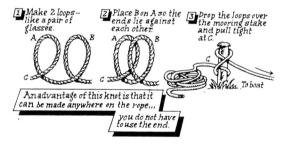

2 *The Round Turn & Two Half Hitches* If this is the only knot in your repertoire, you will come to no harm. It is precisely what it says it is. You can tie up with a plain rope's end or with a loop, if it is too much trouble to pull yards of rope through each time. You can add further hitches, if you do not feel confident about what you have done, and you can pass the final loop over the mooring stake when you have finished, as an added security. It is very reliable, provided that you lock the two hitches together as you make them.

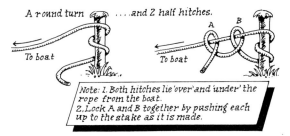

A round turn ....and 2 half hitches.

To boat

To boat

Note: 1. Both hitches lie 'over' and 'under' the rope from the boat.
2. Lock A and B together by pushing each up to the stake as it is made.

Apart from these two knots, you will come across mooring rings and bollards at most public moorings. With a ring, the best solution is to pass your rope through it and make it fast to your own bollard, on board, using locking twists over the arms. You can tie directly to the mooring place bollard, or pass your rope under its arms and back to yours. At a busy mooring, this is more acceptable socially, because it does not clutter up the bollard for someone else. (Bollards are discussed more fully under 'Locks and Locking'.)

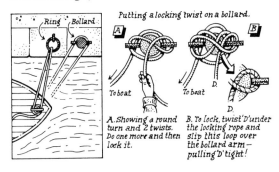

Ring   Bollard

Putting a locking twist on a bollard.

A   B

To boat   To boat

D.

A. Showing a round turn and 2 twists. Do one more and then lock it.

B. To lock, twist 'D' under the locking rope and slip this loop over the bollard arm — pulling 'D' tight!

Lee Out of the wind. The side of a boat which is downwind. A lee shore is that against which a wind is blowing a boat, and can be difficult to get off. (See MOORING)

Life-ring See MAN OVERBOARD!

Life-jacket If you cannot swim, wear a life-jacket. If your crew are young, even if they can swim well, always put life-jackets on whenever the boat is travelling. Make the rule simple and have no exceptions. 'I am going below to read' is the obvious one. Be firm. When you want your crew at mooring stations, which is the moment of maximum risk, the crew below will either forget to put it on, or take so long coming on deck as to mess up the whole manoeuvre.

Locker Cupboard.

Locks and Locking *Approaching the lock* If you have never been through a lock before, try, if at all possible, to go downstream at the start of your voyage, even if you only pass through one lock in this direction. This is because you will then be running into a full lock and out of an empty one, which is very much easier, given reasonable conditions of wind and stream, than the other way round, as we shall see.

As you draw near the lock, make early preparations for landing. Slow down. If you have lifted your fend-offs, drop them. Have your crew at mooring stations, making sure the ropes are untangled. When you are about 100 yards from the lock, you should be assessing whether you will be tying up before the lock, or going straight in. If the gates are open, you will go straight in, making sure nobody is coming out before you do. At this point, look for the lock-keeper. If he does nothing, or is not in sight, you are probably free to go in. Or he may wave you in, in which case acknowledge by raising your arm. He may also indicate which side he wants you (if there is another craft there already), in which case acknowledge.

Probably the gates will not be open. In this case you can look for boats in the lock. If you cannot see any, it is either because they are at the bottom of the lock, which means there will be a delay of at least five minutes, or because there are not any. If there are boats, are they going up or down? If, for instance, you are going downstream and there is a boat in the lock and the lock-keeper is at your end, working the machinery, he is either about to open the lock, or has just closed it, so you would be better to stooge, dead slow, until you know which it is, than to tie up, with all the excitement that entails, only to untie again immediately.

Usually you will tie up before using the lock. This is the only occasion when you should not turn round when mooring downstream. This is because the problems of manouvring in a lock cut are greater than those of tying up. There is not usually a current running close to a lock either. The lock will either have a set of vertical white posts, joined together by horizontal ones, known as pilings and walings respectively, or a hard stand, or both. They are both equipped with bollards, to which you can tie up. Your ideal approach to these landing points is at minimum steerage speed and at an angle of incidence of about 20 degrees. That should ensure that your bow is going to touch, or be close enough for your bow crew to loop his rope over a bollard, or step off.

When you are sure you have your bow in, put the rudder hard over to bring in the stern, put the gear in neutral and, as she lies up to the mooring, go astern to stop the boat. If you have got it right, both crew will slip their ropes over the nearest bollards, or step onto the pilings and hold the boat neatly in position. If you have got it wrong, at least your bow crew will have done this. If he puts his rope round a bollard or piling and holds on, leaving say three ft of loose rope between the bollard and the boat, there should be no difficulty for you in putting the rudder hard over and driving the stern in. The loose rope is crucial, for if the bow is tightly held, there is no way you will get the stern to swing.

Incidentally, proper rivermen never step onto the lock pilings. They always judge their approach to perfection and simply slip their ropes over the waiting bollards. I sometimes manage this too, and no doubt so do you. Nevertheless, lock pilings are usually crowded with people who have failed to be as accurate as this and have stepped off to make sure of their landing. Let us suppose you failed to get your bow in. Either your stern crewman must pass his rope round a bollard and hand the loose end to you, while he hurries up to the front end for your bow crew to throw him the rope, or you must stop the boat and rush to receive it yourself. Again, for it is the usual beginner's

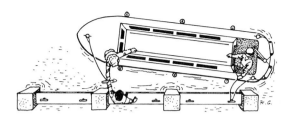

mistake, the stern rope must not be pulled tight until you have the bow rope ashore.

Which brings me to the snag, which you may already have spotted. The pilings are 24 ft apart and the horizontal bit for walking on is about 1 ft wide. There are bollards every 8 ft for you to trip over. There is water on both sides. The only way round an upright is to hug it to you while you swing out round it. So, rushing along 30 ft of this is a purely relative term! Mind you, the vertical bits are awfully comforting if you are inclined to be dizzy, or need some leverage. (Thames Water have now started fitting walkways to pile moorings, which will be a great help.)

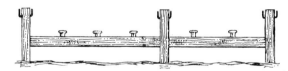

There may be a moment when you decide that you have made such a mess of the whole thing, you will have to abandon the attempt. In this case, collect such ropes as have gone ashore, and any crew that you can easily recover, back off until you are far enough away, and start all over again. This moment will be when you are too far away to put either crewman ashore, or when you have a stern rope ashore but cannot reach the bow rope. Leaving a crewman on the mooring is a good idea, since it is easier to throw a rope ashore to someone than to step ashore clutching it.

Incidentally, where Thames Water own the river bank, the pilings are slowly being removed as they wear out and replaced by concrete hardstands. These make life much easier, although they do not look so attractive. The basic technique does not change though.

Please remember when you come to a lock mooring that the three cruisers behind you are going to have to use it as well. One frequently comes across people who are so appalled at the prospect of tying up to the mooring posts, that they grasp the first bollard they come to. It is much more difficult to pass such people and moor above them than to come straight in, particularly as they usually throw a temper tantrum if you go past, on the grounds that you are queue-barging. So stand bravely on up towards the lock, and moor as far up as you reasonably can. It will actually help you to make fine adjustments to your approach angle, so your final mooring will be more likely to be good anyway.

On the subject of queue-barging, it is very much frowned on and is one of the few things that will upset a lock-keeper. So, even if you do have to pass someone who has moored badly, wave him in ahead of you, and in general look out for others who may be waiting to use the lock as well. They may be stooging, for instance, or they may have stopped on the opposite bank to the lock mooring. If someones carves you up, do not run your boat into danger, give way.

Bollard While we are waiting for the lock to open, a word about bollards. We have discussed tying up to them. In a lock, or on a lock piling, they are more often used for leverage, or simply to hold on to. For a temporary hold, pass the rope round the bollard and hold on to the free end. If you are ashore, stand over the bollard, and you will have applied enough leverage to hold the boat while the lock is working. If you need more help, take another half turn round the bollard. To hold this position, while you help someone, or switch off the engine, jam the end.

When in a lock, the simple loop method,

either from on board or ashore, is perfectly safe and manageable, and bears no relationship to trying to hold on by the chains on the lock wall. If the boat pulls your arms out, a child of ten could hold it without difficulty, using the second method. In this case, take great care that the loose end is not jammed by the fixed end as it passes under the arm of the bollard. Never leave a fixed rope in a lock while this is filling or emptying. If you do, the effect may be similar to that shown below which is not desirable!

Lastly, when working through a bollard in a lock, never bend down to it, or let your hand come near it. There is a notice about this in every lock, but the automatic reaction to a problem at a bollard is to take your hand to it, and this is something you must teach your crew not to do. Stand over the bollard and work the rope from above. It is a technique you will soon master.

Entering the lock Whether you have tied up before the lock or not, your final approach will be the same. Turn off any radio or tape recorder. Secure the dog. Post crew at bow and stern. Your speed should be such that you have good steerage way but slow enough to give you time to sort out disasters. This means that you should have finished slowing down before you get to the lock, and the only momentum is what you have applied for the purpose of locking.

Position yourself so as to approach the gates in mid-stream, unless you are the last boat in to a crowded lock and must simply edge in as best you can. This will give you a good view and leave you room to manoeuvre. Never allow yourself to creep round the edge of the opening.

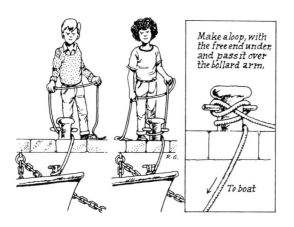

Make a loop, with the free end under, and pass it over the bollard arm.

To boat

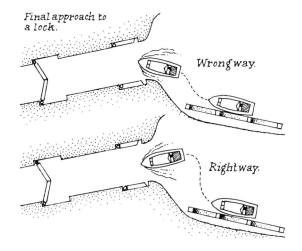

Final approach to a lock.

Wrong way.

Right way.

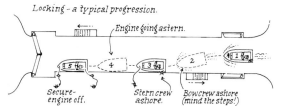

Locking – a typical progression.

Engine going astern.

Secure-engine off.

Stern crew ashore.

Bowcrew ashore (mind the steps!)

It may seem simpler, but you are bound to hit something and bounce off across the lock at the worst possible moment.

As you pass the gates, steer for the side and put the gear lever in neutral. If you are steering on the left of the boat, you will moor naturally on the left, because you can see the exact relationship between the boat and the lock side. Circumstances, like a boat already in on the left, instructions from the lock-keeper, or even a high wind, may make you vary this approach, in which case remember to tell your crew of your intentions in good time, particularly as your stern crewman will probably have to use a different rope.

Your approach to the lock-side should be at a fairly sharp angle, to make sure the bow goes into the side. Once you are confident of this, hard right rudder to drive the stern in and, when it is in properly, full astern until she stops moving forward; neutral; check that the crew are both ashore and holding you to the correct bollards. (Is there anyone to come in behind you?) Switch off engine. You must always do this in a lock, the lock-keeper will ask you to if you do not.

The above is a typical locking procedure. *Your* boat may need power all the way, to keep steerage way. You will probably need a short burst of engine and lots of rudder to push the stern in, in any case. Do not worry how early your crew step off. They can easily walk beside you as the boat runs up the lock, but the sooner they are ashore, the sooner you will know you have done a good job.

Notes:

1 The cruiser is in mid-stream. It can go left or right.
2 The bow crew is ashore early.
3 The stern crew is ashore. Note the bow crew is not pulling his rope tight, leaving the stern free to move.
4 The engine is going astern in plenty of time, in case of emergency.
5 Secured fore and aft. The perfect locking manoeuvre.

Normal locking problems The things that are liable to go wrong and which a skipper should think about beforehand are:

1 Too slow and therefore without steerage way at critical moments. Maintain good steerage way.

2 Failing to bring the bow in close enough for the bow crew to step ashore. This is either because the stern has come in too early, or because the approach is too flat to the side of the lock. In this case it may well be the boat's own displacement that is keeping it off the side! Remember that it takes a good deal of movement of the stern to alter the position of the bows, and at slow speed, in a narrow space, you do not have the steering room you need. Get the bow in, even if you have to hit the side with it.

3 Failing to get the stern in. This is because the bow crew is pulling too tightly, or because of loss of steerage way. Check that the bow is held loosely, put the rudder hard over and give a quick burst on the engine.

4 Failing to stop. This is particularly embarrassing in a lock, but it happens all the time if you let anyone else steer for you. The helmsman is so uptight about steerage way, getting the bow in, driving the stern in and being sure everyone is ashore, that he forgets about the throttle, and proceeds at about three

knots, straight for the end doors, with the crew running alongside. If a beginner is on the helm, be close enough to shout 'Stop!', or 'Reverse'. The other reason for failing to stop is stalling the engine. This is probably through going straight from forward to reverse without pausing in the neutral position. Exercise yourself in panic starting procedures. Then, you will not go numb with shock when it happens. As long as the crew are ashore, no great harm should result anyway. But, crew do need to be instructed beforehand, or they will simply stand and watch, instead of catching you on a couple of bollards and pulling.

Locking up Locking down is easier than locking up, because in the latter case you are at the bottom of the lock when you enter it. In a shallow lock, 4 ft or less, this is not all that dramatic, since one can still scramble ashore, even from a small cruiser. In deep locks, the problem is one of precision.

The need is to put a crewman onto the steps cut in the lock side. Since these are certainly going to be wet, and possibly slippery, it follows that you should stop exactly, so that the crewman can step gingerly onto the steps. Once ashore, he secures his rope to a bollard and then comes back for the other one, which therefore has to be thrown to him. This is where a crew that has not sorted out its ropes and practised throwing them ashore, is going to have egg on its face.

Most locks have two sets of steps, one on each side. (The rest have three or four.) Since the most usual, and certainly the most crucial time for these to be used is when a boat is locking up, you would think that these would be placed to make life easy. In other words, you would expect them to run the same way as you are. Alas, this is often not the case. So, you have not only to place your boat so that the crewman can step onto the steps, he may well have to climb up 8 ft of lock wall back towards you before he can look for a bollard or take action to stop you. This is why the direction of the steps is shown on the diagrams of the individual locks, and why the locks are shown as shallow or deep. It is noticeable that all the latest locks, and all those subject to major repair, are equipped with steps running the correct way, so clearly

Thames Water are aware of the problem.

There will be times when you cannot come alongside the steps, because someone is already there. In this case, you will have to lie alongside and hold onto the chains that have been thoughtfully provided for that purpose. Do not allow the lock to fill while in this situation. Holding several tons of boat in a boiling lock by means of slippery chains is not to be recommended. Often the lock-keeper will take your ropes, wrap them round bollards and drop them back down to you. Other lock users may also help in such cases. Failing that, someone is going to have to lever himself onto the lock side.

For this reason, I usually send one crewman up to the lock, when I have stopped below it. It is a great comfort to have a friendly face smiling down at you as you run into the lock. Brief your crew to watch you approaching though, in case you have to change sides on the way in.

Working the lock oneself From time to time, you may arrive at a lock to find that the keeper is off duty. If this is one of the manually operated locks, above Godstow, working the lock yourself is rather fun and should not delay you. If it is not, your best bet would be to stop for lunch or tea yourself, if your schedule allows. The modern locks are not technically difficult to work manually, but they require prolonged, heavy, physical effort, and the larger ones will take at least half an hour to lock through. The rule is that the lock must be left empty, with the gates closed. If you are travelling upstream, the first part should therefore be relatively easy. You will find instructions on the control console, and there is a sort of gear lever, to pull up or down, labelled 'Gates' or 'Sluices' respectively, and a large wheel, labelled 'Open' and 'Close' and indicating which way to turn to have this effect. So, unless the labels are back to front, as they are at Sandford, for instance, the idea is simple enough. Nor are the gates difficult to open and shut.

Having opened the gates, put your boat in and closed them, make sure the sluices are closed. There are bellows on top of the gates, and these should be wound down tightly. Only then should you start to open the top sluices. Incidentally, do not worry if the gates do not shut completely. The incoming water will do

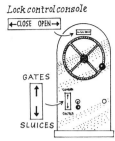

Lock control console

this automatically. The gearing for the sluices is very low, so you have to wind and wind to make any impression. Keep going, even when the water starts to run in, or it will take all day.

Once the lock is full, the gates will 'give', springing slightly apart. Then move the switch to 'Gates' and open them, take the boat out, shut the gates, close the sluices and open the lower sluices. By which time you will be absolutely shattered! (Thames Water tell me they are experimenting with means of improving this system.)

One tip. You will find it easier to move the lock gates if the sluices are open.

You have to do the same exercise with a manual lock, but this is much easier, because it is designed to be worked in this way. Here the sluice mechanism is on the gates themselves. There is a big wheel to turn, and this will move two vertical indicators, one up and the other down. The indicators have a red and white top, respectively. When the red one is up, the sluices are open. So, make sure that only one set of red indicators is up at once. When the reds are up, the sluices have been pulled up, so secure the wheels with the rope loop provided, or they will shut as soon as you let go.

The gates are opened by pushing against the wooden beam, which is counterbalanced, so the process is quite easy, even for a smallish child,

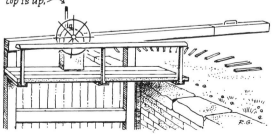

Manually operated lock gate.
N.B. The sluice is open; the indicator with the red top is up.

as long as the sluice is open. If you are doing this alone, you will find a long pole attached to one of the gates, with which you can push the other one open, and save yourself a walk round the lock.

As long as you think what you are doing before you do it, this is quite a jolly exercise. Indeed, children of all ages frequently like to help the lock-keeper, even when he is on duty. But always ask first.

Man overboard The life-ring is another item, like the anchor, which you will probably never use in earnest. Likewise, if you do, somebody's life may depend on it. The life-ring should be in easy reach of the person at the helm. The rope attached to it should be neatly coiled, and checked regularly in case it has become tangled. The life-ring must be kept clear of obstructions like somebody sitting on it, or using it to trap a drying swimsuit under. *Do not tie* the rope to the boat, but remember you have not when throwing the life-ring. If it is tied you can bet it will be in the only place where you cannot reach it from where you want it.

In the event that anyone should fall off your boat when it is under way, this is what you do:

1 Whoever sees the accident, or is first to notice that there are fewer people aboard than there were, shouts 'Man Overboard!' It does not matter if it is Aunt Ethel or baby Sam, or the dog, that is what you shout. If the person involved can retain the presence of mind to shout it himself, so much the better, especially if nobody saw him go. It has an excellent effect, that shout. You can be sure of the total attention of the remaining crew.

2 The helmsman immediately puts the drive in neutral, to ensure there is no danger of injury from the propellor. The resultant loss of way is also helpful, as it reduces the suction of the boat through the water.

3 The next step is to locate the body, which will presumably be somewhere astern. Unless he is unconscious, it is bad policy for anyone to jump in to help. This simply means you have to make two rescues, instead of one.

4 Throw the life-ring, using the same technique as you would for mooring, including the

bit about not throwing it at the person, but slightly to one side. Remember to hold on to the end of the line, you may need to have two goes at it. If the victim can swim at all well, he should make for the shore, from where recovery is much easier.

5 If he cannot swim well and is too far away for the ring to reach him, or to make things easier once he has the belt in his grasp, you can now manoeuvre to come broadside to him. Do not come too close, because of the propeller, suction and fear of hitting him, and keep him in sight at all times. It is also helpful, particularly if he panics, to tell him what you are doing.

6 When you are in position and stopped, you can pull him up to the boat with the line. Again, unless he is a child, or cannot swim, he would do better to swim ashore, with the aid of the life-ring and with you in support. But *never* attempt to tow him ashore, or you will either pull him under and drown him, or cut him to pieces on the propeller.

7 Once he is alongside, it is a simple matter to haul him in, providing he only weighs four or five stone. When you have tried pulling a twelve stone, soaking wet, fully clothed man three feet vertically out of water, you will appreciate why he should have swum ashore. A fend-off can be helpful to the swimmer, if he can grab it, and so can a rope with a couple of strategically placed knots, and the other end fixed.

Mooring (See also ROPES). Apart from locking, mooring is the most testing activity for any crew. It is important for the helmsman to give reasonable warning to the crew to man bow and stern ropes, and for the crew to respond readily. Here are some basic rules:

1 Always moor facing upstream. If you do not, and there is any sort of a stream running, you will overshoot and arrive in a heap, instead of stopping precisely and quietly. In the middle of nowhere, when there is nobody but yourself to observe the shambles, you will only damage your pride in your watermanship. When attempting to move into a space two feet longer than your boat, at a busy wharf, you will be made terribly aware of your inadequacy. Mooring bow down is absolutely unwatermanlike, and instantly recognisable.

2 Do not moor on a bend, at the bottom of somebody's garden or where there is a notice asking you not to.

3 Do not moor in a lock cut, unless you are using the lock or sanitary station, and then only for that purpose.

4 Never allow your crew to jump ashore (or to jump aboard). Such action is bound to lead to an accident, and if someone is sandwiched between the boat and a wall, or if you cannot stop the propeller in time, it could be a very nasty one. If the boat is not close enough for the crew to step ashore, the helmsman must reposition the boat until they can.

5 Make sure your crew never run to do anything. Running about on a small boat is as dangerous as jumping ashore. It is just as irritating. There is nothing worse than placing the boat absolutely right for a mooring and then having to stop and fool around fishing for some enthusiast who ran overboard.

6 Check fend-offs before mooring, to ensure they are all there. If you normally cruise with them raised, do not forget to lower them.

The crew's first task is to make sure the ropes are free, properly coiled and ready to use. They should then sit down, or brace themselves properly, in case the boat stops suddenly.

The helmsman brings the boat into the shore (facing upstream), as slowly as possible, whilst still steering properly. Ideally, the boat will run up parallel to the shore and not more than a foot away from it, so that the crew can step ashore and secure it. (See KNOTS.)

For a number of reasons, the ideal only happens infrequently. Incompetence is the main cause of error, but eccentricity of the stream and, particularly, wind, can upset the most careful planning. When the helmsman realises he is wrong, what does he do?

Well, at worst he takes the boat round and tries again. Usually, he will be able to make at least one end go ashore, probably the stern, by using lots of rudder and power. One crewman will then land and walk towards the other end of the boat. The other crewman throws his rope ashore and the first crewman takes hold of both and waits to be relieved of one of them. Do not pull hard on the rope from the end of the boat that is ashore, because this will only force the other end further away until it is so far away that the other rope cannot reach. This is such a common fault that, if the boat seems to have stopped obeying the rules, always check that the landing ropes are not the reason.

Throwing a rope ashore When there is a need to throw a rope ashore ('heave a line' is the term), the crewman picks up the coil, recoils it, and holds it in his left hand. He takes a good quantity, say two thirds, in his right hand, checking that he has taken consecutive loops and not left an early loop in his left hand, and stands facing the shore. At the appropriate moment, he swings his right arm a long way back and, with a long, lazy throw, sends all the coils in his right hand ashore. If more is needed, it will unloop easily from the left hand, as long as it is crooked between thumb and first finger,

not grasped tightly. The usual beginner's error is to throw too early, without checking that the rope is coiled properly and, for both reasons, throwing short. This is an exercise that any crew will do well to practise before setting out.

Do not throw the rope *at* the person ashore. It is 6–4 on he will fail to catch it and it will bounce off his chest and fall into the water, and all the preparations will have been wasted. Throw it to the side of the receiver. If he catches it, well and good. If not, it will go straight past him and give him plenty of time to put his foot on it and then secure it. If it does go wrong, the crewman must retrieve the rope and coil it in his left hand again, as if he had all the time in the world, and then repeat the process. This is where practice comes in. The inexperienced or unpractised crewman will gather up an armful and chuck it ashore again, and this will certainly fail. It follows that, if you can be in a position to throw the rope 20 ft before you need to, there

will be time to have two goes at it while you have a chance to keep the boat on station. A crewman who knows what he is doing will certainly be able to re-coil and throw in less than ten seconds from his first miss.

Tying up Two ropes are usually sufficient to hold a boat comfortably. They should be secured a few feet ahead and astern of the boat, respectively. Do not tie up too tightly. The boat may 'work against the bank, because of wind or wash, and be damaged. Or, the level of the water may change considerably during the night, and tight ropes will not allow for such movement, also causing damage.

Changes of river levels at night come about because, staff being off-duty, there are no weir movements, necessary corrections being made in the morning. So it is possible to moor up for the night and find someone has pulled the plug out while you are asleep, and you are aground. If possible, try to moor with at least a foot of water under you. If not, and you have to push her off in the morning, this is what has happened. (Thames Water recommend two feet, but this is not often possible.) It is particularly important not to moor over old pilings!

In boisterous conditions, or at an awkward mooring, you may find the boat moves uncomfortably. The answer is not to tighten the ropes, but to use a Spring. This is a rope which is made to run from one end of the boat to a point ashore roughly amidships. Adjust this until it balances the ropes already out, and you will find the boat rides much more easily. This is a single spring. In extreme conditions, you may need a double spring, which is achieved by running a rope from the other end.

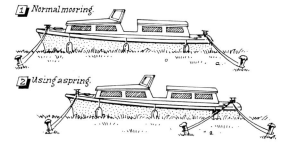

Wind When landing against an offshore wind, do not underestimate the strength needed by your crew to hold the boat ashore. I once had an interesting experience when trying to moor in the teeth of a gale. I succeeded in landing two adults with their ropes, only to find that their combined strength was insufficient to hold the boat against the bank. She literally pulled the rope out of their hands. The human instinct was to walk off the bank rather than let go. You must guard against this, I almost lost a perfectly good daughter at Abingdon because she fell in rather than let go. However, I persuaded this crew to abandon their ropes, recovered these before they wrapped themselves round the propeller, drove round the next bend and was driven ashore with a resounding crash. She did not move an inch all night in that wind, the mooring ropes were quite superfluous.

On the other hand, getting off a lee shore against a gale can be an awkward problem. Since your stern is against the bank, you cannot steer off, and the normal method of pushing the bow out does not work, because the wind promptly pushes it in again.

The answer is to turn *towards* the bank. Put the wheel hard over and drive the stern out into the river, pressing the bow against the bank. Once the stern is facing the wind, go astern to lift off the bank. You will probably be facing the wrong way by now, but turning round in the river is not a problem.

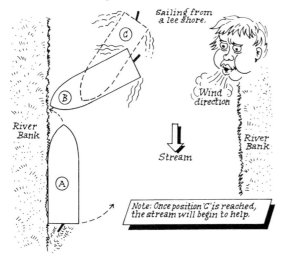

Sailing from a lee shore.

Wind direction

River Bank

River Bank

Stream

Note: Once position 'C' is reached, the stream will begin to help.

Neutral See GEAR LEVER

Piles/Piling Piles are now usually interlocking metal sheets driven into the river bed to protect or straighten up the bank. The somewhat sharp tops of these are clad in concrete or wood, typically at public moorings or lock lay-bys. These should be regarded slightly suspiciously, if you propose to moor against them, because at certain river levels and with certain pilings, it is possible to slide your gunwale *beneath* this capping, thus causing damage to your deck. This applies mainly to narrow-boats and small launches, which have a relatively low freeboard.

Piles used to be wooden posts, similar to those which still figure prominently at locks. They are traditionally of seasoned heart oak, and last almost indefinitely below the waterline.

The lock pilings are an unforgettable part of the river scene, smartly painted in black and white, and offering a refuge from the weirs.

Port Left. The left side of the boat. Anything on the left is 'to port'. Port is conventionally coloured red. It used to be called 'larboard'. This was dropped because it could easily be confused with starboard in a screaming sou'wester. The origin of port is obscure. The *OED* suggests that, since the steering-board (before rudders were invented) was on the right (hence starboard) side of the ship, it would have been sensible or convenient to go ashore from the other side, particularly against a wharf, in port. Although it was not officially prescribed by the Admiralty until 1844, it was in recorded use two centuries before that, and was probably used colloquially even earlier. My own feeling is that the word referred to the entry port of the ship, rather than to a harbour. Given that it was originally on the left because of the steering oar, perhaps it was there on naval ships as a matter of policy, so that visiting officers would always know where to approach a strange ship.

Punt A flat bottomed, square-ended pleasure boat, to be propelled by a long pole or by paddles. It makes an excellent camping boat, being much more stable than a skiff and having large areas of flat, unencumbered space for lying down on. It is easily the slowest form of river transport.

'Put up/down' See STEERING.

Quarter The area which lies to port and starboard, abaft the beam, but which is not ASTERN.

Reach A stretch of river, typically that between two locks, and taking its name from the lower one. Often named after a town or feature instead, e.g. Henley, Cliveden.

Ropes See MOORING. Ropes are more than useful items for tying up with. They can be crucial to your safety and should always be used with this in mind. You will have at least two, one at each end. Proper rivermen, using soft ropes, wind these down on the deck, starting with the loose end in the middle, until they finish up with a sort of large dinner-mat. Nylon rope does not usually lend itself too well to this (it depends how expensive it is), and you may feel it is too much effort anyway. Apart from looking smart, such a practice has the advantage of ensuring that the rope is never tangled, and this is the end to which a crew should work ceaselessly. Most people do not bother to keep their ropes free, and one of the most regular forms of amusement to the casual onlooker is the sight of a boat's crewman finding the need to heave a line ashore and standing holding a bundle of spaghetti, two or three coils of which have encircled his legs as he picked it up. Fortunately, this is not usually fatal, but it probably means another shambles at a lock.

The art is simple, so long as a crew knows what it is trying to do, and practise it a few times. Whenever you are not using a rope and at the moment when you stop using it, so that it is always ready for instant use, coil the rope as follows:

1 Take the fixed end in your left hand (if you are right handed), a convenient distance from the deck bollard, say 3 ft.

2 With the right hand, make a loop about 18 in deep. Twist the rope in your fingers, half a turn and lay the loop in your left hand.

3 Repeat this process until all the rope is in your left hand, making sure by twisting it, that each loop lies flat against the others, without kinks. That last is the most difficult part. When you have a neat coil of rope, place it carefully on a piece of deck that is not used for anything else—over the bollard to which it is attached is best, though not always feasible. Make sure nobody kicks it, sits on it, or interferes with it in any way, and it will be ready for use. At least, that is the theory. In practice, it is always best to re-coil any rope immediately before using it. This is because even the best coiled and laid ropes seem always to manage to entangle themselves the moment they are left alone!

The term: 'Take a turn round that tree-/bollard/piling', means: 'Pass the rope round it once and then hold the free end.' It would be used when leverage was needed to hold the boat still, as for instance, in a lock.

Rudder (See STEERING) A moveable, vertical flap at the stern of the boat, which steers it. A rudder works by interrupting the smooth flow of the water past it. Thus, if you turn the rudder to the left, the flow of water to the right of it speeds up, and the rudder is sucked to the right, taking the stern with it, and thus shifting the line of the boat in the water to the left:

Rule of the road The basic rules of the road on the river are these.

1 *Drive on the right* The best position is slightly to the right of the middle, unless you are pushing against a strong stream, when you are better off well over to the right. You will pass oncoming craft port side to port side, and when a boat is approaching, it is better to move further to the right.

When an approaching cruiser helmsman uses your side of the river, do not move further to the right. He will only move further to his left, and it will all get rather nasty. Give him the widest berth you safely can.

2 *Overtake on the left* When a power-craft is overtaking another boat, it must do so on its left; i.e. in the middle or left side of the river. It follows that the overtaking helmsman must be ready to give way to oncoming craft and should only overtake in a wide stretch of the river, where he can plainly see it is safe.

This rule is not nearly so well known as is keeping to the right. A surprising number of skippers will pass to your right, even in quite a confined river space. Sometimes they will make you a sandwich boat, as they strive to overtake the boat that is overtaking you. Both these practices are risky, and the second is foolhardy in the extreme.

The obvious riposte is that, if someone *can* pass on the right, you are too far out. While this is true on a road, it does not follow on the river, where a helmsman is entitled to make use of the current. At the same time, keep a good watch astern, and make life as simple as you can for any overtaking boat.

3 *Upstream gives way to downstream* This is an 'if in doubt' rule. It does *not* mean that downstream boats can force all upstream boats into the bank by claiming a right of way.

The rule is based on the relative lack of control of downstream boats, which have not only to stop, but also to counter the effects of the stream, whereas upstream boats can use the stream to help them to stop and to hold steady.

The obvious place for this rule to have effect is at bridges with only a single navigation arch, Sonning Bridge being a good example.

4 *Power gives way to sail or muscle at all times* In effect, cruiser helmsmen should give way to everybody else. This rule is based on straight forward common-sense. A cruiser is more mobile and more easily controlled than other boats, including large passenger launches, which have to worry about their draught, as well as normal considerations. A sailing-boat frequently cannot go where it wants to, and rowing-boats and punts frequently do not know how to go anywhere. This last applies to small launches, hired by the hour. You will also sometimes come across cruiser helmsmen who have not heard of the rule of the road, or who could not care anyway.

In all these cases, especially when you come across non-power boats, slow down or stop until you can see how best to proceed, or until they are past. With a sailing-boat, you will soon see the pattern of his progress, and can probably run under his stern when he turns ahead of you and moves off across the river.

With these boats, you can also assume the

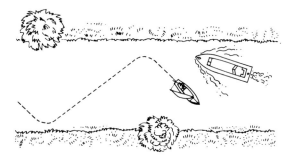

helmsman knows what he is doing and is aware of your presence. You will soon see if a rowing-boat is similarly proficient, and can then proceed normally, but slowly. When this is clearly not the case, all you can do is hang around and wait for it to hit you or get out of the way. Even if it appears to be getting out of the way, be very careful. Such boats have a distressing habit of turning suddenly, blissfully unaware of your existence, and dashing across

'...will turn and dash across your bows.'

your bows, just at the moment you have decided it is safe to proceed. For reference, you will find this sort of boater at Windsor, Maidenhead, Cookham, Henley, Reading, Abingdon and Oxford. The small launches behave in the same way, only more quickly, with the added excitement that their engines stall regularly.

5 *Watch your wash* (See WASH AND SPEED) Apart from general considerations relating to wash, discussed elsewhere, the cruiser skipper must ensure that his wash causes as little inconvenience as possible to small boats. Skiffs and punts have a freeboard of about 4–6 in. Therefore, a 6 in wash will actually cause great distress to such vessels, and could sink them.

6 *Make your intentions clear to others* (See HAND SIGNALS) If you are doing something strange, likely to concern others, keep them informed. For example, while examining moorings for this book, I was frequently on the wrong side of the river, heading upstream. By raising my left arm, I was able to advise approaching helmsmen that I knew I was in the wrong place, had seen them and was not about to turn across them.

7 *Never run your boat into danger* It is not enough to be doing the right thing in the right place. A helmsman has to judge and allow for the ignorance or lack or skill of all other boaters. The cardinal rule is that a captain will never hazard his ship.

Saloon Living-room.

Scull To row, using two oars per person. The oars themselves.

Screw The screw, otherwise called the propeller, is what drives a boat through the water.

Shell A word of American origin, now widely adopted here, denoting an ultra lightweight boat, for racing. See EIGHT.

Skiff A light rowing-boat, usually to be sculled by one person, and steered from a comfortable seat in the stern. The double-sculled version is nowadays the most common form of camping boat.

Sluice A device used to control water flow, by being opened or shut. Gate sluices are to be found in all locks, for instance. Ground sluices are fitted to some of the larger ones.

Speed The rule on the Thames is that speed shall not exceed a brisk walking pace. Maximum should therefore be 4 knots, or roughly $4\frac{1}{2}$ mph. See RULE OF THE ROAD, WASH.

A way of checking your actual speed is to establish the time taken to travel a measured mile or two, taken from a convenient point on the map. Apart from anything else, such information is useful when planning an itinerary.

In addition to and connected closely with your speed, is the noise of the engine. Normally, this is unimportant, but early in the morning or late in the evening, when you may be the only craft moving, it is a kindness to remember that a boat at speed can be noisy. So, if you decide to set off in that marvellous time in midsummer when all is new and sparkling, and the sun is high in the heavens, say 7 am, please remember that everybody else is still asleep, and revolutions for 2 knots, rather than 4 are more likely to leave them that way.

Splits The classic beginner's error in boating is doing the splits. All cruisers can be easily pushed off the shore by one hand or foot, and this is the cause of much distress to the unwary. Once the boat has moved beyond one's centre

Doing the splits!

HEREWEGO

of gravity, there is no way back, only down! The knack is always to step onto and off the boat without pausing between foot movements.

Spring See MOORING.

Starboard Right. The right side of the boat. Anything to the right is 'to starboard'. Conventionally coloured green.

Starting/Setting off When you are ready to set out, start the engine and make sure it is running smoothly. Let it idle and then engage the drive mechanism. Never cast off first and then start the engine. People do it all the time, and it is dreadful watermanship. Nine times out of ten if will not matter, but the riverman is never caught out by the occasion when the engine refuses to start.

Preparing to cast off.

Post crew forward and aft, unless you are going to work the stern rope yourself. It is sound policy to put the most reliable crewman at the end further from you. Have the crew untie the ropes securing you to the bank and then hold the boat, either by standing on the bank, or by leaving the rope round whatever it has been tied to and holding the loose end firmly from on board. This will be determined in practice by whether you are tied to your own mooring posts, which of course you will want back, or to something like a tree or bollard, which you intend leaving behind. (And whether your rope will reach back on board!) Note also, if there is a high wind off the bank, the boat may 'take off', pulling the crew into the water if he is not strong and quick. (cf. MOORING)

Make sure both ropes are free and then issue the order that has launched Drake and Frobisher, Nelson and Beatty and a million others on epic voyages down the ages: 'Cast off forr'ard' (pause while this is done and while the bow swings gently away from the shore; 'Let go aft' (pause while this is done); shift the gear lever to 'slow ahead,' make sure you are not pulling out in front of somebody and are clear of adjacent moored boats, and off you go.

Once free of the bank, the crew should coil their ropes properly, ready for next time. Then it is time to lift fend-offs, if you are going to.

A few things to watch for:

1 Make sure your crew know to ready their ropes for casting off and then wait for the order to do so. Otherwise, you will find one end of the boat swinging blithely and uncontrollably out into the river, while the other is still firmly tied to the bank.

2 Always check with your rope crew that they have undone the ropes and freed the mooring-stake, if appropriate, before telling them to cast off, or you will have the same problem as at **1**!

3 On a crowded mooring, or if there is a strong stream running, you may well need to go slow ahead *before* one or both ropes are released. This will give you the necessary control to stop the boat running back onto the boat astern.

4 This is another time you will be glad you moored facing upstream. If you were moored bow down, the bow would not swing out and you would have great difficulty avoiding any boats moored close to you.

Steerage See WAY.

Steering On most cruisers, the steering position is on the left of the cockpit. This is because of the rule of keeping to the right of the river. Narrow boats are steered from the stern, centrally, but their controls are usually on the left.

Steering is normally done with a wheel, which in many boats is remarkably similar to a car steering-wheel, and has the same effect, in that you turn the wheel to the left, if that is the

direction in which you want to go. When going astern, you must remember to turn the wheel the opposite way, also, just as in a car. The problem arises only in the way a boat turns.

Since the rudder, which makes the boat turn, is at the stern, it is the stern that moves when you steer, not the bow, as it would be in a car. If you wish to change direction therefore, you move the stern round the bow until this is pointing in the new direction. It follows that, if your stern is close to something like the side of a lock, the bank, or another boat, you will not be able to turn away very quickly, and if you try to you will simply clout whatever it is and come back to your original position. In such circumstances remember to steer gently away until you clear the obstruction. Also, when turning right round in the river, say to the left, do not move close to the right hand bank before starting to turn.

Another characteristic of turning on water is that a boat moves through it in all directions, and the effects of wind and stream are continually present. So, although the stern is being moved, the whole boat follows this movement, the final effect being that it swings about a point roughly amidships. On the other hand, if you manoeuvre correctly, you should be able to turn right round in the river without moving from where you started. This is an advantage a boat has over a car, it does not need a turning circle. Any boat can turn almost in its own length, given suitable depth of water at each end.

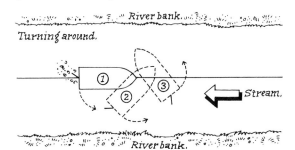
River bank.

Turning around.

① ② ③   Stream.

River bank.

If your boat is a narrow-boat, it will usually be steered by a tiller, a horizontal piece of tubular steel projecting into the steering position from the stern and directly connected to the rudder. So, the steering position is necessarily at the stern. Since the connection between rudder and tiller is direct, you have to do the opposite to what you want to happen, i.e., you push the tiller to the right in order to turn left and vice versa. This is a cause of endless excitement to the beginner, who moves the tiller the wrong way, finds the boat moving the wrong way and *always* pushes the tiller further the wrong way!

A rudder works more efficiently the faster the water is caused to flow past it. So, if you are turning round and the boat is making a circle instead of spinning on itself, you should accelerate to make it turn more sharply, at the same time making sure you have turned the wheel as far as it will go in the desired direction. This takes a little believing, so practise in a safe place and prove to yourself it is so.

Steering Astern Most cruisers steer perfectly well astern, although less well than they steer ahead. Narrow-boats are notoriously difficult to direct at all.

The problem with narrow-boats is that they have a lot of windage. That is to say, they are very long for their width and can be blown sideways rather easily. What usually happens is that, while you are steering the back of the boat, the front is taken off somewhere else, this movement normally being irreversible. The only response is to go full ahead on full rudder, to move the stern sharply round without pushing the boat forward, and then to go astern again and endeavour to steer. Even in a light breeze you will probably have to repeat this exercise several times in order to finish up where you want to be.

Two tips. She will probably steer best on about half rudder. You will feel the rudder start to fight you when you are in the right place. If you are brave enough and have room, she will steer better the faster she goes.

'Put up/down' This applies to a boat with a tiller. 'Put up the tiller' means pull it towards you, 'put down', push it away.

Stem The extreme front of the boat, the bow-post.

Stern The rear of the boat, see ASTERN.

Stop A confusing word. The command 'STOP' means 'put the gear lever in neutral. It does not mean 'stop the boat' and it certainly does not mean 'stop the engine'. Make sure the crew know this.

'Stop' knob A device used on a diesel engine to cut the fuel supply and thus stop the engine. It is usually a simple push/pull knob. Remember to push it back once the engine has stopped, or it will not restart. If a beginner is steering and cannot restart the engine, the stop knob is the first thing to check.

Stopping A boat has no brakes. If you move the gear lever from 'forward' to 'stop' (neutral), the boat will lose speed steadily, at a rate depending on the weight of the boat and the strength of the stream and wind. A narrow-boat, which is typically made of $\frac{1}{4}$ in steel plate, and weighs anything from 9 to 20 tons, will continue to run forward in slack water for quite a long way before it stops. A plastic boat, weighing 2–6 tons, will stop rather more rapidly. However, you will want to stop at a definite point, and to do this you simply put the drive astern. You do not have to wait, as you would in a car, for the boat to stop. The drive can be transferred from 'full ahead' to 'full astern', allowing only enough time for the engine to slow down in neutral on the way (say three seconds). The reaction you will get from the boat will be in the same ratio to its weight as it would be if you just let it run. In other words, even with the engine going full astern, a narrow-boat will take much longer to stop than a four berth plastic cruiser. It is always a good thing to experiment with this, before you need to know in earnest.

If you have been moving astern, the boat is stopped by the propeller being driven 'ahead'.

'Take a turn' See ROPES.

Tiller A steering lever, mounted at the stern of a boat and connected directly to the RUDDER.

Throttle See GEAR LEVER.

Turning See STEERING.

Waling Horizontal lengths of timber. Originally used to describe these on the top of dams. On the Thames, the horizontal pieces between the PILES at lock lay-bys.

Wash See SPEED. Wash is the V-shaped wave formation that follows a boat and spreads from bank to bank. The amount of wash for a given speed varies from boat to boat. Broadly, short, fat boats make more wash than long, thin ones; keel boats less than flat bottoms. Note your wash and compare it with others, adjusting your speed from these observations.

A boat's speed, unlike that of a wheeled vehicle, is of direct concern to everybody else, all the time. Your wash scours every inch of river bank and causes every floating thing to move. In narrow or shallow waters, this effect is greater than in deep, wide places. So, your speed should always be adjusted to the circumstances of the moment, unless you want to be very unpopular.

The response to the order 'full ahead', is to move the throttle to the point where the boat is moving at the maximum speed for the comfort and safety of everybody else, and the preservation of the river bank.

Way A boat moving under power is said to have way on her. At a certain speed, this movement becomes fast enough for the rudder to become effective, and the boat has 'steerage way'. What this is varies with the length, shape, weight and power of the boat, the size of the rudder and propeller. Thus, all boats behave differently. My narrow-boat steers quite reasonably at about $\frac{1}{2}$ mph, but I once hired a large, plastic boat that seemed to lose all steerage way at any speed below 4 mph.

It is the speed of the water passing the rudder that works this, and only the water flow caused by the power of the craft itself, not any stream in the river. So, if you are stationary and then go full ahead, the boat will steer well before it gathers speed. For this reason, it is important to discover at what speed a boat stops steering satisfactorily *after* you have shut off the power, or reduced to dead slow.

Weir A structure built across a river to hold up the stream and thus control the depth and rate of flow of the river.

Wheel See STEERING.

PLANNING
A CRUISE

The Chaperone

Let us tow mamma

This is charming

Poor Mamma is very much upset

The world forgetting, and the Chaperone.

MAKING A PLAN

There is little doubt that anticipation of a special event can be almost as much fun as the event itself. Planning a cruise is full of delight, whether it be for a weekend or two weeks. How better to spend January and February evenings than savouring in advance the days of summer to come? Thus would the Norsemen have dreamt of going a-viking. They were, to the best of my knowledge, the first people to make a habit of summer cruises on the Thames, although their impact on the natives was much more the equivalent of the present day Easter rugby tour than will be your gentle progress! For this chapter, you will need to consult the map and, unless you have your own boat, the holiday brochures. Having obtained these things, you will be in a position to determine where you wish to cruise, where to start from and which boat will best suit your needs.

There are those whose idea of a cruise on the Thames is to set off from one end, travel as quickly as possible to the other end and then rush back again. With a great deal of effort, totally ignoring the speed limits and therefore at maximum disturbance and inconvenience to everyone else, it can be done in a week. This attitude is surprising. Surely a Londoner, for instance, would find it simpler to take a car down the M4 to Maidenhead, A423 to Oxford, A420 to Faringdon and A417 to Lechlade? Leaving at 11.00 am, there would be ample time for drinks and lunch by the river at Lechlade, and to return home for tea. Furthermore, he would cross the river at Bray, Henley, Wallingford and Shillingford (by a small detour) and Oxford. He would see almost as much as he would by boat, and all the other river users and residents would be spared his company!

In practical terms, if you want time for shopping and sightseeing; for leisurely breakfast and unhurried lunch; for walking the dog, or not moving at all when the weather is foul; and to be sure of mooring by 4.30; 17 miles a day is the distance on which to base your planning. At $4\frac{1}{2}$ miles an hour, that is about 4 hours' cruising. To this must be added an average of six locks, each of which will take at least 15 minutes to pass. So, you would typically set off at 9.30, stop for lunch from 12.30 until 2.00, and moor up at or before 4.30. (To remain cruising any later in the high season will mean missing all the best moorings, and sometimes *all* the moorings.) This sort of schedule will allow those who wish to do nothing to have quite long periods when they can, the energetic to walk without being left far behind, and children to do childish things like buying ice-cream and fighting. In short, you may end up with a contented crew.

If you hire a cruiser for a week, you will find it comes down to six days, with a couple of hours on the first afternoon to shake down your crew. So, your range is roughly 50 miles from the departure point. There are boatyards that operate a 'pick it up here, drop it there' system, which gives you up to double the range. I am not sure this carries any real advantage. The Thames is quite different when viewed from opposite directions. There will be things you would like to see again, or did not have time for on the outward journey. There may well be a mooring that you or your children want to use again, or noticed but did not use before.

Cruise planning depends on two premises: where to go and which boat to hire. If the boat you want is in range of your favourite cruising area, you are in business. If not, you will have to change your boat, destination or length of holiday. For example: if Lechlade is your goal, then you are only interested in boatyards from Wallingford upwards; if you are most anxious to see Windsor, then Wallingford is the highest point from which to hire. It is probably unwise to hire from a yard at the extreme end of your range, for then you have no margin for losing a day for bad weather or engine-trouble. Thus, in the above examples, Oxford or Reading would be more suitable starting points.

By all means plan a route, day by day. Be prepared to change it as circumstances dictate. Life on the River usually makes a nonsense of the most carefully laid plans. If it were only for you, planning might well be superfluous. The more normal situation is one in which you have to communicate your enthusiasms to others, who may or may not be convinced that a river holiday is a good idea. In that case, you must be seen to be willing to make allowance for their views. If, for instance, your favourite person is delighted to be going on the river, so that two days can be spent exploring Oxford, it is as well to know this before making final arrangements to hire from a Windsor boatyard! A boat carrying four adults is also carrying four opinions on how to spend the time, and a meeting or meetings in the planning stage will give everyone a chance to air his thoughts. It will also give you a very good idea from which quarter trouble is most likely to come and how best to nip it in the bud. In all these cases, a PLAN is a most useful basis for discussion.

If you have not done it before, you should not underestimate the difficulty of keeping four people (let alone six or eight) in a confined space and some discomfort for a week or more, and yet remaining friends. Certainly, whatever plan you start out with, you should be prepared to abandon and rethink your schedule from day to day. I have found a crew to be at its most amenable after supper, when members sit about quietly and discuss the day's adventures. That is the moment to pull out the map and say: 'What shall we do tomorrow? I thought we might ...' With any luck at all, you will then get your own programme through almost unopposed.

What you must avoid is the danger of running the boat like a democracy. A captain must be a dictator if his crew is to feel safe and happy. By all means be a benevolent dictator and sound out everyone's opinion before making a decision, but then tell them what they have decided. If it was your idea to go on the river, you will be the one holding the buck in the minds of your crew as to the success or failure of the holiday, so you may as well take the decisions.

CHOOSING A BOAT

Boats are unlike other means of transport in one major sense. They are not mass-produced. True, most of them on the Thames are nowadays made of plastic (or glass reinforced plastic, GRP, to be more accurate), and many hull shapes are reasonably standard to a number of different boat-builders. Nevertheless, there are no large fleets, comprising identical models, as is the case with cars, or even caravans. They are much more like houses in this respect, and just as people buy houses for all sorts of reasons, many of them subjective, so do they choose

boats. There is, fortunately, no ideal boat for everyone, and there are a number of factors influencing choice, whether for keeps, or for a week's holiday. Here are a few of them.

There are three major design types: traditional cruisers; the so-called broad beam cruisers and narrow-boats. Traditional cruisers are further divided into those with the steering position aft and those that are controlled from amidships.

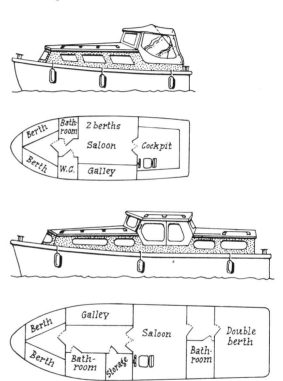

While some of them have keels (usually because they were designed as coastal boats), most have flat bottoms. They come in size from about 22 ft in which two people who like each other a lot can live in reasonable discomfort, fairly primitively, providing it does not rain too much, to over 40 ft in which six people can live in a high degree of comfort, whatever the weather.

The traditional type is the most pleasing to the eye. It looks like a boat, for a start. It has a pointed and flared bow. Its lines are usually raked, to look fast and businesslike. It is steered from a raised position, a bit like the bridge of a naval ship. Such craft should stir your blood if you are in the least interested in boats. The snags inherent to the design are these: the curves of the hull are reflected in varying widths and heights inside; the forward accommodation comes to a point, usually where two bunks meet, head to head, or feet to feet; wide decks, raked windows and the need to raise the helmsman and yet pass under bridges, tend towards banging your head in a variety of places. Practically, this last tendency means that boats that are designed to minimise head-banging will not pass under Osney Bridge, limiting your cruising to the river below Oxford.

Head-banging is a feature of all boats, the design thing is purely a matter of degree.

This type of cruiser is the easiest to use and the easiest to use well. It would be surprising if this were not the case, since the modern cruisers are the latest in a long line of boats designed to behave well on the River. For this reason, the traditional shape is the answer for rivermen and non-rivermen with remotely sporting crews. Although you will frequently have dual usage of space (for eating and sleeping), this can often be avoided. Since their design bears their element very much in mind, they are not as comfortable as either of the other types. On the other hand, the saloon, cockpit and galley areas are usually perfectly civilised.

Not even its greatest admirer would call a broad beam cruiser a thing of boating beauty. This type, known affectionately, if disparagingly, as a Tupperware boat, is the driest form of river locomotion. You sit at the front, for all the world like a country-bus driver, with the main cabin all round you. And you will only bang your head getting in and out.

Broad beam cruisers are designed primarily for the comfort and convenience of their living-space. The living-room (saloon) is scarcely smaller than that of a cottage. They usually have cabins that are purely bedrooms, so the beds can be made up just as they would be at home. Even when you need to use the saloon as a bedroom, they come with a bed that folds against the wall during the day. The galley has a space to itself too, in the larger ones, and they have wash-basins scattered about the place like confetti. If there is anyone the least bit iffish about 'camping' in your party, this is your boat.

The broad beam cruisers vary in length from about 24 ft to 45 ft. They are essentially self-propelled floating caravans. The snag with them is that, since the total effort in their design has been concentrated upon things that appeal to land people; space, comfort, headroom etc., they are not good boats in the pure sense. They handle rather as you would expect a floating caravan to handle.

This type does not steer well at low speeds. Indeed, it does not steer at all unless the propeller is turning. It will make a nonsense of all your best laid plans. On the other hand, all rivermen and lock-keepers know this and thus nobody will be in the least surprised when you create the usual mayhem in a lock. And think of the odd occasion when luck and good judgement coincide!

Narrow-boats vary in length from about 30 ft to 70 ft, but their chief characteristic is width, 6 ft 10 in. This is because they are designed as canal-boats and have to fit the locks on the narrower canals. Their other main features are that they are usually made of steel, that the helmsman has to be outside when it rains and that they are underpowered when used on the river, because rivers have currents and canals do not.

A narrow-boat certainly looks pretty and has a continuous, flat floor area and full length, full width head-room, like a broad beam cruiser. Again, you only bang your head getting in or out of it. It is the least private of the types, because it is little more than a wide passage along which everyone has to pass. Dual-purpose space is the norm on this type, for the same reason. Because it is made of steel, it can

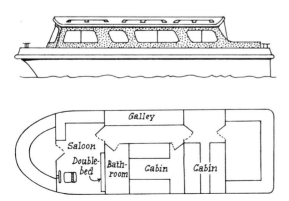

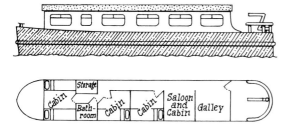

be properly insulated. So, for living in, there is nothing to beat a narrow-boat. For a summer week or two on the Thames, you can do much better for the same money.

Narrow-boats look out of their element on the River, which they are. Being underpowered means you have greater than usual problems when there is a strong stream running. I frequently take twice as long going upstream as I do going down, in these conditions. This means that you would be well advised to go up river to start with, unless you want to risk having to cruise flat out for 14 hours a day to get back in time. Another peculiarity which is unimportant on a canal but can be most embarrassing on a river, is that they will not steer satisfactorily astern, without a great deal of practice and a flat calm day. On the credit side, they are capable of being steered ahead accurately when almost stopped, which makes them highly manoeuverable in confined spaces.

The remark about taking longer to go up river than to come down applies to all craft, of course, to some extent. If the weather is, or has been, wet, be prepared to make up to half a day's adjustment for the effect of the stream. In particular, do not risk going too far down from base in these conditions.

COMFORT AND ACCOMMODATION

If you accept that all boats are slightly damp and that all furnishings have to be able to spend their lives being damp, without distressing side-effects, then modern cruisers are really remarkably comfortable. If you are hiring, you will find that the brochures show the layouts of the boats clearly and honestly, giving you every opportunity to choose the design that fits your needs. Decide what these are and study the brochures carefully. Here are some thoughts to bear in mind.

If the brochure indicates that the boat is for 2–4, 7–8, etc, people, take the lower figure if possible. If you can fit your crew into a boat that comes within your budget, without using the saloon to sleep in, I strongly advise it. The exception to this is where there is a fold-up bed in the saloon, which is always so marked.

As a rule, the available space will be less than you think. You can do a rough check on each boat, by multiplying the length by the breadth (beam) and dividing the answer by the number of your crew. If the resulting figure is less than 85, you will not have much room to rattle.

The fig. below shows what might be described in a brochure as a 2–4 berth cruiser. The dining-table lets down to form a double berth. If the suggested space factor is applied to it, the result is 112 for two people but only 56 for four. A couple with two smallish children would be comfortable but four adults would feel cramped.

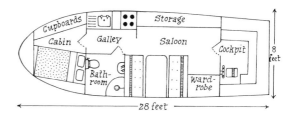

Privacy is difficult to achieve on a boat. The walls between cabins are normally constructed of $\frac{1}{2}$ in plywood. There are usually 2 in gaps above and below the doors. As to comfort, a single bunk is, typically, narrower than a single bed, though not always.

A centre-cockpit cruiser or large broad beam cruiser makes the best choice for a family with teenage children, or for two couples. Sleeping accommodation can then be at opposite ends of the boat. Parents can sleep happily, while the children can be up, walking the dog, making breakfast or playing games. With two couples, each can be detached from the other when they want to be, so important after two or three days

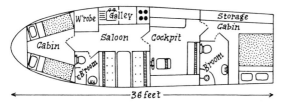

in close proximity. Two bathrooms are also highly desirable in these circumstances.

The fig. overleaf shows a 4–6 berth centre cockpit cruiser, ideal for two couples, or for a family of four. At 36 ft × 9 ft 6 in, she has a factor of 85.5 for space.

BUYING A BOAT

It is not practicable in a book like this to cover the whole subject of boat purchase adequately. It is too large and complicated a matter. Apart from the general comments made above, however, there are a few other useful points to be made.

On the Thames, where to keep a boat is usually more important than which boat to have. Mooring and storage facilities are in increasingly short supply. Your search for a boat may be as simple as walking into your nearest boatyard, or the yard in your favourite Thames centre, and asking which boats are for sale which already have moorings and/or winter storage booked. If you do not live near the Thames, it is worth thinking about the cost of mooring when deciding where to buy. Mooring charges are much lower in the upper river than they are in the lower reaches. Do not buy a boat in any circumstances unless you know where you are going to keep it.

Choosing your boatyard is also helpful in another way. The owner of the yard is going to have you as a customer, once he has sold you a boat. It is not in his best interests therefore, to sell you a bad boat. While he will obviously charge you as much as he can reasonably hope to obtain, it will often pay you to listen to his advice as between one boat and another. As to price, you can arrive at a fair estimate of what you *should* pay by reading the advertisements in the periodical magazines.

If it is your first boat, your prime concern may well be the price. If money is of secondary importance, then the best advice is probably to buy something standard and relatively modest to start with. Then, if you decide you do not like boating after all, you know there is a ready market for resale. The best way to progress as a boat owner is by developing your own 'feel' for a boat, which can only come with experience. You will meet other crews and their boats, the River is a remarkably friendly place, and learn the merits and snags of the various models available. You will often find people who have owned boats for twenty years or so have done precisely that. Or, they may fix on a particular boat and wait until the owner wishes to sell it.

HIRING A BOAT

If you wish to hire a boat, there are various ways of doing it. You can go down to your local yard, choose the boat that takes your fancy and book it. You can telephone or write to the Thames Hire Cruiser Association, 17 Chudleigh Court, Clockhouse Road, Farnborough, Hants GU14 7UA and ask for brochures. You can answer advertisements in the national press. Or you can obtain brochures from the three agencies which act for the boat-owners.

On paper, the only difference between these methods is that the agencies are slightly cheaper. This is because they include bedding in their terms, whereas when yards let directly they invariably seem to charge for this.

The agencies are to be thanked for causing a significant and sustained improvement in standards, over the last twenty years or so. The main ones originally functioned for the boatyards on the Broads, where standards were considerably higher than those on the Thames. Now, the facilities offered for both cruising areas are equal. So it is no bad thing to support the agencies, particularly while there is a cost advantage in so doing.

The hire agencies are:

Hoseasons Holidays Ltd
Sunway House,
Lowestoft, NR32 3LT

Blakes Holidays Ltd
Wroxham
Norwich NR12 8DH

Boat Enquiries Ltd
43 Botley Road, Oxford OX2 0PT

It is important to remember that agencies act for the boat-owner, as his servant. While they can refuse to offer boats for hire unless these meet their published standards, they cannot compel an owner to behave in an ethical fashion. There are rogues in the boat business, as there are in any business. The hirer can only take care of his interests. There are a few things to consider:

1 *Serviceability*. The best yards take their boats out of the water each winter and completely overhaul hulls, engines, controls and on-board facilities. The bad yards do none of these things. They wait for something to break and then repair it. The difference in convenience to customers is, of course, considerable.

The hirer's best insurance is to call on the yard of his choice and look at the way the owner prepares his boats. If they look clean and the cordage and fend-offs are in good condition and properly secured, the chances are that the works have been looked after too.

2 *Pump-out* If possible, hire from a yard which has its own, working, sewage pump-out facility. You can find out if it is working by telephoning the yard and asking what they charge for pumping-out. When you take delivery of the boat, ask if the tank has been pumped out. There is a distressing tendency with some yards not to bother. This is usually where they have not their own facility, or where it is broken down. The new hirer sets off, and finds he cannot use the lavatory because the tank is full. A tank that is properly used will only need pumping out every three or four days with a full crew. So you should only have to pump out once during a week's cruise.

3 *Fuel* Always dip the tank while the yard is doing the hand-over check with you. You will insult nobody who is honest and you could save yourself a good few pounds. The tank should be full, according to the dipstick. If it is not,

have it topped up. You are charged according to the amount of fuel the tank will take when you return from your cruise. So, be sure it is full to start with, and be there when it is filled on your return. You would be amazed at the number of unsuspecting hirers who leave with half a tankfull of fuel.

4 *Water* Sloppy yards often send boats out without topping up the water tank. It is not only the cost to you of having to fill the tank, that is small. It is not having water in the depths of nowhere at 9 o'clock at night that raises one's ire.

WHEN TO GO

Any month except October and February may be reckoned to be equally wet, according to the Met. Office! So you takes your choice. The only helpful advice is that, whilst August is usually wetter than February, it is often rather warmer as well!

At one time I had a theory that it was better to hire at the beginning of the season than at the end, because the boat would be newly overhauled. This thinking received a knock when I hired a boat in the first week of the season, only to find it had no engine at midday on the day of hire, and no electricity until 4.35! During the whole of this time we stood about, without information or so much as a cup of tea on offer. Three days later the drive shaft sheared at Bray Lock and almost caused us to run over the weir. In the first week of the 1986 season, a boat arrived outside my house, two days out, without water and with a full pump-out, in high stream conditions, which made movement difficult, and with six people aboard.

Nevertheless, the River can be a delight in April. There are only a few boats out, so you have no great problems finding pleasant moorings and plenty of room to be alone. Stream conditions can be severe, so it is not the best time for a complete novice.

If you are without children, May, June or early July are lovely. The water chicks are hatching, and nobody can fail to be moved by the clutches of ducklings, cygnets, goslings and coot chicks that cluster and clamour around the mooring places.

For most people, the school summer holidays are the only practical time. The Thames is then at its busiest, particularly in the lower reaches. If you do not mind longish waits at some of the locks and if you are careful to moor early, it is amazing how little the 'crowds' seem to matter. The essence of a boat is that it is free and private territory for its crew. Even the act of tying it to the shore does not make it part of the land.

There is therefore no need to feel the busyness will spoil your fun. It will not, unless you are in an enormous hurry.

As for the autumn, it can be enchanting to cruise in late September and October. The nights are cold and you need good, warm clothes, even on a sunny day, for it is always cool on water. Otherwise, it is an excellent time to be afloat, and once again uncrowded.

PEOPLE AND OTHER CURIOSITIES

Morning Scenes

The early bird catches the worm

LARK'S NEST

(Lively lad) O my eye!
Here's a livin' Pears soap advertisement—
ans don't he love washin' for hisself

"Good Morning Susan"
"Selina Matilda if"
you please, I
aint no Susan

"Looks Cold"

THE SWIFT DITCH

Almost halfway between Abingdon Lock and Nuneham Railway Bridge, on the south bank, are two small weirs, set roughly two hundred yards apart. They mark the entrace to an historically important yet strangely enigmatic stream, known as the Swift Ditch. It runs for $1\frac{1}{4}$ miles from here to the top of Culham Reach, emerging under the beautiful Culham Bridge at its lower end.

The Swift Ditch is now a quiet, sleepy little stream, a soothing place to wander and to wonder. From about 1060 to around 1550 and again from about 1630 to 1790, this was the main channel for river traffic. It still contains the remains of one of the first three Thames pound locks, the only one still in its original position.

The enigma centres round whether the Swift Ditch is the natural course of the Thames and the present course man-made, or vice-versa. Fred Thacker, in his book *The Thames*

The upstream arm of the Swift Ditch. The weir can just be seen at centre right.

Highway, was convinced that the Thames used to run exclusively in what is now the Swift Ditch. This has since been echoed by others. I think Thacker was wrong.

We know that the Abbey at Abingdon was founded in or about 695, probably in the village of Senekesham. The monks had been forced, for some reason not recorded, to leave their first foundation, near Oxford. These were troublous, lawless times and monks were a prime target for looters. The abbey was attacked several times in the next 300 years. It seems certain therefore, that they would have regarded defensibility as a prime requirement for their new foundation. Secondly, they would have looked for a safe water supply, which could not be cut off. With the Thames where it presently runs, the siting of the abbey makes sense for both these requirements (as does that at Dorchester for instance). If the Thames had been half a mile away to the south east (i.e. the Swift Ditch), it would have made more sense to have placed the abbey closer to the Ock, or on the hill round which the Swift Ditch runs.

The confusion starts somewhere between 955 and 965. Thacker quotes Leland, writing in

about 1535: 'Ethelwolde ... caused a Gut to come out of Isis by force to serve and purge thofficis of thabbay.'

Thacker says: 'The monks very probably caused the traffic to use this channel in place of the Swift Ditch'. He is not entitled to say that. Firstly, there is no evidence of a flash-weir at this time, and without some form of 'stop' how could the monks 'cause' the traffic to do anything? Secondly, Leland uses the word 'Gut'. The *OED* defines this as 'a narrow passage of water' and gives 1538 as the date of first reference. I believe it was dug to provide a cleaner source of running water than that into which the inhabitants of Abingdon chucked all their garbage and sewage, a mains water supply and sewage disposal facility. That is, after all, what Leland says it was for. It is still in existence and is called the Abbey Stream. It runs from the side of the present weir to rejoin the river at Abingdon bridge.

To avoid confusion, the fig. attempts to show what the waterways looked like in 963, with the present situation in diagram 1, Thacker's suggestion at diagram 2, and the alternative to this at diagram 3. Note firstly that Thacker's 'Gut' in diagram 2 is $1\frac{1}{2}$ miles long, whereas in diagram 3 it is a quarter of a mile. Secondly, joining up the river Ock and the Thames as Thacker would have it could have led to serious problems with levels. Thacker blithely ignores the Ock. It does not even appear on his map.

The event that causes the most difficulty occurred in 1052 (Thacker says 1060). A reference I found in Abingdon Museum says that Abbot Ordric, taking note of pressure from Oxford and London to improve the river through Abingdon, where there was considerable blockage below the abbey walls, allowed a new channel to be dug through the meadow to the south, and that this remained for centuries the navigation channel.

Thacker translates the Latin from the Abbey Chronicle:

> Abingdon monastery has the Thames flowing along its southward parts, up and down which navigation is conducted. In the days of Abbot Ordric, beyond the precinct of the church, at a place called Barton, next the hamlet of Thrup, the wide bed of the river used to cause rowers no little difficulty. For

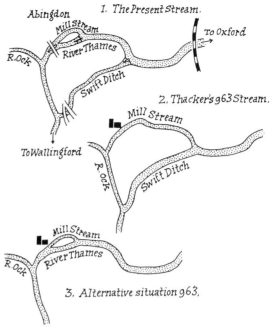

the land below being steeper than that above often made the said channel slack of water. The citizens of Oxford, therefore (having most traffic there), petitioned that the course of the river might be directed through the church's meadow further south. ...

Since the Swift Ditch commences opposite Thrup and runs further south than the present

The downstream end of the old pound-lock.

channel, that quotation appears to make perfect sense. The channel built in 1052 was what came to be known as the Swift Ditch. My own reference seems to confirm this, since it was the blockages beneath the abbey walls which had created the need for the new channel further south.

However, Thacker prefers to rely on two other sources, Leland and Harrison, writing in 1535 and 1577 respectively. Leland wrote:

The chefe Streme of Isis ran afor betwixt Andersey Isle and Culneham, even where now the South End is of Culneham.

Harrison:

No part of (the Thames) at the first came so neere the towne as it doth now, till a branch thereof was led thither from the maine streme, thorough the industrie of the monks.... Some write, that the maine streme was brought thither which ranne before betweene Andredesie and Culenham.

Leland was writing 500 years after the events he described, almost as distant from them as we are from his time. Harrison was writing a 'Description of England', in which the Swift Ditch can hardly have figured prominently. So he probably relied on Leland for his source.

When one considers how much was written down in the sixteenth and subsequent centuries, compared to how little was recorded before, the problems facing Leland in making an accurate appraisal must have been acute. Fifty years after Leland, the plays attributed to Shakespeare were written. Yet controversy rages over who actually wrote them. We simply do not have absolute evidence to support any of the theories. How much less chance had Leland, about a subject much more obscure?

Leland was actually relying on tradition. Thacker says, perfectly reasonably, that tradition is usually reliable. This time I think it fails us. The siting of the monastery, the length of the mill-stream, the problem of the Ock, the naming of Thrup, the evidence from the Abbey Chronicle and lastly, the very name of the channel of 1052, all indicate the opposite.

Why Swift Ditch? Its length is $1\frac{1}{4}$ miles. The bend it cuts off is a little above two miles. Thacker suggests the resulting relative swiftness of its current may have caused its name.

He says there are numerous other instances of the name, in quite different circumstances. He quotes a suggestion that it might be a corruption of a Saxon personal name, Swaefe. He does not offer what I consider the simplest explanation. For Swift Ditch read Short Cut. It was a quicker route because it was shorter and it was a ditch because it had been dug.

Whatever the answer to the puzzle really is, we are left with one certainty and some interesting speculation. It is certain that the channel of 1052 was the earliest man-made navigation channel on the Thames. What is not clear is why a channel needed to be dug. The reason given in the chronicle, rapids causing shallows, is a classic case for a weir. Indeed, there must have been a weir in the Swift Ditch or at Abingdon or both, as soon as the new channel was opened. Probably, the general rubbish below the abbey walls and the difficulty of dredging satisfactorily was the decisive factor.

There is also the question of the Abbey Stream. This served Abbey Mill for hundreds of years. Had this been its original purpose however, there would have been a need for a weir, to keep the head of water at the correct level. Yet there is no record of a weir at the time it was cut. Since the Abbey had been in existence for almost 300 years before the cut of 963, it is more than likely there already was a mill, presumably on the Ock, where a dam was no hindrance to navigation, another indication that the cut was originally a domestic water supply only.

The Swift Ditch now looks as shown on p. 173. It appears to be about half as wide as it once was; the line of its old banks can clearly be seen.

The old pound lock, built sometime between 1630 and 1638, and last used in 1790, is still clearly visible near the top. It has a footbridge across its tail, so that both sides may be examined, after some argument with the bushes that surround the lock basin. When Fred Thacker saw it, in 1910, there was a brick wall at the tail, so that the lock was full. This wall has been largely removed, so that the whole structure of the lock can be seen, including the recesses for the tail doors. There used to be an overflow weir immediately above the lock. This was at some time repaired with sandbags and is now shuttered in steel.

About halfway down the quiet, gently

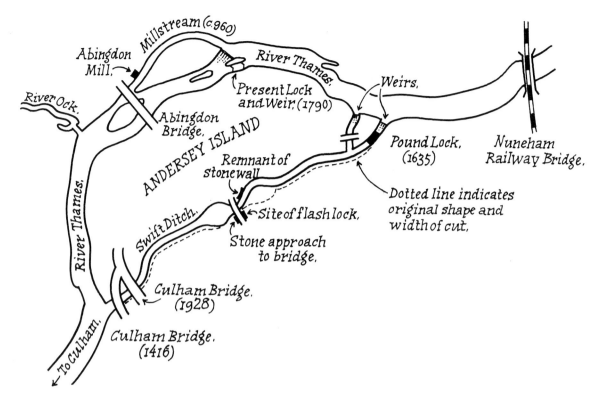

The recess for the gate can still be seen.

meandering course of the stream there stood a flash-lock, which was removed when the main channel was made in its present course, in 1790. The site of the weir is now marked by a foot-bridge. In 1910 the stones which used to support the beam were still in place, but I have found no sign of them. When the lock was in use, there was a considerable barge port here. The bed of the ditch was cut out to form a sort of hour-glass, with the lock in the waist. The lower pool, though now greatly reduced in width, is still of considerable size, the upper one is largely silted up.

Thacker says that stone was taken from the site for two years from 1790, to repair Sandford and Iffley locks. This suggests that the port had stone sided wharves. The remnants of these will doubtless be mostly underground now, but I found some fragments above the bridge, running for perhaps 100 ft. I also found signs of a stone paved or cobbled approach to the bridge, from the Culham side.

The earliest record Thacker could find for the flash-lock, then known as 'Collombe Weare', was 1580–85, which was during the period when the river was largely impassable in this area. It seems inconceivable that it was not in position much earlier. How else could the two streams have been used effectively? In high stream conditions the Ditch would have become a mill-race, whilst in times of drought, all the water would have run this way, leaving Abingdon high and dry. There is record of a complaint against the weir at Abingdon in 1316, which was then raised too high (to create a better head at the mill). So it must have been there before that and the weir in Swift Ditch presumably matched it in antiquity. It would be quite reasonable to suppose that both were there from 1052, or shortly after, when the monks had had a chance to study the effect of the Swift Ditch. Equally, there was probably a bridge across the Ditch at the weir, for we know there was at least a ferry at Abingdon a long time before the bridge of 1416, and there would be no point in that if one could not cross the Ditch.

Lack of historical evidence of these things is not altogether daunting. There is no historical evidence for the barge port, but it is still there for the eyes to see. It probably developed piece-meal as trade and the importance of Abingdon increased, and it never occurred to anybody to record the fact.

The weir continued in use after the pound lock was built above it. It would have provided a deep anchorage in the upper pool and the necessary flashes to carry traffic over the notorious shallows below Culham Bridge.

The stream below the half-way bridge and lower pool is much straighter than it is above, and has a definite appearance of being a canal.

Here then passed all the main traffic on the River, from before the Norman Conquest until (and perhaps because of) the Dissolution of the Monasteries under Henry VIII. Again, this was the principal course from the opening of the earliest modern locks in the 1630s, until the beginnings of the Industrial Revolution that marked the end of the Thames as a trading river. Now, the old channel is slowly being reclaimed by nature. The flash-lock is gone without trace, the pound is heavily overgrown and gradually collapsing. The course of the cut is considerably silted up. The Swift Ditch survives now, away from the modern Thames, as a memorial to all those countless men and women who made their lives and their livelihoods upon and beside the river through the centuries. Above all it reminds us of the resource and energy of those unknown hewers of the soil who made it, 900 years ago.

SWANS

Almost all the popular knowledge of swans is based on misconception, long since refined into folklore, of learned comment. As far as I know, they *do* mate for life. Certainly they are touchingly considerate of their mates and their young. Otherwise, it is all bunk.

For a start, Thames swans are called mute swans. They are many things: white, orange-beaked, black-legged and common (in the ornithological sense), all leap to mind. Mute they are not. A swan is not chatty, like a goose, but you can have a serious conversation with one, which you cannot with a duck, for instance.

Someone once observed that a swan was so strong that he could break a man's arm with his wings. The chap was trying to be helpful, in giving to those who knew not swans some idea of the power of this remarkable bird. It has turned out quite differently in practice. Generations of people have grown up in the certain belief that all swans spend their waking hours looking for likely arms to break. I have never seen a good word printed in defence of the creature.

Being a perverse individual myself, I have spent a lifetime looking for a genuine, arm-breaking swan, with extraordinary lack of success. I have been hissed at, often; I have been cascaded with water (aimed at my dog); I have fed innumerable swans from my fingers; I have had my fingers chewed; I have had much tapping on the side of my boat and jumping up, to see if I was in; but no swan has ever essayed

Swans need wide water for flying. These are on the regatta course at Henley.

to cause me bodily interference, let alone harm, unless I have inadvertantly cornered him. I have, on the other hand, occasionally been allowed the privilege of coming really close to a wild animal, in a situation of equality. It is a joy well worth the effort.

The swan is easily the largest and certainly the boldest wild creature you will meet on the Thames. The important point here is that he is wild, despite appearances to the contrary. A swan uses the Thames because it is a wide stretch of water, full of good things to eat. He needs wide water because it takes him 50 yards to gain speed for take-off, and a similar distance to achieve cruising airspeed, so that he can rise out of danger. Because of all this effort, he only flies if he is going somewhere, or in dire emergency. In all other circumstances he relies on his size and aquatic ability to keep him out of danger. Perforce, he spends a good deal of time in close proximity to man. Consider also that he is king of his chosen environment. Nothing on the river that knows what is good for it pushes the swan around. He is quite fearless, and will always confront an attacker rather than run away. Thus, you have a wild creature that is prepared to treat man at best as an equal, and who therefore gives the impression of being tame. It is this mixture that people sometimes fail to understand, which leads to a bad press for swans.

Life for a swan among men is far from easy. His chief enemy is the angler who, until they were banned in 1987, left lead weights all over the bank for the beast to swallow and thus poison itself, and who leaves nylon line, often with barbed and barbarous hooks attached, in a filmy network along the water-margins, where the swan feeds. Then, especially at breeding times, there is the budding (or actual) football hooligan, whose idea of a Sunday afternoon's entertainment is chucking rocks at sitting swans. The latest menace is the manic 'animal rights activist', who releases vicious predators like mink into the wild, with catastrophic effect on British wildlife, who have no defence and no understanding of the need to organise one. All six cygnets at Hambleden in 1986 were destroyed by mink thus released.

Do not expect gratitude, respect or consideration from any swans you feed. They have the same attitudes as cats. Be firm and quiet,

and keep your hand still if you want the swan to feed from it. The sensation of being bitten is a bit like being rubbed with a plastic dish-scourer, and leaves no mark. Large swans will usually take from your fingers with great delicacy. Cygnets have co-ordination problems, and are liable to nibble half your arm before they find the edible bit. Swans cannot take from a flat palm, that is for horses. Nor should you give them large pieces of food, because they have thin throats and will choke. If you do not want them to be boring, do not feed them while feeding yourself, on deck or river bank. They have no appreciation of your need to feed, and will challenge your right to do so, if they can see your food. It is in such circumstances that swans gain their reputation for being vicious brutes.

Swans have a tendency to gather in large groups, at certain times. I have twice, years apart, while moored at Remenham, witnessed the arrival of perhaps a hundred of them, in pairs and small groups, early in the evening. They left shortly after dawn, like great bombers, turning into the wind and lumbering into the air, one by one, circling briefly and then flying off. Pairs live on, and return to, the same stretch of river, which is clearly defined for the benefit of neighbouring swans looking for excitement.

OARSMEN

In an earlier chapter I discussed rowing-boats in relation to navigation. There is a particular form of rowing-boat, that used for racing, which needs special mention.

The racing shell is the elite Thames boat. An eight, seriously rowed, is the fastest thing afloat. They can be found all over the river, but most particularly at Oxford and Henley, at Eton during the summer term, and in the Kingston and Molesey reaches. In addition to eights, there are fours and pairs, as well as the sculled boats, single, double and four. Oars or blades are described as sculls when each rower holds two of them.

The most important thing about them is that power-boats have to keep out of their way. I have heard complaints, voiced by non-rivermen in Oxford, that College boats row about as if they own the place. This is taken by some as symptomatic of elitism, social division etc. It is important to make clear that the behaviour of racing-boats on the river has nothing to do with that. They are allowed right of way for these reasons:

A racing shell is built for speed. It is fragile and expensive to repair.

They cannot be easily manoeuvred. In particular, they can turn only slowly and are difficult to drive astern. They are also vulnerable to being blown sideways by wind, when at rest.

Oarsmen have relatively short stretches of river to practise on, usually between two locks, while cruisers have the whole river. They are therefore entitled to elementary courtesy, including minimum wash, even at some minor inconvenience to others.

From the point of view of the cruiser helmsman, the major headache is caused by the fact that oarsmen always proceed in the opposite direction to that which they face. Nor should you be misled into thinking that boats with a cox in the stern can see you. They cannot. The range of view of the ordinary cox is 60 degrees to port and starboard. This leaves the 60 degrees dead ahead as a fairly formidable blind-spot. Nowadays they have headphones to enable them to listen to advice from the coach ashore, and microphones and loudspeakers to broadcast their instructions to the crew. Add the racket set up by eight large men hurling themselves back and forth while shifting pro-

The Thames is synonymous with rowing and rowers deserve courtesy.

digious quantities of water, and you will appreciate they cannot hear you either.

You may recall Cambridge running into a massive barge a year or so ago, simply because it had not been there the day before. I almost had the same experience the year before. I had been watching an eight coming up behind me, through three large bends, for over half a mile. I was tucked into the right bank, as close as I dared but, when it was ten yards astern, I realised I had not been seen and was about to be rammed. My cry of 'Ahead eight!' must have sounded jolly close, because eight oars stopped in mid stride and fell into the water. The boat stopped very suddenly, but not half as suddenly as it would have done two seconds later. The lasting picture I have is of the cox's head suddenly darting out from the huge bulk of stroke ahead of her, as she strove incredulously to see what she had just missed.

Such things apart, racing crews normally know what they are doing and can be relied upon not to act strangely, unless you think it strange to indulge in the sport in the first place.

ANGLERS

It was my father's firm opinion that anglers never fished in order to catch anything, but simply to get away from home. There must be a good deal in this. To begin with, nothing that comes out of the river is edible. It is caught, put in a net and then, if it survives the pain and shock, not to mention tissue damage from the hook, chucked back in the river again. Secondly, nobody who has experienced the physical discomfort and sheer boredom of sitting in steady rain or freezing sleet for seven or eight hours, watching a little red float, would ever do it again without very compelling reasons. So, an angler can be as certain as any man of being left alone in his misery. (This, incidentally, is the only time in this book where, when I write 'he', I mean male, rather than human. Women do not angle.) One can only marvel at the depth of misery that drives men to angle, week in, week out, almost all year. But they do, in their thousands at week ends, in their scores and hundreds during the week.

The term for angling on the Thames is, I

understand, Coarse Fishing. This has nothing to do with the fish. I imagine it comes from that excellent series of humourous books by Michael Green, of which *The Art of Coarse Sailing, The Art of Coarse Bridge* and *The Art of Coarse Rugby* are three other excellent examples. Whether this is so or not, you should on no account approach an angler. They are quite capable of stuffing your teeth halfway down your throat, and always give the impression that they are just about to. The usual way of establishing contact with another human being, smiling and speaking calmly, brings such an expression of loathing to the face of an angler as to turn your heart to stone. That is, if he is prepared to acknowledge you have addressed him. You are just as likely to be looked straight through, for all the world as if you did not exist.

It was my father's further observation that anglers never caught anything. This must be an interesting commentary on the pollution level of the river, which has greatly improved since the war. For I have observed that they do often catch fish. Or, at least, they do catch some fish, which appear to be called perch.

After a few years, the fish learn about anglers and stop being caught. So the fish that are caught are always the little ones, from 2 in to 6 in, and weighing from one to five ounces or so. The same fish are caught at least once a week in high summer, and their mouths become so

Anglers always sit on the far side of a bush!

damaged and swollen that their faces become fat in relation to their bodies. It appears that these fish are called 'chubby', reduced by those in the know to 'chub', and are rarely caught because they have learned wisdom. In angling circles it is considered clever to catch a fish that is wise, although since the same bait seems to catch anything that is foolish or unlucky enough to take it, luck would seem to play the biggest part. Be that as it may, an angler who has caught chubby fish will mention the fact particularly to his friends. 'I got three perch and two nice chub', he will say.

You may think I am making this up. 'If they will not speak, how does he know all this?', you will ask yourself. The answer is simple, any boater can do it. It is like observation of wild animals. If you are in a vehicle you will be ignored, the smell of the car drowns your own scent. The same applies to boats. All you have to do is moor in the vicinity of some anglers and keep out of sight and reasonably quiet, and you will find they become quite bold after a bit. I have even had them sitting on my boat, on several occasions, which is just like having a tiger on the car roof in a safari park. You will be amazed what you hear in these circumstances, if there are two or more of them about.

Whilst you should never approach one, anglers are not normally openly aggressive. You are unlikely to be attacked by one, unless you inadvertently trip over any of the ton or so of assorted equipment he finds essential to his misery, and needs to have scattered over the tow-path. On the river, you will frequently come on one suddenly, for they always sit on the far side of a bush from any vessel using the correct side of the river. Nor will they see or hear you in good time. This is clear because their lines are always withdrawn at the last moment, often too late to avoid being wrapped round the propeller. This last is a damn nuisance, because it is the very devil to unwind, but it does have the effect of causing the greatest show of emotion you will see from an angler. They leap up, call cheerily, and often even wave as well. However cross you are about the tangled web under your boat, you should always wave back and make yourself smile. If you feel strong enough, you might even shout something witty, although: 'And you sport' will normally suffice.

Do not moor for some distance after such an incident however. The angler may be so overcome with emotion at having made contact with another human, that he calls to see you, and then you are in for cups of tea and goodness knows what else. To feel the full effect of these displays of camaraderie, you should try navigating the upper Thames, which is narrow, when an angling competition is on. Then they sit, cheek by jowl, on both sides of the river, often for miles on end. The day is then full of leaping up and down, calling and waving, while you can only grit your teeth and hold to the centre of the river as best you can.

ANAS BOSCAS

It is a curious phenomenon of human nature that we tend to pay least attention to that which is most familiar. The most successful and therefore commonest creature on the Thames is the mallard. Everyone knows what a mallard looks like; most of us feed them from time to time. That is about the extent of our interest. Let us consider then *Anas boscas*, common duck, the Mallard.

Fiercely independent to the exclusion of any thought but of self, manically sexual in the spring and early summer, possessed of an unquenchable optimism and insatiable appetite, mallard is one of nature's great characters. Furthermore, although remarkably stupid, *Anas boscas* would figure in any shortlist of the most efficient creatures on earth.

What other animal has such complete mastery of three elements? He is slightly ungainly on land, it is true, although much quicker than most water-birds and big enough to drive land birds away from any food. On the water he is completely at home, apparently unaffected by cold, a tireless swimmer, reasonable diver, big enough to deter attack from pike and other predators. It is as a flying machine, however, that he becomes supreme.

The power available to a Mallard is almost beyond belief. He is quite capable of rising vertically 20 to 30 ft, and then accelerating while climbing at an angle of 20 degrees! His straight and level flight is fast and direct and his lightning reflexes and superb aerobatic abilities

Anas boscas *in his ideal habitat, cruising with an eye on the main chance.*

make him a leading exponent of formation flying. Since he is relatively heavy, his glide angle is rather steep, but this fits well with his general air of ceaseless hurry and enthusiasm.

The Mallard's confidence in the air frequently approaches recklessness. When he is relaxed and thinking about what he is doing, he can land with the lightness of swan's down; head stretched forward, body arched upwards, air-brakes open, tail spread, legs braced as they kiss the water and drop his body gently onto the surface. Perfection. More typically, landing is precipitated by an urgent need to beat 20 of his fellows to a tasty bit of food, suddenly espied. In these circumstances all rules are instantly and totally discarded. The air is spilt frantically, wind direction is ignored and, side-slipping crazily, he hits the water with a mighty splat. This performance is frequently followed by a single 'quarck' and the shake of his head. One can only assume he is unwinding himself and clearing the tears out of his eyes! Truly, the river would be a much poorer place without this lovable, scatterbrained extrovert.

THE PASSING OF THE FLASH-LOCKS

Nowadays, we take locks as a matter of course, without a second thought. In fact, they make the Thames what it is, or at least the weirs do. These hold back the water for extraction, control land drainage and ensure a deep channel. The Thames without weirs would be fast flowing in rainy seasons and inclined to be rather narrow and shallow in the drier months. Furthermore, there would be rapids in places.

Exactly when efforts began to regularise the flow is not known. There are small clues in the names of river places: Windles ora, Weir grove, Lockstigle, which I have discussed earlier and which, being Anglo-Saxon, suggest that weirs or navigational aids were there certainly in the tenth century, and possibly earlier still. The Thames must have been vital as a communications and trading link in those times, in the absence of roads. Even so, the earliest barriers were most probably fish-weirs, which would only have blocked part of the stream. Penning up the water for milling must have followed soon after.

Both these activities would have the same, accidental, effect, that of slowing the flow and providing a more uniform depth in the reach above the weir. In the beginning the weirs would have been crude affairs, comprising a few trees laid across the stream, filled in with brushwood, stones and mud, a beaver dam in fact. Such structures had one, crucial, disadvantage. It was not possible to pass them by boat. There must have been some interesting discussions over the years, between boat-owners and weir/mill owners, before the latter became bored with continually rebuilding their smashed weirs and began to build them with a section which was easily removable.

Thus was the flash-lock invented. It was so called because the opening of the removable part caused a flush or flash flood. A down-going craft would use this to carry it over shoals and fords, and down to the next weir. At the height of the system, in the eighteenth century, times of flashes were prescribed, so that a barge starting from St John's could, in theory, run right down to the tideway on the flash it started with. Returning, against both stream and flash, was a much more awkward and strenuous business. Both ways were fraught with difficulty and physical peril.

The system was by no means perfect, causing sudden surges and equally sudden drops in river levels as the weirs were flashed. Also, the mill owners could charge a fat fee for their services, or become awkward when boats wanted to pass. The cost and difficulty of running a cargo were a continuous cause of friction and complaint. From as early as 1215, and frequently thereafter, there were decrees from the King against obstructions to the navigation. Mostly these seem to have been unlicensed or unlawfully enlarged fish-weirs. As frequently, mill owners were required to reduce the height of their weirs, which had been raised such as to cause flooding and to increase the difficulty of navigation. No sooner were matters put right than the process of rebuilding and heightening began again.

The first pound (pond) lock, which is the sort we use today, was operating at Iffley by 1633. The advantages are enormous. Because the amount of water held in each pound is small, the working of the lock has no noticeable effect on the river level. The weirs for controlling the flow can be worked quite separately. Boats can run up or down with equal ease and without danger of capsize. So the idea caught on, and

The winch at Hurley. Was Windsor named after something like this?

flash-locks were displaced. Since the last one went in my life-time, 1938, the process was hardly hurried!

There are records of some 70 locks between Lechlade and Teddington, of which 44 now remain. Flash-locks are now no more. Four of them survived into the present century. Twenty eight of them are now pound locks and five have been replaced by pound locks at different sites. Of the remainder, the sites of several are still provable by observation, as I have shown in an earlier chapter. I now endeavour to draw their history together.

The first problem with any history of flash-locks is that it is impossible directly to date them. Not until the Thames Commissioners, in the eighteenth century, did anyone bother to record the building of a Thames lock. This even applies to the Oxford/Burcot Commission and their three pound locks. The reasons for this state of affairs are themselves obscure.

For several hundred years it is most unlikely that anyone intimately connected with a flash-lock could write. Nevertheless monks could write, and yet monastries like St John's, Oseney and Abingdon all had flash-locks and their origins are as obscure as any. Locks were generally unpopular with farmers, whose lands were constantly being flooded, and with bargees, who thought them damnably expensive and time-consuming obstructions. The same bargees also understood their merits of course, but that did not stop them complaining. So perhaps it was prudent to keep quiet about a lock, lest the fact of it should be used to make you remove it.

The first serious effort to list the locks was not made until 1585, when one John Bishop petitioned the Queen to have them removed. He was not in the least successful, but the preservation of his list gives vital proof of the existence of all the locks between Maidenhead and Oxford. That he had to make a list at all is surely proof that there was no official record. It seems incredible nowadays that nobody concerned himself with keeping an eye on the country's most important trade route on anything approaching a regular basis. But so it was.

In 1585 then, we can place all the flash-locks between Maidenhead and Oxford. Fred Thacker, who prints Bishop's list, moves on as late as 1746 before he finds a list of the upper

river flash-locks, made by Roger Griffiths, a water bailiff. Apart from these lists, one can only infer a lock from other information, or hear of one mentioned in connection with another matter.

If we accept that 'Old' Windsor was 'windlass shore', then we know that the Saxons were hauling boats up a steep incline at the time the village came to be named. Was it simply a rapid that caused the problem, or was it a weir? We do not know. The earliest reference is to the king's weir being repaired in 1300. If the site of Hart's weir at Basildon was Lockstigle in 1181, then we know there was a lock there at that time. The next reference to it is 1401! As for Wargrave, 'weir-grove', Bishop's list is the first reference to two weirs at Wargrave, neither of them definitely on the river itself. Since his list is of impediments to the navigation however, it seems reasonably safe to assume they were.

The earliest historical reference is two weirs at Shifford, in 1005. Thacker thinks one was probably Duxford and the other the precursor of Shifford old lock. Tantalisingly, there is nothing about St John's until 1775, although I feel there must have been a flash-lock here for most of the time since the twelfth century, because of its importance as a port. Similarly, we can surely assume a flash-lock in the Swift Ditch in 1052, or soon after.

There was a lock at Sandford in about 1350, but quite possibly in 1294. Osney dates from 1227, but there must certainly have been a lock at the Oxford Castle Mill for nearly two centuries.

The Thames mills are the surest proof of associated flash-locks. Thus, there was one at Iffley by 1220, and Sutton Courtenay mills were turning in 1374. Shiplake mill had a weir, in all probability, before Domesday, 1086, and certainly before 1404, which is also the date of the first reference to Marsh. In about 1285, the mill weir at Mapledurham was stated to have been there in 1215. Hambleden Lock could well have been there at Domesday, the mill was. We know for sure it was there in 1338. Boulter's probably had a lock in position by 1346, and the predecessor to Bell Weir seems to have been there in the thirteenth century.

After Bishop, the only new flash-lock on his stretch of river would seem to be Haule's weir, between Shiplake and Sonning. On the upper river, Ten Foot does not appear in any surveys until 1771. This meagre list illustrates more than anything the accuracy of judgement of the people who first erected weirs. The possible sites are limited by the lie of the land and the angle of incline of the river bed, and this state of affairs seems to have been understood a thousand years ago. The final proof of this is provided by the considerable number of old lock sites still in use. The modern river authority, backed by an overall view of the river and the benefits of modern engineering and hydrological expertise, cannot usually improve on the strictly rule-of-thumb methods of their early predecessors. Where they have, in places like Shifford, Culham and Clifton, the modern locks have not contradicted the concept of the original placing. It is more that the bed of the river has been straightened to cut off inconvenient bends.

To be specific, 21 of the original 31 main sites listed by Bishop are still in use, or their necessity, if not their actual site, is recognised. Above Oxford, twelve locks, including Osney, now serve where 23 locks once did. The record here is not so good.

Medley Weir in 1890 from the Minn collection at the Bodleian Library, Oxford. Note the boat-slide.

St John's has not changed. Buscot takes the place of Farmer's, which was one mile lower. Grafton serves for Eaton Hastings as well as the flash-lock it replaces, Lower Hart's. Radcot replaces Clarke's, Rushey is in stead of Old Man's and Old Nan's. Shifford takes over from Tadpole, Thames, Ten Foot, and Duxford, and is one of the deepest on the Thames as a result. Limbre's, Ridge's and Ark are served by the 'new' lock at Northmoor. Pinkhill replaces a flash-lock and Skinner's. Eynsham is instead of Bolde's. King's also takes the load of the rather obscure Clay Weir, as well as its ancient flash-lock. Godstow was built in 1790, presumably because Medley did not give sufficient depth up to King's. Once it was built, the importance of Medley declined since, when the reach was properly dredged, Osney could effectively control the channel to Godstow.

The reason for the relative plethora of upper river flash-locks is perhaps that it was easier to erect a weir in the narrower stream, and less difficult to maintain it against the reduced volume of water at this stage of the river's development. No doubt a low weir was easier and less wasteful to negotiate than a high one. There would certainly be no question of a flash-lock as deep as Shifford Lock, 7 ft 4 in, or Rushey, 6 ft.

Within the marvel of the long history of the early locks, reality was not all roses, of course. Weirs subject to individual initiative and

energy necessarily suffered the vicissitudes of individual incompetence, old age, idleness and financial difficulty. Bishop speaks of two 'ruynous weares' in his survey, at Sonning and in Sutton parish. Later travels are full of comments like 'tackle all out', and observations about the state of some of the locks and their keepers which are less than complimentary. Most flash-locks had their ups and downs.

The weirs attached to the Thames mills have been the best looked after over the centuries, although they have been the subject of greatest abuse from the public. The higher a miller could raise his weir, the greater the head of water to drive his mill. Unfortunately, above a certain height, raising the weir caused floods for miles in all directions, which upset the farmers. Equally, having raised a good head, millers down the ages have been reluctant to release it in a 'flash'. This essentially quite reasonable attitude caused endless delays and expense to the bargees, who were never by nature particularly long-suffering.

In all the circumstances, considering the enormous benefits to everybody of pound locks instead of flash-locks, exactly why none of the former were built for 150 years after the first three, is one of the great mysteries. Lack of

money must have been a reason, but lack of foresight and initiative on the part of the grossly unwieldy Thames Commissioners makes them in all probability the chief culprits.

The four flash-locks still in use at the beginning of this century were, in order from the top of the river, Eaton Hastings, Eynsham, King's and Medley. Of these, the most important was Eynsham. Eaton Hastings was so remote that not many boats needed to pass it, and you could avoid King's and Medley by running down the Oxford Canal, via the Duke's Cut, rejoining the river just above Osney Bridge.

The most disreputable was the lock at King's, which Thacker reports had a pair of gates similar to those at one end of a pound lock, unique, apart from the last lock at Nuneham. He does not say when he last saw these but a photograph of 1925 shows no sign of them, nor indeed of a boat-pass of any kind, except the rollers. On July 11, 1927, the Navigation Committee of the Thames Conservancy reminded the Board that money was put aside for reconstruction of King's Weir, and that a decision had been made to provide a pound lock in

King's Weir in 1870. One of the gates can be clearly seen. Henry Taunt.

January, 1926. The committee minute proceeded:

> As the Board are aware, the existing flash-lock is in a very defective condition and the depth of water on the sill is only 2 ft 1½ in, which is insufficient for navigation purposes.

The plea was answered, for on November 14, 1927, the Committee are:

> ... pleased to report that very rapid progress has been made with the construction of the new pound lock at King's Weir. . . . now completed and the gates fitted.

They still had to dig the cut, but were so pleased at the cost, which was considerably below the sum they had allowed (£10,000), that they were going ahead with the construction of a similar lock at Eynsham. Here also the water level at the sill was only 3 ft, and insufficient for navigation. The estimate for the lock was £7500, which gives some indication of what King's had cost.

On February 13, 1928, they decided 'forthwith' to build a new lock house at Eynsham.

On May 14, 1928, the Committee reported that work on both locks was nearing completion and they would be ready for navigation early the same month. And so they were.

This left Eaton Hastings and Medley.

On November 11, 1929, the Conservancy

Eynsham 'Old' Lock 1886. The last flash-lock on the site was more elaborate. Henry Taunt.

raised the wages of its lock staff, and I note that the keepers at Eaton Hastings and Medley each had a raise of 9d (4p) per week. No other comment is made until June 16, 1930, when:

> ... the removal of the superstructure of the navigation pass at Medley Weir, Oxford, was completed on April 30, and that there is now a free navigation channel between Osney Lock and Godstow.

Precisely why this was done does not appear, although the annual meeting on December 31 reports:

> In completion of the scheme of improvements to the navigation above Oxford, which comprised the abolition of King's and Eynsham flash weirs and the construction of pound locks in substitution therefor, Medley flash weir has been entirely removed and extensive dredging has been carried out in that part of the river.

There has been an unfortunate confusion apparent in several recent books, as to whether Eaton Hastings or Medley was the last flash-lock. Indeed, three books I have read make claims for each of them, in different places. There is actually no doubt that Eaton was the last.

On November 16, 1936, the Navigation Committee noted the continued sickness of the lock-keeper at Eaton Hastings, W. Prowton, and decided to continue paying him, albeit half-pay.

Eaton Hastings flash-lock 1883. Henry Taunt.

At the annual meeting on December 31, 1937, again without prior comment in the minutes of the committee, I find:

> The abolition of Eaton Weir and the construction of a new footbridge is in hand.

And on June 13, 1938:

> The removal of Eaton flash lock and weir and the construction of a new bridge ... completed on 13 April, 1938, and that there is now a free navigation channel between Buscot and Grafton locks.

Thus ended quietly a feature of Thames life that had been fundamental for at least 900 years. And thus did Eynsham lock end the process commenced almost exactly 300 years before, at Iffley, by becoming the last pound lock to be built. For, though it opened at the same time as King's, it was not started until King's was almost finished.

As for the present, the site of the lock at Medley is clear and obvious, especially with the cottage still extant. It actually crossed in line with the upstream end of the cottage. The sill of the weir on the old course of the river can still be seen under the footbridge which crosses to Port Meadow at this point.

The site of the old lock at King's was exactly

in line with the present weir, because the old boat-roller channel is still there, by which light craft could be manhandled round the weir.

At Eynsham I can find no trace of the lock, but it appears from Taunt's map to have been at or just below the position of the present weir.

At Eaton Hastings, the bridge crosses to the lock island at exactly the position of the flash-weir. There is an old mill-stream on the other side of the little island, and you can still see the grooves in the masonry made by the wheel, and the remains of its bearings. The mill became the Anchor pub, and this was destroyed by fire in 1979/80, and has been razed to the ground. Only an outhouse remains.

I asked Ethel Hambridge, who has lived in Kelmscott all her life, if she could remember when the lock was removed, and she had no doubt. '1938', she said at once, 'the year my daughter was born. We took her over the bridge to the pub when she was three weeks old!' So there you are. Eaton ended the old era by surviving nine years longer than any other Thames flash-lock. Incidentally, old Kelmscott people still confuse foreigners like me by referring to the Anchor as the Weir. 'When was the weir taken down?' '1980'!

BIBLIOGRAPHY

The following books have provided me with source material:

The Book of the Thames, by M C and S C Hall, 1859 Re-printed 1983

Taunt's Illustrated Map of the Thames—6th Edition, 1897 Henry Taunt of Oxford

The Thames Illustrated, by John Leyland, 1901 Re-printed by Town & Country Books Ltd, 1983

The Thames Highway, by Fred S Thacker, Vol I, 1914 and Vol II, 1920 David & Charles, 1968

The Thames from Mouth to Source, by L T C Rolt B T Batsford Ltd, 1951

Derivation of Place Names I found in the following:

Place Names of Berkshire, Margaret Gelling. Cambridge University Press

The Place Names of Buckinghamshire, Allen Mawer and F M Stenton, Cambridge University Press

Maidenhead and its Name, E A S Brooks, Stretton

Oxfordshire Place Names, H Alexander, Clarendon Press

Place Names of Oxfordshire, M Gelling, Cambridge University Press

Place Names of Middlesex, J E B Gover, A Mawer and F M Stenton, Cambridge University Press

Place Names of Surrey, Gover, Mawer and Stenton, Cambridge University Press

The following were also on my reading list:

Sweet Thames Run Softly, Robert Gibbings, J M Dent & Sons, 1940 Chivers Press, 1980

Time on the Thames, Eric de Maré, Architectural Press, 1952 Flare Books, 1975

Portrait of the Thames, J H B Peel, Robert Hale Ltd, 1968

Holiday Cruising on the Thames, E & P W Ball, David & Charles, 1970

Victorians on the Thames, R R Bolland, Midas Books, 1974 Evans Bros, 1983

A Thames Companion, Mari Pritchard and Humphrey Carpenter, Oxford University Press, 1975 (1981)

The Making of the Middle Thames, David Gordon Wilson, Spurbooks Ltd, 1977

The Country Life Book of the Thames, Gordon Winter, Country Life Books, 1982

The Thames from Source to Tideway, Peter H Chaplin, Whittet Books Ltd 1982

Punts & Punting, R T Rivington, 1982

The Book of the Thames, Alan Jenkins, Macmillan, 1983

Apart from *Stanford's Map of the Thames*, I consulted the following Guides:

Nicholson's Ordnance Survey Guide to the River Thames

The Thames Book, Link House

Discovering the Thames, Leon Metcalfe, Shire Publications Ltd

Upper Thames Valley To-day, Harry Knights

INDEX